Astrological (
Freedom Through Divination

Astrological geomancy is an ancient art, derived from the practice of the wisemen of the Middle East who divined the future from the marks made in the desert sands by people seeking enlightenment and resolution of problems. Geomancy, or earth divination, later was naturally combined with the other ancient science borne of the clear skies of the deserts—astrology.

Geomancy proper derives from the contact of humans with the earth, a powerful relationship. Humans are "earthbound" materially and, in many cases, spiritually. Geomancy gives guidance in dealing with the bond between humans, the unconscious mind, and Mother Earth. Astrology provides the heavenly overview which lifts earthbound sights to concepts of freedom generated by the power of the soul. Astrology marks the pathway to acceptance of the conditions of material life and its limitations and opportunities, while offering a broader perspective to higher attainments on the astral, mental and spiritual planes.

Astrology is not truly complete without geomancy, which always describes the individual and his or her talents and problems, opportunities and pitfalls, at a given moment in time. In focusing on the individual, geomancy is not complete without astrology, which gives the individual his or her universal placement, his or her role in the cosmos. The person of the moment becomes the person for all times. Together, astrology and geomancy give the most complete guide to development and success in both immediate material terms and eternal spiritual terms.

About the Authors

Priscilla Schwei was born April 2. She is the creator of *The Wisdom of Solomon the King* divination kit. An astrologer for over 30 years, Schwei became attracted to geomancy because it added the unique input of the individual to the impersonal and objective influences of the stars. In addition to writing, Schwei exhibits her talents at psychic fairs, where she gives both geomantic and card readings.

Ralph Pestka was born February 3, 1950. As a professional astrologer and member of the American Federation of Astrologers, he consults with individuals, writes books and articles, and lectures. Pestka has made major astrological predictions regarding business, government, social trends and natural phenomena, and has a good record for insight and accuracy. *The Complete Book of Astrological Geomancy* reflects his interest in the intuitive/psychic possibilities within astrology.

To Write to the Author

We cannot guarantee that every letter written to the author can be answered, but all will be forwarded. Both the author and the publisher appreciate hearing from readers, learning of your enjoyment and benefit from this book. Llewellyn also publishes a bi-monthly news magazine with news and reviews of practical esoteric studies and articles helpful to the student, and some readers' questions and comments to the author may be answered through this magazine's columns if permission to do so is included in the original letter. The author sometimes participates in seminars and workshops, and dates and places are announced in *The Llewellyn New Times*. To write to the author, or to ask a question, write to:

Priscilla Schwei and Ralph Pestka
c/o THE LLEWELLYN NEW TIMES
P.O. Box 64383-704, St. Paul, MN 55164-0383, U.S.A.
Please enclose a self-addressed, stamped envelope for reply, or $1.00 to cover costs.

Llewellyn's Modern Astrology Library

The Complete Book of Astrological Geomancy:

The Master Divination System of Cornelius Agrippa

Priscilla Schwei
and
Ralph Jordan Pestka

1990
Llewellyn Publications
St. Paul, Minnesota 55164-0383, U.S.A.

FIRST EDITION

Library of Congress Cataloging-in-Publications Data

Schwei, Priscilla.
    The complete book of astrological geomancy : the master divination system of cornelius agrippa
    by Priscilla Schwei and Ralph Pestka.
        p. cm. — (The Llewellyn modern astrology library)
    ISBN 0-87542-704-9
    1. Astrological geomancy.   I. Pestka, Ralph, 1950-
II. Title.   III. Series.
BF1779.A88S28   1990   90-6224
133.5'8133333—dc20   CIP

90 91 92 93   10 9 8 7 6 5 4 3 2 1

This book is printed on acid-free paper

Llewellyn Publications
A division of Llewellyn Worldwide, Ltd.
P.O. Box 64383, St. Paul, MN 55164-0383

The Llewellyn Modern Astrology Library

Books for the *Leading Edge* of practical and applied astrology as we move toward the culmination of the 20th century.

This is not speculative astrology, nor astrology so esoteric as to have little practical application in meeting the needs of people in these critical times. Yet, these books go far beyond the meaning of "practicality" as seen prior to the 1980's. Our needs are spiritual as well as mundane, planetary as well as particular, evolutionary as well as progressive. Astrology grows with the times, and our times make heavy demands upon Intelligence and Wisdom.

The authors are all professional astrologers drawing from their own practice and knowledge of historical persons and events, demonstrating proof of their conclusions with the horoscopes of real people in real situations.

Modern Astrology relates the individual person in the Universe in which he/she lives, not as a passive victim of alien forces, but as an active participant in an environment expanded to the breadth *and depth* of the Cosmos. We are not alone, and our responsibilities are infinite.

The horoscope is both a measure and a guide to personal movement—seeing every act undertaken, every decision made, every event, as *time dynamic*, with effects that move through the many dimensions of space and levels of consciousness in fulfillment of Will and Purpose. Every act becomes an act of Will, for we extend our awareness to consequences reaching to the ends of time and space.

This is astrology supremely important to this unique period in human history, when Pluto transits through Scorpio, and Neptune through Capricorn. The books in this series are intended to provide insight into the critical needs and the critical decisions that must be made.

These books, too, are "active agents," bringing to the reader knowledge which will liberate the higher forces inside each person to the end that we may fulfill that for which we were intended.

—Carl Llewellyn Weschcke

Also by Priscilla Schwei

The Wisdom of Solomon the King (Kit)
    (includes book and divination card deck)

Forthcoming

Ra: The Egyptian Oracle (Kit)
The Astrological Geomancy Deck

To Our Mother,

Wanda Pestka

Contents

Preface

Astrological geomancy is directly related to horary astrology. The ancients instructed people to draw marks in the earth. The geomantist then combined the numerological and symbolic meanings of these markings with the positions of the planets, signs and houses at that moment. The principle behind horary astrology is that the planetary influences affect the querent's framing of a specific question, and his or her seeking guidance at that particular moment. The deeper principle behind this is that we hold, within ourselves, the necessary keys to answering the question, or to discovering the best course of future action.

By having the querent manipulate some physical object (marking stick, cards, dice, etc.) the geomantist brings the querent into direct participation with the chart. This participation is unconscious and intuitive. In the usual horary reading the querent asks a question and the astrologer gives an answer. The addition of symbolical manipulation brings in chance. This takes astrological geomancy one step beyond the usual horary astrology. Physicists now understand that chance and chaos are a basic part of existence; even chance and chaos show predictable patterns. The geomantic manipulations of the querent penetrate these realms and make them understandable within the order and cycles of the universe.

Through the horary chart we perceive that which is orderly, cyclical and obvious. If we do not use an actual horoscope, we use the houses of astrology to obtain this order. Through geomantic manipulation we tap into what is chaotic, changeable and hidden. In combination, astrology and geomancy offer a means of harnessing the logical and intuitive powers of human foreknowledge and prediction. The rational and psychic powers of the individual are drawn upon, blended together and interpreted. The possibilities of this area of astrological practice are vast. They are only limited by the particular talents and techniques of the individual. Experimentation and practice will help you develop your abilities to fuse your intellectual and psychic powers for the purpose of foreknowledge and divination.

Ralph Jordan Pestka

Introduction

Cornelius Agrippa:
The Foremost Geomantist

Astrological geomancy is a method of predicting the future. It combines the astrological factors of the moment with the interpretations derived from the questioner's manipulation of symbols. Geomancy was originally practiced by making points or marks in the earth, and interpreting their meaning from the combinations they formed. This is the simplest form of marking, dating from earliest humans' attempt to symbolize the forces of nature and their influence.

The method of astrological geomancy used in this book is derived from the system developed by the 16th century scholar, Cornelius Agrippa. He was born September 14, 1486, at Cologne, and was baptized into the Roman Catholic Church as Henry Cornelius Agrippa von Nettesheim. He had a notable career in the service of the German Emperor, Maximilian the First, founder of the Hapsburg dynasty. Agrippa acted as secretary, messenger, military commander and spy in the service of the Emperor. He was an accomplished physician, theologian and linguist, having mastered eight languages. His occult philosophy and magical practices were rooted in the ancient Hebrew scriptures and the secret teachings of the Hebrew sages. Agrippa was one of the earliest European scholars to expound on the original Hebrew texts and the teachings of Cabala.

Agrippa was born into the caldron of the Reformation when the powers of the Roman Catholic Church were shaken and the people of Europe fought horrible religious wars. In the midst of this, Agrippa wrote about the practice of magic, expounded the secrets of the Hebrew scriptures and tried to reconcile true magic with the Christian faith. As a result, Agrippa was suspected of being a sorcerer, or evil magician. In his preface to *The Philosophy of Natural Magic,* he answered his critics, " . . . a Magician doth not, amongst learned men, signify a sorcerer or one that is superstitious or devilish; but a wise man, a priest, a prophet; . . . that Magicians, as wise men, by the wonderful secrets of the world, knew Christ, the author of the world, to be born, and came first of all to worship him; and that the name of Magic was received by philosophers, commended by divines, and is not unacceptable to the Gospel."[1]

Agrippa's work has been influential in the development of subsequent occult philosophy and practice. Many writers on magic drew on the original work of Agrippa. These included Francis Barrett, Eliphas Levi and A. E. Waite. The present authors hope you will practice astrological geomancy with the same high standards of divination as those held by Cornelius Agrippa.

---

[1] Henry Cornelius Agrippa, *The Philosophy of Natural Magic.* (University Books, Inc., 1974), page 27.

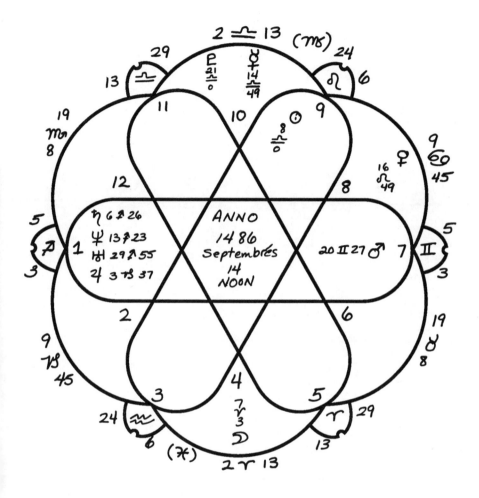

Cornelius Agrippa
Geomantist, Astrologer,
and Occultist

2

Explaining the Geomancy
Chart Form

Those of you who are familiar with astrology will recognize the general layout of the chart, which features the 12 houses; however, instead of the modern circular form, we are using the chart associated until recently with astrology and geomancy. This is to emphasize that it is *not* an astrologically generated chart. The sign rising and planetary house placements do not arise from a given time, place and date, but from the lines of dots drawn by the querent. The rising sign is dictated from the first symbol drawn, and while the planets are given for the date the geomancy dots are drawn, we do not use the exact degrees, merely the sign. Thus the geomancy chart is not an accurate picture of the heavens for a particular time and place, but a generally accurate picture of the emphasis and relationships between the planets for a given focus of interest or question, from which the lines of dots originate.

For example, a chart drawn for 2 p.m. on a November afternoon might have any one of the twelve signs of the zodiac rising as derived from geomancy; a horoscope would have the Sun in Scorpio (or early Sagittarius) in the Eighth House, with Aries or Taurus as the only possible Ascendants or rising signs for that time of day.

We would like to emphasize the difference between a geomancy chart and a horoscope by using the older form of the horoscope chart. You will notice that the house numbers move in the reverse direction from the modern horoscope chart, with houses 1, 2, 3, 4, 5, 6 above the horizon; this is in keeping with the fact that these are the houses associated with the signs of the zodiac when the days are the longest. It is thought that the modern form derives from the ease of following the house numbers descending and moving to the right, as our eyes move in reading.

5

Astrological Geomancy

Name:_____   Date:_____

Mothers

I	1	II	10	III	7	IV	4

Daughters

V	2	VI	11	VII	8	VIII	5

Nephews

IX	9	X	6	XI	3	XII	12

Witnesses

I	II

Judge

3

The Scope of Questions

The scope of questions that can be answered by geomancy is very broad. Nevertheless, there are some questions which rightly belong to one of the astrological specialties, that can only be answered partially or in general terms. For example, geomancy can answer questions about possible job or business success, your income in the near future, opportunities in gambling or sales, etc. The *choice* of a career, however, requires more information from the querent, and accordingly deserves analysis from the natal horoscope of the individual. Geomancy can tell a person if his or her love life is active, and about close relationships. Geomancy cannot pick a wedding date or give extensive details of a person's nature; for this, the querent needs an electional horoscope or a compatibility horoscope.

And, of course, neither an ethical astrologer nor geomantist will ever answer any questions about the death of a specific individual.

As you practice geomancy, you will be amazed at the specific, relevant information you can derive from the geomancy chart, with or without the analysis of the transiting planets. You will also learn to *define* questions clearly so that they *can* be answered. Recalling the preceding questions on determining the choice of a career, ask for some possible interests, which can be identified in the geomancy chart and accurately prognosticated. Areas of marital conflict or shared interest can also be pinpointed, although the *total* picture can only be given through astrology as applied to individual natal charts.

4

Geomancy's Starting Point: The Question

Unlike most astrological charts, but in common with the divinatory arts, geomancy always starts with a *question*, generally an important question to which the querent really needs an answer. Even practice geomancy charts require some kind of definite query as a starting point. All other questions can be answered after the chart is constructed, but a specific question is necessary to start the process. Here the art of divination comes into play. Geomancy assumes that the Earth spirits are guiding the hand of the querent in drawing up the 16 lines of dots. The earth spirits need a specific goal—the answer to a specific question—to in turn guide *their* efforts. We can also apply psychology in suggesting that the question stimulates the unconscious mind, the genuine source of answers to all questions.

Once the question is defined, and the chart erected, you will need to have a basic understanding of the meanings of the astrological houses in order to get a pertinent and well-defined answer. Very basically, the two Witnesses and the Judge can give a yes-or-no answer with some specifics of the process, as discussed elsewhere. However, a complex question may require examination of the symbol associated with that particular question. This requires a knowledge of the meanings of the houses. Further analysis of the question requires placing the planets for the date of the question in the chart, and this in turn requires a basic understanding of the meanings of the signs and the planets.

All questions should be directed to one or another of the *houses* of the geomancy chart once you have examined the meaning of the Judge and two Witnesses for a general answer. The house involved will give a more detailed answer by adding the meaning of the sign on the cusp, its ruler (if you are using astrology as well as divination), the symbol within the house, and any planets. While every house of the geomancy chart holds one symbol, not all houses will hold a planet.

Almost any question directed to geomancy can be related to one house or another. For example, all money questions can be directed to the Second House; all credit, tax, joint financial questions, to the Eighth House. In the following paragraphs, we list the most useful rulerships of each of the twelve houses of the geomancy chart. We also give the meanings of the planets and their rulerships, some description of the ways the signs of the zodiac act on the house cusps, and a brief description of the sixteen geomancy symbols. For a full discussion of the symbols, Judges and Witnesses, consult the interpretation section at the end of this book.

HOUSE RULERSHIPS

First House (Ascendant): personality of the querent and his or her personal tastes, likes and dislikes, general attitude, modes of self-expression; any new projects or contacts with new people; general physical well-being; the head.

Second House: money, income, possessions, sense of values, resources; the neck.

Third House: brothers and sisters, neighbors and relatives, short trips, means of transportation such as car or bicycle; means of communication such as telephone, two-way radios; messages and communications in general; travel within 300 miles of home base; involvement in local government, politics or groups (with Eleventh House); arms and lungs.

Fourth House: the home, family, security, real estate, agriculture, mining, second half of life, one of the parents, usually the mother; the stomach.

Fifth House: love affairs, children, creativity, speculation, recreation; the heart and chest.

Sixth House: health in general, regular employment, service given and received, working conditions, relationships with coworkers; small and large intestines.

Seventh House: marriage, partners, close friends, open enemies, competition, legal disputes; kidneys.

Eighth House: sexual relationships and general relations with the opposite sex, death, the occult, joint finances, legacies, taxes, credit; the sexual organs.

Ninth House: long-distance travel, higher education, religious views, philosophical beliefs, long-range planning, in-laws; the thighs.

Tenth House: career, status, reputation, independent business, dealings with government, appearances in the public eye, relationships with supervisors; the knees.

Eleventh House: friends, group affiliations, general social life, professional ties, hopes, wishes; the calves and ankles.

Twelfth House: illness, secrets, sorrows, the unconscious mind, dreams, sleep; the feet.

These are the most significant house rulerships, and the ones you are most likely to find useful. Rex Bill's book *Rulerships* is the ultimate source for all types of rulerships, by house, planet or sign.

THE PLANETS

The Sun: power, authority, the soul, spiritual energy, ego, creative drives; the center of being and existence, life itself. The Sun adds power, energy and success to any area of life it touches.

Occupations: advertising, all positions of authority, managerial and executive, all positions related to organizational ability, acting, banking, finance, government, jewelry, law, public relations.

Hobbies: community work, civic action, volunteer services, exercise and outdoor sports.

Activities: advertising, buying, selling, speculating, short trips, meeting people, anything involving groups or showmanship, putting up exhibits, running fairs and raffles, growing crops and taking care of health matters.

The Moon: personality, circumstances of this lifetime, fluctuation, moods, children, women, the home and family, the public and public attention; people as a group.

Occupations: caterer, domestic science, home economics, nursing, fisherman, navigator, sailor.

Hobbies: collecting stamps, antique furniture, anything to do with the sea and sailing.

Activities: any small change in routine, asking favors, borrowing or lending money, household activities such as baking, canning, cooking, freezing, washing and ironing, cleaning, taking care of small children.

Mercury: conscious thought, reasoning, speech, writing, power to learn and teach others, dexterity and manual skills, short travels.

Occupations: accountant, ambassador, bookkeeper, brokerage, clerk, critic, craftsman, debtor, disc jockey, doctor, editor, journalist, inspector, lecturer, librarian, linguist, medical technician, scientist, secretary, student, teacher, writer.

Hobbies: writing stories, watching TV, anything dealing with communication and the mass media.

Activities: bargaining, bookkeeping, dealing with lawyers or literary agents, publishing, filing, hiring employees, learning languages, literary work, placing ads, preparing accounts, studying, telephoning, visiting friends.

Venus: love, beauty, the arts, culture, individual affections, co-operation, charm, grace, desires, music, harmony.

Occupations: architect, artist, beautician, chiropractor, dancer, designer, domestic work, engineer, entertainer, fashion marketing, musician, painter, poet.

Hobbies: embroidery, making clothes, music, painting, sculpture, sewing, landscape gardening.

Activities: amusement, beauty care, courtship, dating, decorating homes, designing, getting together with friends, household improvements, planning parties, shopping.

Mars: sexual drives, physical energy, war, combat, competition, initiatives, courage and daring.

Occupations: barber, butcher, carpenter, chemist, construction worker, dentist, metal worker, surgeon, soldier.

Hobbies: anything that involves work with tools or machinery such as repairing cars, gardening, grafting, household improvements, wood working.

Activities: good for all business matters, mechanical affairs, buying or selling animals, dealing with contractors, hunting, undertaking study.

Jupiter: luck, bounty, optimism, generosity, truth, justice, expansion.

Occupations: counselor, doctor, educator, guardian, horse trainer, hunter, jockey, judge, lawyer, legislator, merchant, minister, pharmacist, psychologist, public analyst.

Hobbies: social clubs, travel.

Activities: activities involving charity, education or science, correspondence courses and self-improvement, reading, researching, studying.

Saturn: age, wisdom, experience, the past, history, government and politics, bones and teeth, the spinal column, conservatism, delays, caution.

Occupations: agronomist, builder, civil servant, excavator, farm worker, magistrate and justice, mathematician, mine worker, osteopath, plumber, politician, real estate agent, repairperson, shoemaker, printer.

Hobbies: dealing with public matters, farming or working with the soil, papermaking.

Activities: anything involving family ties or legal matters such as wills and estates, taking care of debts, dealing with lawyers, financing, joint money matters, real estate, relations with older people.

Uranus: change, suddenness, surprises, information from sources beyond the five physical senses, as in clairvoyance and revelation; astrology and astronomy; electricity, the future, impulses.

Occupations: aeronautics advisor, aerospace technician, broadcaster, electrician, government official, inventor, lecturer, radiologist, computers.

Hobbies: electronics, experimenting with ESP, novel ideas, the occult, studying, computer programming.

Activities: air travel, all partnerships, changes and adjustments, civil rights, new contacts, new ideas, new rules, patenting inventions, progress, social action, starting journeys.

Neptune: psychic phenomena and abilities, the sea, perfumes, oil, confusion, illusion, charity, universal love, the astral plane, idealism, sympathy, romance.

Occupations: chain store manager, character actor, chemist, diplomat, photographer, psychiatrist, secret agent, wine merchant, working with religious institutions, the shipping business and the sea.

Hobbies: acting, pets, photography, music, movies.

Activities: advertising, dealing with psychological upsets, health foods and resorts, large social affairs, night clubs, psychic healing, travel by water, restaurants, visits, welfare, working with institutions.

Pluto: fate, death and rebirth, renewal and rejuvenation, groups, unions, obsessions and compulsions, psychology, the occult.

Occupations: acrobatics, athletic manager, field of atomic energy, research breakthroughs, speculation, sports, stockbroker.

Hobbies: any purely personal endeavor, working with children.

Activities: anything dealing with energy and enthusiasm, skill and alertness, personal relationships, original thought, and pioneering.

THE SIGNS OF THE ZODIAC

Aries on a house cusp inclines to daring, energetic, pioneering, hasty, impatient, competitive action and plenty of it in the areas ruled by that house.

Taurus on the cusp of a house inclines to placid, calm, persistent, tenacious, inert, fixed attitudes in the areas ruled by that house, and a love of comfort and beauty.

Gemini on a house cusp inclines to curiosity and discussion about the areas ruled by the house, with many ideas and conversations, and action that is sporadic, and less of interest through boredom.

Cancer on a house cusp inclines to a strongly emotional attitude toward the areas ruled by the house, tenacious, sentimental, fluctuating in action, restless, protective and clannish.

Leo on a house cusp inclines to domineering, egocentric, but creative and courageous action in the areas of life ruled by the house. There is a demand for praise and attention.

Virgo on a house cusp inclines to perfectionism, criticism, attention to detail, willingness to serve, and concern for health in the areas of life ruled by the house.

Libra on a house cusp inclines to tact, refinement, harmony, intellectuality, and indecision in dealing with the affairs ruled by the house.

Scorpio on the cusp of a house inclines to passion, intensity, persistence and secretiveness in dealing with the affairs of the house involved.

Sagittarius on the house cusp inclines to optimism, generosity, adventurousness, and restlessness in dealing with the affairs of the house. Friendliness is a predominant characteristic.

Capricorn on the cusp of a house inclines to caution, conservatism, adherence to tradition, ambition, diplomacy in relation to the affairs of the house.

Aquarius on a house cusp takes a detached, independent, intellectual, impartial, scientific, experimental attitude in relation to affairs of the house.

Pisces on a house cusp takes an emotional, sensitive, intuitive, sympathetic, idealistic, sometimes vague or confused attitude toward affairs of the house in question.

THE SIXTEEN GEOMANCY SYMBOLS

Now that you have browsed through the astrological information, we present a brief description of the symbols used in geomancy, which are also astrologically oriented to the planets and signs of the zodiac.

The *Sun*-ruled symbols are Fortuna Major (Greater Fortune) and Fortuna Minor (Lesser Fortune).

O O	O
O O	O
O	O O
O	O O
Fortuna Major	Fortuna Minor
Sign Aquarius	Sign Taurus

The *Moon*-ruled symbols are Populus (People) and Via (Way, Pathway, Method).

O O	O
O O	O
O O	O
O O	O
Populus	Via
Sign Capricorn	Sign Leo

The *Mercury*-ruled symbols are Conjunctio (Union) and Albus (Wisdom).

O O	O O
O O	O
O	O
O O	O O
Albus	Conjunctio
Sign Cancer	Sign Virgo

The *Venus*-ruled symbols are Puella (Female) and Amissio (Loss).

Puella
Sign Libra

Amissio
Sign Scorpio

The *Mars*-ruled symbols are Puer (Male) and Rubeus (Anger).

Puer
Sign Aries

Rubeus
Sign Gemini

The *Jupiter*-ruled symbols are Acquisitio (Success) and Laetitia (Joy and Happiness).

Acquisitio
Sign Aries

Laetitia
Sign Taurus

The *Saturn*-ruled symbols are Carcer (Bondage) and Tristitia (Sorrow).

Carcer
Sign Pisces

Tristitia
Sign Scorpio

The symbol Cauda Draconis (Tail of the Dragon) is the South Node of the Moon.

```
    O
    O
    O
    O O
```
Cauda Draconis
Sign Sagittarius

The symbol Caput Draconis (Head of the Dragon) is the North Node of the Moon.

```
  O O
    O
    O
    O
```
Caput Draconis
Sign Virgo

A complete description of geomantic symbols is given in the section on interpretation at the back of this book.

A Note on the Outer Planets

The outer planets were unknown when geomancy was developed; therefore, the symbols relate only to the seven ancient planets, Sun through Saturn. If we were to assign a new planet as partial significator or ruler of a symbol, the following relationships would probably be the most acceptable: Pluto, the higher octave of Mars, would likely be associated to some extent with the symbol Rubeus. Neptune, as the higher octave of Venus, would probably have affinity with Amissio, or Loss, partially in material and partially in spiritual terms. Uranus, the higher octave of Mercury, would likely be connected with the symbol Wisdom, as Uranus rules sudden enlightenment and knowledge from sources beyond the senses. Rubeus reflects the angry side of Mars, just as Puer represents positive masculinity, and Mercury is related to wisdom, the kind gained through experience and understanding. Venus pertains to Amissio as this is the negative side of desire, the lack of fulfillment of that desire, much of the old saying, "Better to have loved and lost than never to have loved at all." One only feels a sense of loss if the object or person that is considered "lost" has been strongly desired. No one misses or feels the loss of anything *un*desirable.

In the process of interpretation, Rubeus and Pluto in a house can be considered a double dose of Rubeus, similar to Rubeus and Mars; Uranus and Albus in a house can be considered a double dose of Wisdom, similar to Mercury with Albus in a house; and Neptune with Amissio in a house can be considered a double dose of Loss, similar to Venus with Amissio in a house.

5

Constructing the Geomancy Chart

Every geomancy chart originates in the sixteen lines of dots drawn by the querent. From these dots, the four initial symbols (Mothers) are drawn up, and thence is the rest of the chart constructed.

Here is an example of 16 lines of dots:

Dots	Total	Symbol
. . . .	13	o
. . . .	7	o
. . . .	12	o o
. . . .	11	o
		—
. . . .	13	o
. . . .	13	o
. . . .	14	o o
. . . .	4	o o
		—
. . . . .	5	o
. . . . . .	6	o o
. . . .	9	o
. . . .	15	o
		—
. . . .	18	o o
. . . . .	5	o
. . . .	12	o o
. . . .	14	o o

The next step is to add up the number of dots on each line, as above.

For each *even* number, place *two circles* on the line next to the number.

For each *odd* number, place *one circle* on the line next to the number.

Remember to count the dots a second time to make sure the number is correct. Also remind the querent to make the dots large enough to be easily visible and distinguishable. Some like to make little circles.

Each group of four lines makes up one of the geomancy symbols. You now have the following four symbols with which to construct the remaining symbols, the two Witnesses and the final Judge of the question.

	Puer (Male)	Fortuna Minor (Lesser Fortune)	Puella (Female)	Rubeus (Anger)	
1.	o	o	o	o o	Heads
2.	o	o	o o	o	Necks
3.	o o	o o	o	o o	Bodies
4.	o	o o	o	o o	Feet

Note that next to each line of the symbols we have placed the descriptive terms "Heads," "Necks," "Bodies," and "Feet." These are the lines used to create the next four symbols, the Daughters:

Line 1 consists of o, o, o, o o. Arranging them in order, the symbol becomes:

o

o

o

o o

This symbol is Cauda Draconis, the Dragon's Tail.

Line 2 consists of o, o, o o, o. Arranging these circles in order, the symbol becomes:

o

o

o o

o

This symbol is Puer, or Male.

Line 3 consists of o o, o o, o, o o. Arranging these circles in order, the symbol becomes:

$$
\begin{matrix}
\circ & \circ \\
\circ & \circ \\
& \circ \\
\circ & \circ
\end{matrix}
$$

This symbol is Albus, or Wisdom.

Line 4 consists of o, o o, o, o o. Arranging these circles in order, the symbol becomes:

$$
\begin{matrix}
\circ & \\
\circ & \circ \\
\circ & \\
\circ & \circ
\end{matrix}
$$

This symbol is Amissio, or Loss.

To recap, in addition to the Mothers, the first four symbols, you now have the Daughters, symbols 5 through 8:

Cauda Draconis (Dagon's Tail)	Puer (Male)	Albus (Wisdom)	Amissio (Loss)
o	o	o o	o
o	o	o o	o o
o	o o	o	o
o o	o	o o	o o

The next four symbols, 9 through 12, are called the Nephews and are constructed by adding up the previous eight symbols in the following manner:

Mother 1	+	Mother 2	=	1st Nephew (Symbol 9)
Puer	+	Fortuna Minor	=	Tristitia (Sorrow)
o		o 2		o o
o		o 2		o o
o o		o o 4		o o
o		o o 3		o

Please note that we are adding the circles and using two circles for the even numbers and one circle for the odd numbers, just as we did with the original 16 lines of dots.

Mother 3	+	Mother 4	=	2nd Nephew (Symbol 10)
Puella	+	Rubeus	=	Via (Way, Path, Method)
o		o o 3		o
o o		o 3		o
o		o o 3		o
o		o o 3		o

Daughter 5	+	Daughter 6	=	3rd Nephew (Symbol 11)
Cauda Draconis	+	Puer	=	Fortuna Major
				(Greater Fortune)
o		o 2		o o
o		o 2		o o
o		o o 3		o
o o		o 3		o

Daughter 7	+	Daughter 8	=	4th Nephew (Symbol 12)
Albus	+	Amissio	=	Laetitia (Joy, Happiness)
o o		o 3		o
o o		o o 4		o o
o		o 2		o o
o o		o o 4		o o

In a similar manner, from the four Nephews are derived the two Witnesses. Here are the four Nephews:

Tristitia	Via	Fortuna Major	Laetitia
o o	o	o o	o
o o	o	o o	o o
o o	o	o	o o
o	o	o	o o

Nephew 1	+	Nephew 2	=	First Witness
Tristitia	+	Via	=	Cauda Draconis (Dragon's Tail)
o o		o 3		o
o o		o 3		o
o o		o 3		o
o		o 2		o o

Nephew 3	+	Nephew 4	=	Second Witness
Fortuna Major	+	Laetitia	=	Puella (Female)
o o		o 3		o
o o		o o 4		o o
o		o o 3		o
o		o o 3		o

From the two Witnesses, in a similar manner, we derive the final Judge of the question(s) being asked.

First Witness	+	Second Witness	=	Judge
Cauda Draconis	+	Puella	=	Acquisitio (Success)
o		o 2		o o
o		o o 3		o
o		o 2		o o
o o		o 3		o

On the following page is a geomancy chart in which the symbols have been placed in their correct order and positions. The symbols have also been placed in the correct houses of the horoscope chart, with the rising sign associated with the *First Mother* (first symbol) placed on the Ascendant, and the remaining signs following in order. Examine the chart carefully. The house positions used are those of Cornelius Agrippa. The first four symbols (Mothers) are in the Angular Houses of the horoscope; the second four symbols (5 through 8) in the Succedent Houses; and the final four symbols (Symbols 9 through 12) in the Cadent Houses.

The Angular Houses are 1, 10, 7 and 4; the Succedent Houses are 2, 11, 8, and 5; and the Cadent Houses are 9, 6, 3 and 12. This is the ordering of the symbols set up by the man who codified geomancy, Cornelius Agrippa, and is the method used throughout this book.

Astrological Geomancy

Name:_____ **Date:**_____March 1,1988_____

Mothers

I 1	II 10	III 7	IV 4
Puer	Fortuna Minor	Puella	Rubeus

Daughters

V 2	VI 11	VII 8	VIII 5
Cauda Draconis	Puer	Albus	Amissio

Nephews

IX 9	X 6	XI 3	XII 12
Tristitia	Via	Fortuna Major	Laetitia

Witnesses

I	II
Cauda Draconis	Puella

Judge

Acquisitio

6

Basic Astrology
for the Practitioner of Geomancy

The first necessary items you should memorize are the symbols for the planets and the signs of the zodiac. Here is a table which gives you that information, and also the symbols for the aspects and for direct and retrograde motion of the planets. Throughout this work we will spell out the names of signs and planets, to smooth the flow of comprehension. However, in the charts, only the symbols will be used.

SYMBOL KEY				
PLANETS	☉	Sun	♃	Jupiter
	☽	Moon	♄	Saturn
	☿	Mercury	♅	Uranus
	♀	Venus	♆	Neptune
	♂	Mars	♇	Pluto
SIGNS	♈	Aries	♎	Libra
	♉	Taurus	♏	Scorpio
	♊	Gemini	♐	Sagittarius
	♋	Cancer	♑	Capricorn
	♌	Leo	♒	Aquarius
	♍	Virgo	♓	Pisces
ASPECTS	☌	Conjunction	△	Trine
	ⅴ	Semisextile	⊼	Quincunx
	✳	Sextile	☍	Opposition
	□	Square		
MOTION	℞	Retrograde	D	Direct

25

On the following pages is a guide for finding the aspects between the planets by sign. In geomancy, we use only mundane astrology, which assigns aspects strictly by the signs the planets are in, eliminating the degrees and orbs of influence of modern astrology.

ASPECT FINDERS

Aries

Adverse   _____in Aries is square to_____in Cancer or Capricorn.

Adverse   _____in Aries is opposite to_____in Libra.

Adverse   _____in Aries is quincunx to_____in Virgo or Scorpio.

Favorable _____in Aries is semisextile to_____in Taurus or Pisces.

Favorable _____in Aries is sextile to_____in Gemini or Aquarius.

Favorable _____in Aries is trine to_____in Leo or Sagittarius.

Power   _____in Aries is conjunct to_____in Aries.

Taurus

Adverse   _____in Taurus is square to_____in Leo or Aquarius.

Adverse   _____in Taurus is opposite to_____in Scorpio.

Adverse   _____in Taurus is quincunx to_____in Libra or Sagittarius.

Favorable _____in Taurus is semisextile to_____in Aries or Gemini.

Favorable _____in Taurus is sextile to_____in Cancer or Pisces.

Favorable _____in Taurus is trine to_____in Virgo or Capricorn.

Power   _____in Taurus is conjunct to_____in Taurus.

Gemini

Adverse   _____in Gemini is square to_____in Virgo or Pisces.

Adverse   _____in Gemini is opposite to_____in Sagittarius.

Adverse   _____in Gemini is quincunx to_____in Scorpio or Capricorn.

Favorable _____in Gemini is semisextile to_____in Taurus or Cancer.

Favorable _____ in Gemini is sextile to _____ in Leo or Aries.

Favorable _____ in Gemini is trine to _____ in Libra or Aquarius.

Power _____ in Gemini is conjunct to _____ in Gemini.

Cancer

Adverse _____ in Cancer is square to _____ in Libra or Aries.

Adverse _____ in Cancer is opposite to _____ in Capricorn.

Adverse _____ in Cancer is quincunx to _____ in Sagittarius or Aquarius.

Favorable _____ in Cancer is semisextile to _____ in Gemini or Leo.

Favorable _____ in Cancer is sextile to _____ in Taurus or Virgo.

Favorable _____ in Cancer is trine to _____ in Scorpio or Pisces.

Power _____ in Cancer is conjunct to _____ in Cancer.

Leo

Adverse _____ in Leo is square to _____ in Taurus or Scorpio.

Adverse _____ in Leo is opposite to _____ in Aquarius.

Adverse _____ in Leo is quincunx to _____ in Capricorn or Pisces.

Favorable _____ in Leo is semisextile to _____ in Cancer or Virgo.

Favorable _____ in Leo is sextile to _____ in Gemini or Libra.

Favorable _____ in Leo is trine to _____ in Aries or Sagittarius.

Power _____ in Leo is conjunct to _____ in Leo.

Virgo

Adverse _____ in Virgo is square to _____ in Gemini or Sagittarius.

Adverse _____ in Virgo is opposite to _____ in Pisces.

Adverse _____ in Virgo is quincunx to _____ in Aries or Aquarius.

Favorable _____ in Virgo is semisextile to _____ in Leo or Libra.

Favorable _____ in Virgo is sextile to _____ in Cancer or Scorpio.

Favorable _____ in Virgo is trine to _____ in Taurus or Capricorn.

Power _____ in Virgo is conjunct to _____ in Virgo.

Libra

Adverse _____in Libra is square to_____in Cancer or Capricorn.

Adverse _____in Libra is opposite to_____in Aries.

Adverse _____in Libra is quincunx to_____in Pisces or Taurus.

Favorable _____in Libra is semisextile to_____in Virgo or Scorpio.

Favorable _____in Libra is sextile to_____in Leo or Sagittarius.

Favorable _____in Libra is trine to_____in Gemini or Aquarius.

Power _____in Libra is conjunct to_____in Libra.

Scorpio

Adverse _____in Scorpio is square to_____in Leo or Aquariusn.

Adverse _____in Scorpio is opposite to_____in Taurus.

Adverse _____in Scorpio is quincunx to_____in Aries or Gemini.

Favorable _____in Scorpio is semisextile to_____in Libra or
Sagittarius.

Favorable _____in Scorpio is sextile to_____in Virgo or Capricorn.

Favorable _____in Scorpio is trine to_____in Cancer or Pisces.

Power _____in Scorpio is conjunct to_____in Scorpio.

Sagittarius

Adverse _____in Sagittarius is square to_____in Virgo or Pisces.

Adverse _____in Sagittarius is opposite to_____in Gemini.

Adverse _____in Sagittarius is quincunx to_____in Taurus or
Cancer.

Favorable _____in Sagittarius is semisextile to_____in Scorpio or
Capricorn.

Favorable _____in Sagittarius is sextile to_____in Libra or Aquarius.

Favorable _____in Sagittarius is trine to_____in Aries or Leo.

Power _____in Sagittarius is conjunct to_____in Sagittarius.

Capricorn

Adverse _____in Capricorn is square to_____in Aries or Libra.

Adverse _____in Capricorn is opposite to_____in Cancer.

Adverse _____in Capricorn is quincunx to_____in Gemini or Leo.

Favorable _____in Capricorn is semisextile to_____in Sagittarius or Aquarius.

Favorable _____in Capricorn is sextile to_____in Scorpio or Pisces.

Favorable _____in Capricorn is trine to_____in Taurus or Virgo.

Power _____in Capricorn is conjunct to_____in Capricorn.

Aquarius

Adverse _____in Aquarius is square to_____in Taurus or Scorpio.

Adverse _____in Aquarius is opposite to_____in Leo.

Adverse _____in Aquarius is quincunx to_____in Cancer or Virgo.

Favorable _____in Aquarius is semisextile to_____in Capricorn or Pisces.

Favorable _____in Aquarius is sextile to_____in Sagittarius or Aries.

Favorable _____in Aquarius is trine to_____in Gemini or Libra.

Power _____in Aquarius is conjunct to_____in Aquarius.

Pisces

Adverse _____in Pisces is square to_____in Gemini or Sagittarius.

Adverse _____in Pisces is opposite to_____in Virgo.

Adverse _____in Pisces is quincunx to_____in Leo or Libra.

Favorable _____in Pisces is semisextile to_____in Aquarius or Aries.

Favorable _____in Pisces is sextile to_____in Capricorn or Taurus.

Favorable _____in Pisces is trine to_____in Cancer or Scorpio.

Power _____in Pisces is conjunct to_____in Pisces.

In the next chapter, the planetary positions are given for March 1, 1988:

Sun in Pisces
Moon in Leo
Mercury in Aquarius
Venus in Aries
Mars in Capricorn
Jupiter in Aries
Saturn in Capricorn
Uranus in Capricorn
Neptune in Capricorn
Pluto in Scorpio

Taking the Sun in Pisces as an example, we turn to the section "Pisces" in the aspect finder. Look up and down the signs on the right side for Leo, the position of the Moon. We find that *Sun in Pisces is quincunx to Moon in Leo*. This is a mildly *adverse* aspect, so the influences of the Sun and Moon do not blend well in this chart.

Continuing with the Sun in Pisces, we look at the right hand for Aquarius, and find that the Sun in Pisces is semisextile to Mercury in Aquarius, telling us, since the semisextile is favorable, that the influences of the Sun and Mercury work well together in this chart.

You can continue examining the relationships of the planets given above at your leisure.

7

Charting the Transiting Planets

Using astrological influences in combination with geomancy symbols is much simpler than regular horoscope work, for no calculations are required. The astrology used in geomancy is *mundane* astrology; that is, only the planets in the *signs* are considered both in placing the planets in the chart, and in interpreting any aspects.

Thus, a chart with Aries rising, the Sun in Leo, and Moon in Sagittarius, indicates that the Sun is in the Fifth House, the Moon is in the Ninth House, and the Sun forms a mundane trine to the Moon. You can consult the Aspect Finder outline to determine what aspects are formed once you place the planets in the signs and houses indicated on the date you draw up for the geomancy chart. To use the interpretative material, you need only know the 12 signs of the zodiac, and the names and symbols of the signs and planets. Obviously the experienced astrologer will be able to add quite a good deal to his or her interpretation, yet this book is designed for both the beginner in divination *and* the beginner in astrology.

Mundane astrology was the norm at the time geomancy was codified by Agrippa, for ephemerides of the exact positions of the planets were relatively unavailable, and often the astrologer did not even possess the equipment necessary to find the degree of a planet in the heavens. The impact of the planets was given refinement by the input of the individual querent in the form of the geomancy symbols drawn up into the combined chart.

Once you have determined the symbols that go into the chart, you will put the signs on the cusps of the houses, starting with the sign associated with the first symbol. Here are the symbols and their related zodiacal signs:

Fortuna Major—*Aquarius*
Fortuna Minor—*Taurus*
Via—*Leo*
Populus—*Capricorn*
Conjunctio—*Virgo*
Albus—*Cancer*
Puella—*Libra*
Amissio—*Scorpio*
Puer—*Aries*
Rubeus—*Gemini*
Acquisitio—*Aries*
Laetitia—*Taurus*
Carcer—*Pisces*
Tristitia—*Scorpio*
Caput Draconis—*Virgo*
Cauda Draconis—*Sagittarius*

For example, if the first symbol is Populus, Capricorn is the rising sign on the cusp of House 1, and the signs follow in order: Aquarius on 2, Pisces on 3, Aries on 4, Taurus on 5, Gemini on 6, Cancer on 7, Leo on 8, Virgo on 9, Libra on 10, Scorpio on 11 and Sagittarius on 12.

The natural order of the signs is as follows: Aries, Taurus, Gemini, Cancer, Leo, Virgo, Libra, Scorpio, Sagittarius, Capricorn, Aquarius and Pisces. No matter what sign you start with, you continue down the list and then go back to the beginning for the remaining houses; just as we did when Capricorn, Aquarius and Pisces were placed on Houses 1, 2, and 3, and we went back to the beginning, Aries, for House 4.

Once the house cusps are in place by sign, you are ready to look at a page in an ephemeris and find the date on which the geomancy chart was started, when the querent drew up the 16 lines of dots. Below is a table from *Llewellyn's 1988 Daily Planetary Guide*, showing the planetary positions for the month of March, 1988.

Day Jour		S. T.			LONGITUDE for 0h										
					☉	☽	☿	♀	♂	♃	♄	♅	♆	♇	☊ True
		h	m	s	° ′ ″	° ′ ″	° ′	° ′	° ′	° ′	° ′	° ′	° ′	° ′	° ′
T	1	10	36	04	10 ♓ 37 26	11 ♌ 43 34	14 ♒ 39	23 ♈ 51	05 ♑ 06	28 ♈ 27	01 ♑ 12	00 ♑ 32	09 ♑ 43	12 ♏R 31	23 ♓R 08
W	2	10	40	00	11 37 37	23 32 15	15 16	25 00	05 47	28 39	01 15	00 33	09 45	12 30	23 05
Th	3	10	43	57	12 37 47	05 ♍ 22 04	15 57	26 08	06 27	28 51	01 19	00 35	09 46	12 30	23 03
F	4	10	47	53	13 37 54	17 15 08	16 42	27 16	07 08	29 03	01 23	00 37	09 47	12 29	23 03
Sa	5	10	51	50	14 38 00	29 13 26	17 31	28 23	07 48	29 15	01 26	00 38	09 48	12 28	23 D 03
Su	6	10	55	46	15 38 03	11 ♎ 18 59	18 23	29 31	08 29	29 27	01 30	00 40	09 50	12 28	23 03
M	7	10	59	43	16 38 06	23 33 52	19 19	00 ♉ 38	09 09	29 39	01 33	00 41	09 51	12 27	23 04
T	8	11	03	39	17 38 06	06 ♏ 00 23	20 17	01 45	09 50	29 52	01 37	00 43	09 52	12 26	23 05
W	9	11	07	36	18 38 05	18 41 01	21 18	02 52	10 30	00 ♉ 04	01 40	00 44	09 53	12 25	23 05
Th	10	11	11	33	19 38 02	01 ♐ 38 22	22 21	03 59	11 11	00 17	01 43	00 46	09 54	12 25	23 05
F	11	11	15	29	20 37 58	14 54 51	23 27	05 06	11 51	00 29	01 46	00 47	09 55	12 24	23 06
Sa	12	11	19	26	21 37 52	28 32 25	24 35	06 12	12 32	00 42	01 49	00 48	09 56	12 23	23 R 06
Su	13	11	23	22	22 37 44	12 ♑ 31 59	25 45	07 18	13 12	00 55	01 52	00 49	09 57	12 22	23 05
M	14	11	27	19	23 37 35	26 52 54	26 57	08 24	13 53	01 08	01 55	00 50	09 58	12 21	23 D 06
T	15	11	31	15	24 37 24	11 ♒ 32 31	28 11	09 29	14 33	01 21	01 57	00 52	09 59	12 20	23 06
W	16	11	35	12	25 37 11	26 25 56	29 27	10 35	15 14	01 34	02 00	00 53	10 00	12 19	23 06
Th	17	11	39	08	26 36 56	11 ♓ 26 13	00 ♓ 45	11 40	15 54	01 47	02 02	00 54	10 01	12 18	23 06
F	18	11	43	05	27 36 39	26 25 10	02 04	12 44	16 35	02 00	02 05	00 55	10 02	12 17	23 R 06
Sa	19	11	47	02	28 36 21	11 ♈ 14 20	03 26	13 49	17 15	02 13	02 07	00 55	10 02	12 16	23 06
Su	20	11	50	58	29 36 00	25 46 18	04 48	14 53	17 56	02 26	02 09	00 56	10 03	12 15	23 05
M	21	11	54	55	00 ♈ 35 37	09 ♉ 55 36	06 13	15 57	18 36	02 39	02 11	00 57	10 04	12 14	23 04
T	22	11	58	51	01 35 12	23 39 13	07 38	17 01	19 17	02 53	02 13	00 58	10 05	12 13	23 03
W	23	12	02	48	02 34 45	06 ♊ 56 36	09 06	18 04	19 57	03 06	02 15	00 59	10 05	12 11	23 02
Th	24	12	06	44	03 34 16	19 49 15	10 34	19 07	20 38	03 19	02 17	00 59	10 06	12 10	23 02
F	25	12	10	41	04 33 44	02 ♋ 20 17	12 04	20 10	21 18	03 33	02 19	01 00	10 07	12 09	23 01
Sa	26	12	14	37	05 33 10	14 33 46	13 36	21 12	21 59	03 46	02 20	01 00	10 07	12 08	23 D 02
Su	27	12	18	34	06 32 33	26 34 16	15 09	22 14	22 39	04 00	02 22	01 01	10 08	12 07	23 02
M	28	12	22	31	07 31 55	08 ♌ 26 27	16 43	23 16	23 20	04 13	02 23	01 01	10 08	12 05	23 03
T	29	12	26	27	08 31 14	20 14 48	18 19	24 17	24 00	04 27	02 25	01 02	10 09	12 04	23 05
W	30	12	30	24	09 30 30	02 ♍ 03 26	19 56	25 18	24 41	04 41	02 26	01 02	10 09	12 03	23 06
Th	31	12	34	20	10 ♈ 29 45	13 ♍ 55 56	21 ♓ 35	26 ♉ 19	25 ♑ 21	04 ♉ 54	02 ♑ 27	01 ♑ 02	10 ♑ 09	12 ♏R 01	23 ♓ 07

Planetary Positions for March 1988

Let us examine the planetary positions for March 1, 1988. The Sun is in Pisces, the Moon in Leo, Mercury in Aquarius, Venus in Aries, Mars in Capricorn, Jupiter in Aries, Saturn in Capricorn, Uranus in Capricorn, Neptune in Capricorn, and Pluto in Scorpio. Turn to the sample, which has the house cusps starting with Aries. For the first symbol, Puer, we have the chart on page 34.

You are now ready to look up the interpretations for the two Witnesses and the Judge for the answers to questions in general. Look in the Judge section under Acquisitio made up of the Witnesses Cauda Draconis and Puella, in that order.

You can now also look in the section on Symbol and Planet Interpretations for the combination of symbol with planet in the house, and for symbols alone in the house as follows:

Puer with Venus in the 1st House.
Puer with Jupiter in the 1st House.
Cauda Draconis alone in the 2nd House.
Tristitia alone in the 3rd House.
Rubeus alone in the 4th House.
Amissio with the Moon in the 5th House.
Via alone in the 6th House.
Puella alone in the 7th House.
Albus with Pluto in the 8th House.
Tristitia alone in the 9th House.
Fortuna Minor with Mars in the 10th House.
Fortuna Minor with Saturn in the 10th House.
Fortuna Minor with Uranus in the 10th House.
Fortuna Minor with Neptune in the 10th House.
Puer with Mercury in the 11th House.
Laetitia with the Sun in the 12th House.

When you have finished looking up the components in all twelve houses, you have the foundation of the General Life Reading, covering all areas of life, for the individual whose chart is represented here. For further refinements, refer to the Aspect Finder section to include the aspects of the planets in your interpretation.

Astrological Geomancy

Name:_____   Date:_____March 1,1988_____

Mothers

I	1	II	10	III	7	IV	4
Puer		Fortuna Minor		Puella		Rubeus	

Daughters

V	2	VI	11	VII	8	VIII	5
Cauda Draconis		Puer		Albus		Amissio	

Nephews

IX	9	X	6	XI	3	XII	12
Tristitia		Via		Tristitia		Laetitia	

Witnesses

I	II
Cauda Draconis	Puella

Judge

Acquistitio

8

Sample Geomancy Interpretations

We will now consider the question on which this chart is based, "Will I get anywhere with my profession this year?"

• •	2	○ ○	
• • • • • •	6	○ ○	
•	1	○	
• • • •	4	○ ○	
		___	
• • • •	4	○ ○	
• • • • • • • • • •	10	○ ○	
• •	2	○ ○	
•	1	○	
		___	
• • •	3	○	
• • • • • •	5	○	
• • •	3	○	
• • • • • •	6	○ ○	
		___	
•	1	○	
• • • • • • • • • •	9	○	
• • • • • •	5	○	
• • •	3	○	

Here we have the 16 lines of dots with the first four symbols:

I		II		III		IV	
	o o		o o		o		o
	o o		o o		o		o
	o		o o		o		o
	o o		o		o o		o
	Albus		**Tristitia**		**Cauda**		**Via**
					Draconis		

The next four symbols are derived from the heads, necks, bodies and feet of the first four symbols:

Heads: o o, o o, o, o, placed in order: V   o o
      o o
      o
      o
      Fortuna Major

Necks: o o, o o, o, o, placed in order: VI   o o
      o o
      o
      o
      Fortuna Major

Bodies: o, o o, o, o, placed in order: VII   o
      o o
      o
      o
      Puella

Feet: o o, o, o o, o, placed in order.: VIII   o o
      o
      o o
      o
      Acquisitio

The next four symbols are derived from combining Symbols I and II, III and IV, V and VI, and VII and VIII, as follows:

```
I      ○ ○      II      ○ ○      4          IX      ○ ○
       ○ ○              ○ ○      4                  ○ ○
        ○               ○ ○      3                   ○
       ○ ○               ○       3                   ○
      Albus            Tristitia                Fortuna Major


III     ○       IV      ○        2          X       ○ ○
        ○       IV      ○        2          X       ○ ○
        ○               ○        2                  ○ ○
       ○ ○               ○       3                   ○
   Cauda Draconis       Via                      Tristitia


V      ○ ○      VI      ○ ○      4          XI      ○ ○
       ○ ○              ○ ○      4                  ○ ○
        ○               ○        2                  ○ ○
        ○               ○        2                  ○ ○
   Fortuna Major   Fortuna Major                  Populus


VII     ○       VIII    ○ ○      3          XII      ○
       ○ ○               ○       3                   ○
        ○               ○ ○      3                   ○
        ○               ○        2                  ○ ○
      Puella          Acquisitio                   Cauda
                                                  Draconis
```

From the last four symbols, IX and X, and XI and XII, we derive the two Witnesses, thus:

```
IX     ○ ○      X       ○ ○      4      Witness  I      ○ ○
       ○ ○              ○ ○      4                      ○ ○
        ○               ○ ○      3                       ○
        ○               ○        2                      ○ ○
   Fortuna Major       Tristitia                       Albus
```

XI		XII		3	Witness II	
o o		o		3		o
o o		o		3		o
o o		o		3		o
o o		o o		4		o o
Populus		Cauda Draconis				Cauda Draconis

From the two Witnesses, we derive the Judge:

Witness I	Witness II		Judge
o o	o	3	o
o o	o	3	o
o	o	2	o o
o o	o o	4	o o
Albus	Cauda Draconis		Fortuna Minor

The completed chart is on page 39.

INTERPRETATION OF THE CHART
FOR QUERENT A

Let us review the question: "Will I get anywhere with my profession this coming year?"

Career relates to the Tenth House of the chart, where we find the symbol Tristitia, denoting some sorrow and sadness. Since this is a Saturn-ruled symbol, it signifies delays. The Sixth House of regular work also has the symbol Tristitia, or sorrow, again denoting problems and delays. The Second House of income, however, has the symbol Fortuna Major, indicating an excellent income from the career or job. The problem, then, is not financial, but emotional, and emotional satisfaction is not indicated by this combination of symbols.

Turning to the astrological interpretation, we find Aries on the cusp of the Tenth with ruler Mars retrograde herein, signifying frustrations. The Sixth House of work has Saturn and Uranus, indicating many ups and downs. Both planets are opposite Jupiter, ruler of the Sixth, in the Twelfth (again of limiting circumstances). The Second House of money has no planets, but has Leo on the cusp, ruler Sun in the Fourth in Libra, conjunct Mercury, trine to Jupiter, and opposite Mars in the Tenth. Sun-Mars indicates money is not the problem, as Sun-Jupiter favors income. Thus we have the same basic interpretation from both symbols and planets, with added details.

Astrological Geomancy

Name: _Querent A_   **Date:** _October 8, 1988_

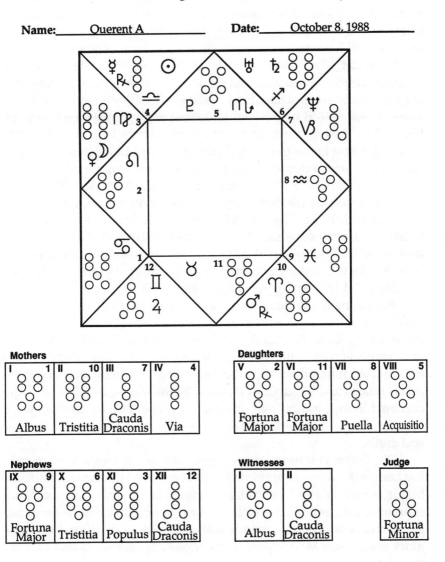

Mothers

I 1	II 10	III 7	IV 4
Albus	Tristitia	Cauda Draconis	Via

Daughters

V 2	VI 11	VII 8	VIII 5
Fortuna Major	Fortuna Major	Puella	Acquisitio

Nephews

IX 9	X 6	XI 3	XII 12
Fortuna Major	Tristitia	Populus	Cauda Draconis

Witnesses

I	II
Albus	Cauda Draconis

Judge

Fortuna Minor

Turning to the two Witnesses and the Judge, we find that the combination of Albus and Cauda Draconis, producing the Judge Fortuna Minor, is adverse for all questions, as the first Witness is good, but the second adverse. The South Node always indicates a drain on resources and a negative influence on events. Therefore, the answer to the question is that the coming year will show many frustrations and you will have to struggle to achieve any kind of satisfaction. We can then add, after glancing at the other symbols in the chart, that while professional interests will show little advancement in the coming year, other areas of life offer great opportunities for advancement. The querent would be advised to devote energy into those areas of life, rather than fighting delaying circumstances in career matters. One important factor in doing readings of any kind is to never leave the querent with a depressing negative answer. Emphasize the other options in life that will prove more fruitful and satisfying if pursued in place of career (or whatever) options that show no promise.

PLEASE NOTE: The two Witnesses and Judge refer strictly to the initial question upon which the chart was constructed. All other questions should be referred to the houses they are ruled by for interpretation. When the Judge section states "Traditionally adverse for all questions," it is referring to *all possible initial questions.*

Returning to the chart, we look for some of the favorable symbols to offset the prognostications for career matters. The First House has the symbol Albus (Wisdom), relating to personality, self-expression, new projects and contacts, all of which provide opportunities for learning, teaching others and communicating knowledge to the public. Albus relates to the sign Cancer, ruled by the Moon, which is in Virgo conjunct Venus, indicating personal happiness and satisfaction with new contacts and projects, and an inclination to self-expression in arts and crafts.

The Second House of money, possessions, income, and resources has Leo on the cusp (as previously discussed) and the symbol Fortuna Major which is the best possible signifier of financial gain and economic prosperity. The querent will be able to achieve financial goals, and desired poossessions with a minimum of effort. Sun conjunct retrograde Mercury suggests money from efforts and investments of the past.

The Third House of short trips and messages, neighbors and relatives, immediate environment, has Virgo on the cusp, ruler Mercury in Libra, and Venus and the Moon herein, giving pleasure in public contacts locally, success in advertising and sales, and opportunities to both learn and teach in congenial circumstances. You get along well with relatives and neighbors, and enjoy local entertainment. Daily routine is smooth and predictable, with Via or Pathway the symbol here.

The Fourth House of home and family, real estate and security, has Libra on the cusp, ruler Venus in the Third, and Sun and Mercury herein. Family harmony and discussions are favored, as are intellectual and mental development, creativity carried on in the home, work in interior decoration and home furnishing, or family counseling. Profits from real estate purchased in the past may be realized now.

The Fifth House of love affairs, children, creativity and speculation has Scorpio on the cusp, ruler Pluto herein, and the symbol Acquisitio (Success) herein, suggesting luck in lotteries and particularly in sweepstakes. Your affections are constantly renewed by contact with a loved one. Watch for possibilities of jealousy, as Pluto is mildly adverse to both Mars and Jupiter. Minor conflicts with career needs are also indicated. However, Aquisitio is Jupiter-ruled and suggests excellent profits from speculative investments. If expecting a child, you are more likely to have a boy than a girl.

The Sixth House of health and work has Sagittarius on the cusp, ruler Jupiter the Twelfth House of illness, and Saturn and Uranus herein, opposing Jupiter, with the symbol Tristitia (Sorrow), denoting tensions and ups and downs on the job, and dealing with unhappy people. Good health can be expected despite the extremes of the job at this time.

The Seventh House of marriage and partners has Capricorn on the cusp, ruler Saturn in the Sixth and Neptune herein, with the symbol Cauda Draconis (Tail of the Dragon), indicating some loneliness because a close relationship is ending or turning sour. Saturn suggests sensitivity, as does Neptune, and the need to be reassured of the affections of a loved one. Anxieties about possible lawsuits may develop. Neptune does trine the Moon in the Third, and cards and letters or a phone call from a distant loved one may cheer up the querent.

The Eighth House of sex, death, the occult and joint funds has independent Aquarius on the cusp, ruler Uranus in the Sixth, and Puella, the female figure herein, giving this person clairvoyant abilities and favoring the practice of astrology. Puella suggests there is some good fortune in joint finances, possibly a sudden windfall under the influence of Uranus. The querent has great charm and magnetic attraction for the opposite sex.

The Ninth House of long-distance travel, higher education, religion and philosophy has Pisces on the cusp, ruler Neptune in the Fifth, and Fortuna Major (Greater Fortune) herein, indicating pleasure in studies and travel, and highly favorable for a long trip in the near future, particularly by sea. Religious mysticism is highly appealing to the querent, and beliefs are based on emotional foundations. There is a great love of harmony and peace.

The Tenth House of career, status, business of one's own has aggressive, combative Aries on the cusp of the Tenth, Mars retrograde herein, and the symbol Tristitia (as discussed previously) indicating many frustrations, delays and disappointments in career matters, but some progress, as Mars trines Saturn and Uranus in the Sixth House of work.

The Eleventh House of friends, hopes, wishes, clubs, social life has placid, calm Taurus on the cusp, Venus ruler in Virgo, and Fortuna Major (Greater Fortune) herein, suggesting the querent will benefit both materially and spiritually from joining a job-related social or professional group, expanding his or her circle of friends and acquaintances, and developing good social relationships. Venus in the Third indicates travel and discussions with friends. Shared local entertainment, is favored. Great popularity can be attained now, as Venus conjoins the Moon, ruling the public.

The Twelfth House of illness, secrets, sorrows, the unconscious mind, dreams and sleep has Gemini on the cusp, ruler Mercury in Libra, and Jupiter herein, trine to Mercury, indicating an essentially positive and optimistic inner spirit, and the likelihood of prophetic dreams in sleep. The content of these dreams may not be the most promising, as Cauda Draconis (Tail of the Dragon) is here, indicating that the unconscious mind is particularly sensitive to negative emotions and events of the future. Many ideas and habits end, but the ultimate results are favorable. Any chronic ailment can be overcome with care and effort now, as Jupiter is highly protective. Jupiter opposes Saturn and Uranus, warning the individual not to overexert or expect to accomplish too much on the job. Jupiter's opposition to Saturn especially augurs poorly for any business ventures, as any adverse aspect between the economic planets, Jupiter and Saturn, augurs poorly for financial gain and economic prosperity.

To summarize, this is a year in which the querent should focus on more personal and social activities, rather than pressing for progress in career matters. Studies and travel, expansion of the mental and physical horizons, and encompassing new people are most highly favored.

We will now consider the question, "What will be the highlights in my life this coming year?" This is a way of expressing a desire for a general life reading.

Dots	Number	Symbol
• • • • • • • •	7	o
• • •	3	o
• • • • •	5	o
• • • • • •	6	o o
		—
• • • •	4	o o
• • • • • • •	6	o o
• • • • • • • • •	9	o
• • • • • • •	7	o
		—
• • • • • • • •	8	o o
•	1	o
• • • • •	5	o
• • • • • •	6	o o
		—
• • • • • •	6	o o
• • • • • •	6	o o
• •	2	o o
• • • • • • • •	8	o o

Here we have the 16 lines of dots with the first four symbols:

I		II		III		IV	
	o		o o		o o		o o
	o		o o		o		o o
	o		o		o		o o
	o o		o		o o		o o
Cauda Draconis		**Fortuna Major**		**Conjunctio**		**Populus**	

The next four symbols are derived from the heads, necks, bodies and feet of the first four symbols:

Heads: o, o o, o o, o o, placed in order:

V
```
    o
   o o
   o o
   o o
```
Laetitia

Necks: o, o o, o, o o, placed in order:

VI
```
    o
   o o
    o
   o o
```
Amissio

Bodies: o, o, o, o o, placed in order:

VII
```
    o
    o
    o
   o o
```
Cauda Draconis

Feet: o o, o, o o, o o, placed in order:

VIII
```
   o o
    o
   o o
   o o
```
Rubeus

The next four symbols are derived from combining Symbols I and II, III and IV, V and VI, and VII and VIII, as follows:

I		II			IX	
o		o o	3			o
o		o o	3			o
o		o	2			o o
o o		o	3			o
Cauda Draconis		Fortuna Major				Puer

III		IV			X	
o o		o o	4			o o
o		o o	3			o
o		o o	3			o
o o		o o	4			o o
Conjunctio		Populus				Conjunctio

V		VI			XI	
○		○		2	○ ○	
○ ○		○ ○		4	○ ○	
○ ○		○		3	○	
○ ○		○ ○		4	○ ○	
Laetitia		Amissio			Albus	

VII		VIII			XII	
○		○ ○		3	○	
○		○		2	○ ○	
○		○ ○		3	○	
○ ○		○ ○		4	○ ○	
Cauda Draconis		Rubeus			Amissio	

From the last four symbols, IX and X, and XI and XII, we derive the two Witnesses, thus:

IX		X			Witness I	
○		○ ○		3	○	
○		○		2	○ ○	
○ ○		○		3	○	
○		○ ○		3	○	
Puer		Conjunctio			Puella	

XI		XII			Witness II	
○ ○		○		3	○	
○ ○		○ ○		4	○ ○	
○		○		2	○ ○	
○ ○		○ ○		4	○ ○	
Albus		Amissio			Laetitia	

From the two Witnesses, we derive the Judge:

Witness I	Witness II		Judge
○	○	2	○ ○
○ ○	○ ○	4	○ ○
○	○ ○	3	○
○	○ ○	3	○
Puella	Laetitia		Fortuna Major

The completed chart is found on page 46.

Astrological Geomancy

Name: Querent B   **Date:** October 8, 1988

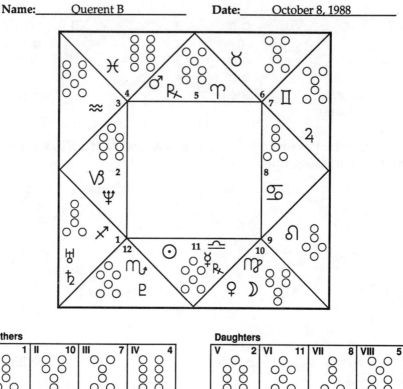

Mothers

I	1	II	10	III	7	IV	4
Cauda Draconis		Fortuna Major		Conjunctio		Populus	

Daughters

V	2	VI	11	VII	8	VIII	5
Laetitia		Amissio		Cauda Draconis		Rubeus	

Nephews

IX	9	X	6	XI	3	XII	12
Puer		Conjunctio		Albus		Amissio	

Witnesses

I	II
Puella	Laetitia

Judge

Fortuna Major

INTERPRETATION OF THE CHART
FOR QUERENT B

Let us review the question: "What will be the highlights in my life this coming year?" This is a good question in that it gives the time-frame for the geomancy chart—it will be in effect for the coming year, in varying degrees for different areas of life.

The general outlook for the coming year is reflected in the Judge, which is Fortuna Major, indicating the greatest good fortune, both materially and spiritually, and indicating that the individual will make much progress in his or her goals in life. The two Witnesses are Puella and Laetitia, reflecting that it is indeed a woman's chart that is being read. The general emotional atmosphere is indicated by Laetitia (Joy or Happiness). For the most part, it looks as if the goals dearest to the heart of the individual will be fulfilled.

The initial symbol is Cauda Draconis (Tail of the Dragon), ruling the sign Sagittarius, which is rising in the chart. At the time the chart was done, both Saturn and Uranus were in the Ascendant, indicating many ups and downs, and the conflict between stability and innovation, security and risk, which create a negative influence on this person's new projects and contacts. There are difficulties in reconciling past experiences with opportunities or hopes for the future. The minor anxieties generated by the Tail of the Dragon are a reflection of the question itself—looking for the high points in order to escape the negative feelings of the moment.

In summary, there is an attraction to new ways of thinking and acting, but past experiences tend to hold the individual back.

The Second House has the symbol Laetitia (Joy and Happiness), denoting sufficient income to keep the person happy and fulfill his or her needs. Neptune is in this house, indicating that spiritual values outweigh the material, so the meaning of Laetitia is transmuted to a desire to give as well as to receive. Good for profits from occult arts (the individual is a professional psychic), and from any interests in the arts and music.

The Third House has the symbol Albus (Wisdom) and no planets, with Aquarius on the cusp of the house and Uranus in the Ascendant, indicating learning experiences of personal value abound for this individual. Impulsive pleasure trips are more frequent than usual, and environmental conditions are favorable.

The Fourth House has the symbol Populus, ruled by the Moon, and no planets herein, with Pisces on the cusp and Neptune in the

Second in favorable aspect to the Moon, indicating a love of privacy which will be satisfied, with peace and harmony in relation to family members, as Neptune also trines Venus with the Moon. The individual may redecorate or express his or her personality more strongly in the home this year.

The Fifth House has the symbol Rubeus (Anger and Frustraton) with Aries on the cusp and Mars retrograde herein, indicating conflicts in love, frustrations in creative efforts, difficulties in dealing with children, and potential accidents in pursuit of hazardous sports or recreation. Mars opposes Mercury and the Sun and squares Neptune in the Second, warning against taking any risks such as gambling or letting social life (Sun and Mercury in the Eleventh) interfere with closer relationships and more appealing personal recreation.

The Sixth House of health and work has the symbol Conjunctio (Union) with Taurus on the cusp and no planets herein. Ruler Venus in Virgo with the Moon, indicates success depending on ability to cooperate and share responsibilities and rewards with others. Good for a working partnership with a woman, and for dealing with women and very young children in general. This area of life offers no problems, but rather opportunities to form closer productive partnerships and thus achieve advancement, as Venus and the Moon are in the Tenth House.

The Seventh House of marriage and partners has the symbol Conjunctio (Union) with Jupiter herein and Gemini on the cusp. Since this person is a palm-reader (Gemini rules the hands) and the Seventh refers to counseling on a one-to-one basis, Jupiter here suggests an increase in the number of readings this individual will be doing, and favors collaboration in producing a book that is of interest to the public. Marriage is a possibility if the individual is interested, as many new and cheerful people will be entering this person's life. Business partnerships are exceptionally profitable.

The Eighth House of sex, death, the occult and joint funds has the symbol Cauda Draconis (Tail of the Dragon), indicating many negative spiritual influences operating in this person's work life—many people with problems who will need a spiritual life, but which will create a drain on this individual. Because the Moon rules Cancer on the cusp, work in the occult area will be profitable and lead to greater public attention and approval (Moon and Venus in the Tenth). The orientation is toward the occult rather than romance. Moon and Venus do square Saturn and Uranus, so the individual's initiatives and personality will sometimes conflict with opportunies for career advancement.

The Ninth House of long-distance travel and higher education has the symbol Puer (Male), indicating a possible meeting of interest with a man from a distant land or different background. It also suggests that initiative is important, since this house also rules publishing; action could lead to the publication of a book. Studies are also highly favored for advancement, as is teaching, for the Ninth has Leo on the cusp, ruler Sun in the Eleventh of groups and social life, with Mercury. Learning and teaching in a social setting thus is highly favored.

The Tenth House of career and profession has the symbol Fortuna Major, Greater Fortune, both materially and spiritually, suggesting that the major focus for the coming year will be on career advancement and prominence in public. Moon and Venus in this house especially indicate that women will be supportive, will work with women, the arts, music, counseling, social work, and will all be highly favored and successful this coming year.

The Eleventh House of friends, groups and social life has the symbol Amissio (Loss) with Sun and Mercury retrograde herein, suggesting that preoccupation with career matters will cut into time for social life. Sun here indicates success, Mercury retrograde many conversations and exchanges with old friends, so Amissio only indicates that there will be a decrease in social interaction this year.

The Twelfth House of illness, secrets, sorrows, the unconscious mind, dreams and sleep has the symbol Amissio with ruler Pluto herein, suggesting some loss of sleep and privacy due to heavy career demands, but also strengthened recuperative abilities and increased spiritual energy to devote to work.

To review, then, the highlights of the year are career success in the two directions that particularly interest this individual, some romantic or social conflicts, good finances, and good relations with the family.

We will now consider the specific question, "Will this job change work out favorably?"

· · · · · · ·	7 o
· · · · · · ·	7 o
· · · · · · ·	7 o
· · · · · · ·	7 o
	___
· · · · · · ·	7 o
· · · · · · ·	7 o
· · · · · · ·	7 o
· · · · · · ·	7 o
	___
· · · · · · ·	7 o
· · · · · · ·	7 o
· · · · ·	5 o
· · · · · · ·	7 o
	___
· · · · · · ·	7 o
· · · · · · ·	7 o
· · · · · · · · · ·	10 o o
· · · · ·	5 o

Here we have the 16 lines of dots with the first four symbols:

I	o	II	o	III	o	IV	o
	o		o		o		o
	o		o		o		o o
	o		o		o		o
	Via		**Via**		**Via**		**Puer**

The next four symbols are derived from the heads, necks, bodies and feet of the first four symbols:

Heads: o, o, o, o, placed in order:
                                        V   o

    o

    o

    o

    Via

Necks: o, o, o, o, placed in order:
                                      VI   o

    o

    o

    o

    Via

Bodies: o, o, o, o o, placed in order:

VII   o
        o
        o
        o o
Cauda Draconis

Feet: o, o, o, o, placed in order:

VIII   o
        o
        o
        o
Via

The next four symbols are derived from combining Symbols I and II, III and IV, V and VI, and VII and VIII, as follows:

I		II			IX	
o		o	2		o o	
o		o	2		o o	
o		o	2		o o	
o		o	2		o o	
Via		Via			Populus	

III		IV				
o		o	2		o o	
o		o	2		o o	
o		o o	3		o	
o		o	2		o o	
Via		Puer			Albus	

V		VI			XI	
o		o	2		o o	
o		o	2		o o	
o		o	2		o o	
o		o	2		o o	
Via		Via			Populus	

VII		VIII			XII	
o		o	2		o o	
o		o	2		o o	
o		o	2		o o	
o o		o	3		o	
Cauda Draconis		Via			Tristitia	

From the last four Symbols, IX and X, and XI and XII, we derive the two Witnesses, thus:

IX		X			Witness I	
	o o		o o	4		o o
	o o		o o	4		o o
	o o		o	3		o
	o o		o o	4		o o
	Populus		Albus			Albus

XI		XII			Witness II	
	o o		o o	4		o o
	o o		o o	4		o o
	o o		o o	4		o o
	o o		o	3		o
	Populus		Tristitia			Tristitia

From the two Witnesses, we derive the Judge:

Witness I	Witness II		Judge
o o	o o	4	o o
o o	o o	4	o o
o	o o	3	o
o o	o	3	o
Albus	Tristitia		Fortuna Major

The completed chart is shown on page 53.

INTERPRETATION OF THE CHART
FOR QUERENT C

Let us review the initial question, "Will this job change work out favorably?"

The Final Judge of the chart is Fortuna Major (Greater Fortune), made up of the two Witnesses, Albus (Wisdom) and Tristitia (Sorrow). This combination is traditionally considered favorable except for questions about inheritance, news or opponents. Therefore, generally speaking, the job change will have favorable results. Although the second Witness is adverse, the Judge's favor acts as atonement. Some anxieties will attend this job change.

The Sixth and Tenth Houses relate to job and career, while the Second House relates to income earned as a result of work. The Tenth

Astrological Geomancy

Name: Querent C   **Date:** October 22, 1988

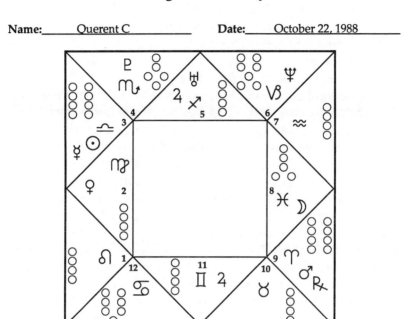

Mothers

I	1	II	10	III	7	IV	4
Via		Via		Via		Puer	

Daughters

V	2	VI	11	VII	8	VIII	5
Via		Via		Cauda Draconis		Via	

Nephews

IX	9	X	6	XI	3	XII	12
Populus		Albus		Populus		Tristitia	

Witnesses

I	II
Albus	Tristitia

Judge

Fortuna Major

House has the symbol Via (Pathway) with Taurus, a fixed sign on the cusp, and no planet herein, indicating that the change is set, and that the querent will pursue the job regardless of this chart's ultimate outcome. The Sixth House has Capricorn on the cusp, Neptune herein, and the symbol Albus (Wisdom), indicating that his or her experience is valuable to future success, and that there are elements of confusion or a lot of mathematical demands, since Neptune rules mathematics (the job involves accounting). Ruler Saturn is mildly favorable from Sagittarius, so the job is likely to last.

The Second House of money has the symbol Via, Venus herein and Virgo on the cusp, indicating clerical efforts, and satisfaction with the income, as well as a standard of performance which will be easy for the querent to follow. Good methods are important in the work itself and the resulting income. Venus is trine to Neptune, so the income will definitely be helpful. In brief, it looks like the job change will be favorable. There may be problems in communications or commuting, as Neptune squares Sun and Mercury in the Third House, or in dealing with customers, as Populus (People) is in the Third House. This is emphasized by Venus opposite the Moon, ruling the public, in the Eighth, which may involve problems with debt collection. Neptune is also square to Mars retrograde in the Ninth, showing impatience and haste in achieving the long-range plans of this job.

In a general life reading, we find that the planets are scattered in a variety of houses, indicating that the querent has his or her fingers in a lot of pies, juggling activities to accomplish many goals. The First House has the symbol Via (Pathway) with Leo rising and the Sun in Libra in the Third, indicating that his or her attention and personal efforts are directed to maintaining some short-range goals, involving a lot of travel and communications. The querent has great personal pride.

The Second House of money and possessions has the symbol Via again, with Virgo on the cusp and Venus herein, suggesting an income from clerical work, work with nutrition and health, and from the arts, music, and crafts. A regular income is indicated, but there may be varied temporary jobs.

The Third House of short trips and messages has the symbol Populus, with Sun and Mercury herein, and Libra on the cusp, suggesting success in the communications and transportation industries, in dealing with community affairs, and in organizing a daily routine that is efficient and smooth. These qualities are exemplified in the ideal secretary, the telephone operator, the translator. Populus as the symbol reinforces success in dealing with large numbers of people in these and other socio-communicative capacities.

The Fourth House of the home and family has the symbol Puer, the planet Pluto, and Scorpio, ruled by Pluto, on the cusp. Together Pluto and Puer, the male symbol, suggest a transition in the domestic setting and initiatives, a move to a new locale, extensive redecorating, or a new direction for the man in the family, in the near future.

The Fifth House of love, children, creativity and speculation has the symbol Via, Sagittarius on the cusp, Saturn and Uranus herein, and ruler Jupiter opposite in the Eleventh House, indicating that the ups and downs in the lives of loved ones have an impact on wider social circles; or that friends will be drawn into the immediate circle of affection and recreation more frequently in the near future. Gambling and speculation should be avoided, along with hazardous recreation, as Saturn and Uranus combine to upset your sense of timing, thereby causing accidents.

The Sixth House of health and work has the symbol Albus (Wisdom), Neptune, Capricorn on the cusp, and ruler Saturn in the Fifth, suggesting some creative type of work, with emphasis on the intuitive and psychic abilities. Success in dealings with the public is not excessive, for Neptune squares Mercury and the Sun in the Third. Clients may be too demanding and create an energy drain. Neptune does favor the Moon in the Eighth of occult activities, supporting psychic development and expression; however, some limits must be maintained. The Seventh House of marriage and partners has the symbol Via, Aquarius on the cusp, and ruler Uranus in the Fifth, restrained by Saturn, and suggesting a continued state of independence, mainly by choice, as the symbol Via (Pathway) indicates a set course. This course is by choice, a pattern developed in the past and held to at this time.

The Eighth House of sex, death, the occult and joint finances has the symbol Cauda Draconis (Tail of the Dragon), Pisces on the cusp, Moon herein, and Neptune in Capricorn, signifying much work in the psychic field, but, as indicated by Neptune square to Moon-Mercury, the presence of the Tail of the Dragon suggests too many dealings with people who are depressed and unhappy, thus creating an emotional drain as well as demanding answers. Pisces increases the emotional reaction and sympathies, but again the negative, receptive side of this sign inclines the person to take the problems home. Sexual relations are romantic, but the querent is easily turned off now.

The Ninth House of long-distance travel and higher education has the symbol Populus, Mars retrograde herein, and Aries on the cusp, indicating the desire for new beginnings and contacts with varied people; but Mars opposing Sun-Mercury in the Third, and all three planets square to Neptune in the Sixth of health, warns him or her to be wary of drunken drivers, and to exert great caution in travel generally. No long trips should be undertaken in the immediate future. This is probably the strongest indication in the chart, as the Sun is involved, ruling the Ascendant of physical well-being.

The Tenth House of career and business of one's own has the symbol Via, and Taurus on the cusp, ruled by Venus in Virgo, ruler also of the Libra planets. Focus career interests on Venus pursuits, such as the arts, music, culture; in Virgo, on the crafts and physical beauty derived from good diet and health maintenance, areas in which this person may teach or sell products successfully. Note that Via shows up frequently in this chart, indicating that this person has already set his or her course in life in most cases, or that there are definite opportunities and openings in various areas of life. Via also can indicate that a choice is necessary, as more than one pathway may appear.

The Eleventh House of friends, social life, group activities, has the symbol Via, Jupiter herein, Gemini on the cusp, ruler Mercury in Libra, and Mercury and the Sun trine to Jupiter, a highly protective and beneficial influence which suggests many social contacts, other than professional, which balance the drains of work with cheer, optimism, supportive friends and group cooperation. Again there may be choices of social life, but the inner pathway will lead this person to ever more positive social contacts.

The Twelfth House of illness, secrets, sorrows, the unconscious mind, dreams and sleep has the symbol Tristitia (Sorrow), Cancer on the cusp, and the Moon in Pisces in the Eighth, indicating too many psychic messages that are depressing in nature, or too many depressing people, particularly as Cancer also relates to the public. Moon squares Jupiter, so there is much optimism and cheer among friends, and family, as the Moon trines Pluto. Home is actually the best cure for the ailments of dealing with the public. There may be some premonitory dreams of events which affect large numbers of people.

In summing up the chart, the lunar symbols, Populus and Via, appear frequently. There is also a T-Square (Mars opposite Mercury and Sun, all square to Neptune) and a Grand Square (Saturn and Uranus square to the Moon, square to Jupiter, and Jupiter square to Venus). All this contributes to tension and scattering of energies. Fortunately, the lunar symbols indicate that these influences are all very transitory. This is a stressful period in the person's life which will not last very long.

We will now consider the question, "Will I win millions in the lottery?"

• •	2	o o
• • • • • •	6	o o
• • • • • • • •	8	o o
• • •	3	o
		—
• • • •	4	o o
• • • •	4	o o
• • • • • • • •	8	o o
• • • •	4	o o
		—
• • • • • •	6	o o
•	1	o
• • • • • • • • • •	10	o o
• • • • • •	6	o o
		—
• • • • • • • •	7	o
• • • • • •	5	o
• • •	3	o
• • •	3	o

Here we have the 16 lines of dots with the first four symbols:

I		II		III		IV	
	o o		o o		o o		o
	o o		o o		o		o
	o o		o o		o o		o
	o		o o		o o		o
Tristitia		**Populus**		**Rubeus**		**Via**	

The next four symbols are derived from the heads, necks, bodies and feet of the first four symbols:

Heads: o o, o o, o o, o, placed in order:

V
o o
o o
o o
o
Tristitia

Necks: o o, o o, o, o, placed in order:

VI
o o
o o
o
o
Fortuna Major

Bodies: o o, o o, o o, o, placed in order:

VII
o o
o o
o o
o
Tristitia

Feet: o, o o, o o, o, placed in order:

VIII
o
o o
o o
o
Carcer

The next four symbols are derived from combining Symbols I and II, III and IV, V and VI, and VII and VIII, as follows:

I		II			IX	
o o		o o	4		o o	
o o		o o	4		o o	
o o		o o	4		o o	
o		o o	3		o	
Tristitia		Populus			Tristitia	

III		IV			X	
o o		o	3		o	
o		o	2		o o	
o o		o	3		o	
o o		o	3		o	
Rubeus		Via			Puella	

V	○ ○	VI	○ ○	4	XI	○ ○
	○ ○		○ ○	4		○ ○
	○ ○		○	3		○
	○		○	2		○ ○
	Tristitia		Fortuna Major			Albus

VII	○ ○	VIII	○	3	XII	○
	○ ○		○ ○	4		○ ○
	○ ○		○ ○	4		○ ○
	○		○	2		○ ○
	Tristitia		Carcer			Laetitia

From the last four symbols, IX and X, and XI and XII, we derive the two Witnesses, thus:

IX	○ ○	X	○	3	Witness I	○
	○ ○		○ ○	4		○ ○
	○ ○		○	3		○
	○		○	2		○ ○
	Tristitia		Puella			Amissio

XI	○ ○	XII	○	3	Witness II	○
	○ ○		○ ○	4		○ ○
	○		○ ○	3		○
	○ ○		○ ○	4		○ ○
	Albus		Laetitia			Amissio

From the two Witnesses, we derive the Judge:

Witness I	Witness II		Judge
○	○	2	○ ○
○ ○	○ ○	4	○ ○
○	○	2	○ ○
○ ○	○ ○	4	○ ○
Amissio	Amissio		Populus

The completed chart for Querent D is shown on page 60.

Astrological Geomancy

Name: _____Querent D_____   **Date:** _____October 22, 1988_____

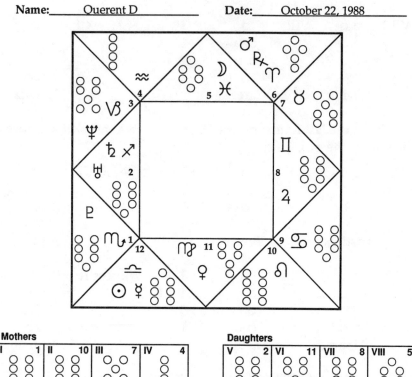

Mothers

I	1	II	10	III	7	IV	4
Tristitia		Populus		Rubeus		Via	

Daughters

V	2	VI	11	VII	8	VIII	5
Tristitia		Fortuna Major		Tristitia		Carcer	

Nephews

IX	9	X	6	XI	3	XII	12
Tristitia		Puella		Albus		Laetitia	

Witnesses

I	II
Amissio	Amissio

Judge

Populus

INTERPRETATION OF THE CHART
FOR QUERENT D

Let us recap the question, "Will I win millions in the lottery?"

The final Judge is Populus, made up of the two Witnesses, Amissio and Amissio. This combination is traditionally adverse for all questions; therefore, in answer to the immediate question, it is unlikely this person will win any money in the lottery. Looking to the Fifth House of the chart, which rules gambling, we find the symbol Carcer (Bondage), suggesting the compulsive gambler, with Pisces on the cusp and the Moon herein, and ruler Neptune in Capricorn in the Third. Moon is part of a Grand Square formed by Moon square to Jupiter in the Eighth (exaggerated hope and optimism), with Venus also square to Jupiter (wishful thinking and extravagance), and to Saturn and Uranus, which also square the Moon. The Grand Square tends to dissipate energies, and is focused in the financial and speculative houses, and the house of hopes and wishes. The planets support the significance of the Judge and two Witnesses, that the person will not win a lot of money on a lottery.

Turning to the general life reading, we find Tristitia (Sorrow) in the Ascendant of personality, self-expression, new projects and contacts, along with Pluto, ruler of the Ascending sign, Scorpio, suggesting transitions in the personal life that are inevitable. Some such changes bring pessimism rather than happiness. Joint finances or debts may be involved.

The Second House of money and income has Sagittarius on the cusp, Saturn and Uranus herein, indicating many ups and downs in finances, and the symbol Sorrow, Tristitia, again, indicating that there is definite worry about possessions and economic affairs, particularly as this house is part of the Grand Square of tensions.

The Third House of short trips and messages, neighbors and relatives, immediate environment has Neptune herein, Capricorn on the cusp, ruler Saturn in the Second, and the symbol Albus (Wisdom), indicating a psychic sensitivity to local events, and the ability to teach others and to spread the psychic word—excellent for the writer, publisher, bookseller in occult subjects. Neptune has a sextile to Pluto, which helps alleviate personal problems; Neptune also has a sextile to the Moon in the Fifth, suggesting pleasurable recreation and fondness for loved ones and children. However, Neptune is part of a T-Square involving Mars in the Sixth, opposed to Sun and Mercury in the Twelfth, square to Neptune in the Third which suggests confusion in travel, ailments such as allergies or kidney problems, and inner tensions which can create health problems.

The Fourth House of the home, family, real estate, security, has the symbol Via, and Aquarius on the cusp, with Saturn conjunct Uranus in the Second, indicating some restraints or restrictions in normal family and domestic activities and the need to economize on domestic expenses. However, Via, or Pathway, suggests a regular home routine, and Aquarius suggests that much of the normal freedom and independence is retained.

The Fifth House of love, creativity and speculation has been discussed in part, with Moon here, Pisces on the cusp, and the symbol Carcer, indicating many continuing responsibilities for children, a comfortable habit pattern in love, and a love of solitude, the arts, music and peace in recreation and creative interests. Moon trine to Pluto indicates that recreation and love are rejuvenating influences, but Moon square to Jupiter suggests excessive generosity and spending on credit for loved ones.

The Sixth House of health and work has Aries on the cusp, ruler Mars herein and retrograde, and the symbol Puella, ruled by Venus, favoring any work in the arts, culture, counseling and beauty. Mars indicates health problems which may be connected to high blood pressure, kidney ailments, headaches and allergies, as Mars opposes Sun and Mercury in the Twelfth, and squares Neptune, creating allergic sensitivities to the environment, and problems with work. Mars is also mildly adverse to Venus, creating some problems in work. The querent should avoid tension-producing situations, disputes in the course of work, and violent people.

The Seventh House of marriage and partners has Taurus on the cusp, ruler Venus in the Eleventh of social life, and Rubeus herein, denoting Anger and Frustration, and some tension in connection with close relationships, perhaps disputes with the spouse. Here a social atmosphere and shared group interests can take the edge off such disputes, as Venus is in the Eleventh House. No planets directly affect this house, but Rubeus suggests the querent be cautious in legal affairs.

The Eighth House of sex, death, the occult and joint funds has Gemini on the cusp, ruler Mercury in the Twelfth, and Jupiter, the Greater Benefic herein, with the symbol Tristitia, indicating that the individual is successful in dealing with unhappy feelings, and successful in any occult interests. There is definitely an improvement in joint finances coming up in the near future. Jupiter opposes Saturn and Uranus, however, warning against too much spending on credit or trust in joint business dealings. The querent should avoid giving others credit.

The Ninth House of higher education, long-distance travel, religion and philosophy has Cancer on the cusp, ruler Moon in Pisces in the Fifth, and the symbol Tristitia (Sorrow) herein, suggesting the desire to travel, study, and expand the mental and physical horizons, but also indicating some pessimism about the future and long-range plans. There is excessive sympathy with problems of others. Travel is not recommended now, nor expensive studies.

The Tenth House of career, status, business of your own, has proud, creative Leo on the cusp, ruler Sun in the Twelfth, and Populus (People) herein, suggesting success in a business catering to the public, in one of the Twelfth House areas, such as metaphysics, mental counseling, or health activities. Sun conjoins Mercury, favoring communications of a private nature, and again, counseling and analysis. Leo suggests a business dependent on the querent's own unique personality and individuality. There are no planets in this house, so influences are indirect, through the ruler, the Sun, which opposes Mars and squares Neptune in the Third, suggesting difficulties with helpers or workers, and with communications or transit involved in business or work. Nonetheless, Sun trines Jupiter, indicating ultimate success.

The Eleventh House of friends, groups, social life, has Virgo on the cusp, ruler Mercury in Libra, and Venus herein, with the symbol Fortuna Major (Greater Fortune), indicating success in any activities that involve social life, social organizations, friends, and cooperative ventures. There is great happiness in social life, which can alleviate some of the problems indicated in areas where the symbol Tristitia, or Sorrow, appears. Mercury and Venus are in mutual reception in each other's sign, similar to a conjunction of power, indicating that the querent has a position of social influence.

The Twelfth House of illness, secrets, sorrows, the unconscious mind, dreams and sleep, has harmonious, balanced Libra on the cusp, ruler Venus in the Eleventh, and Sun and Mercury herein, with the symbol Laetitia (Joy and Happiness), indicating excellent health or a sense of inner well-being, a positive inner attitude despite any external problems, and success in applying counseling methods to resolve the problems of others.

In summation, this querent has a number of areas in life that produce a sense of pessimism or bring disappointments; but the inner self is contented and happy, and solitude is frequently preferred to activities shared with others, however profitable or comforting they may be.

We will now consider the question, "What will my creative energies tap into in 1989?"

Dots	Number	Circles
• • • •	4	o o
• • •	3	o
•	1	o
• • • • •	5	o
• • •	3	o
• • • • •	5	o
• • • • • • •	7	o
• • • •	4	o o
• • •	3	o
•	1	o
• •	2	o o
• • •	3	o
• • •	3	o
• •	2	o o
•	1	o
• • • • • • •	7	o

Here we have the 16 lines of dots with the first four symbols:

I	II	III	IV
o o	o	o	o
o	o	o	o o
o	o	o o	o
o	o o	o	o
Caput Draconis	Cauda Draconis	Puer	Puella

The next four symbols are derived from the heads, necks, bodies and feet of the first four symbols:

Heads: o o, o, o, o, placed in order:

V
```
  o o
   o
   o
   o
```
Caput Draconis

Necks: o, o, o, o o, placed in order:

VI
```
   o
   o
   o
  o o
```
Cauda Draconis

Bodies: o, o, o o, o, placed in order:

VII
```
   o
   o
  o o
   o
```
Puer

Feet: o, o o, o, o, placed in order.:

VIII
```
   o
  o o
   o
   o
```
Puella

The next four symbols are derived from combining Symbols I and II, III and IV, V and VI, and VII and VIII, as follows:

I
```
  o o
   o
   o
   o
```
Caput
Draconis

II
```
   o      3
   o      2
   o      2
  o o     3
```
Cauda
Draconis

IX
```
   o
  o o
  o o
   o
```
Carcer

III
```
   o
   o
  o o
   o
```
Puer

IV
```
   o      2
  o o     3
   o      3
   o      2
```
Puella

X
```
  o o
   o
   o
  o o
```
Conjunctio

V		VI			XI	
	o o		o	3		o
	o		o	2		o o
	o		o	2		o o
	o		o o	3		o
	Caput Draconis		Cauda Draconis			Carcer

VII		VIII			XII	
	o		o	2		o o
	o		o o	3		o
	o o		o	3		o
	o		o	2		o o
	Puer		Puella			Conjunctio

From the last four symbols, IX and X, and XI and XII, we derive the two Witnesses, thus:

IX		X			Witness I	
	o		o o	3		o
	o o		o	3		o
	o o		o	3		o
	o		o o	3		o
	Carcer		Conjunctio			Via

XI		XII			Witness II	
	o		o o	3		o
	o o		o	3		o
	o o		o	3		o
	o		o o	3		o
	Carcer		Conjunctio			Via

From the two Witnesses, we derive the Judge:

Witness I	Witness II	Judge
o	o	o o
o	o	o o
o	o	o o
o	o	o o
Via	Via	Populus

The completed chart is shown on page 67.

Astrological Geomancy

Name: Querent E   **Date:** October 8, 1988

Mothers

I 1	II 10	III 7	IV 4
Caput Draconis	Cauda Draconis	Puer	Puella

Daughters

V 2	VI 11	VII 8	VIII 5
Caput Draconis	Cauda Draconis	Puer	Puella

Nephews

IX 9	X 6	XI 3	XII 12
Carcer	Conjunctio	Carcer	Conjunctio

Witnesses

I	II
Via	Via

Judge

Populus

INTERPRETATION OF THE CHART
FOR QUERENT E

Let us recap the question, "What will my creative energies tap into in 1989?"

The Final Judge of the question is Populus (People), made up of the Witnesses Via and Via. Both are lunar symbols, indicating that the querent will be reaching into the unconscious mind, and into the Akashic Records, where all history, ideas and thoughts of humankind are recorded, and will also be applying intuitive abilities in creative work this coming year. The querent's activities will fluctuate with the waxing and waning of the Moon, and creative ideas need to be grasped immediately and worked upon to avoid losing the opportunity of the moment. People are the greatest source of creative stimulation this coming year, so the querent should make as many new contacts as possible during the period from New to Full Moon. This combination of Witnesses and Judge is traditionally favorable for all activities except career, due to the fluctuating quality of the ruling Moon.

Turning to the general life reading, we find the symbol Caput Draconis (Head of the Dragon), representing new beginnings and the gateway to higher realms, in the Ascendant of personality, self-expression, new contacts and projects, with its related sign Virgo on the cusp, and Moon and Venus herein, highly favorable for any interest in the arts, culture and music, and giving added charm and ability to deal well with the public and gain the cooperation of others for new projects.

The Second House of money and possessions has the Head of the Dragon, with Libra on the cusp, and Sun here with Mercury retrograde, signaling financial success and accumulation of material goods and possessions. Mercury retrograde indicates financial gain from skills of the past which have not been used, but will again be applied. An interest in antiques, historical items and research work is also favored. Money may be earned now through the sale of possessions, or from payments for work done in the past. The Head of the Dragon also suggests new beginnings, and thus new sources of income, from arts, music, counseling, and creative efforts.

The Third House of short trips and messages, neighbors and relatives, and immediate environment, has Scorpio on the cusp, ruler Pluto herein, and the symbol Carcer (Bondage), indicating a heavy daily routine of necessary activities with little time to spare for recreation or simple conversation. Much planning must be done to make the most efficient use of available time. Avoid too many "duty visits."

The Fourth House of home and family has Sagittarius on the cusp, ruler Jupiter opposing in the Tenth of career, and Saturn and Uranus herein with the symbol Puella, ruled by Venus, again suggesting that the querent (a female) dominates her home and domestic situation; but there are many ups and downs in domestic life, due to ambitions and opportunities in career advancement, as Saturn and Uranus oppose Jupiter. The querent enjoys her home, but does not have time to spend there.

The Fifth House of love affairs, children, creativity and speculation has Capricorn on the cusp, ruler Saturn in the Fourth, and Neptune herein with the symbol Puella (Female) related to Venus, suggesting creative expression in the arts, music, and social activities. Although recreation and pleasure are under the influence of Saturn, ruler of Capricorn, the combined Fourth and Fifth suggest creative efforts pursued in the home, and talents developed now will be used more extensively in later years. Neptune suggests romantic ideals, but with Capricorn, a lack of opportunity due to love of career. Neptune is the focus of a T-Square formed by Sun and Mercury opposite Mars, square to Neptune, warning against gambling or speculation, and tense situations in love. Creative painting and photography are highly favorable.

The Sixth House of health and work has independent Aquarius on the cusp, ruler Uranus in the Fourth, and the symbol Conjunctio (Union), suggesting that joining a union or work-related professional group is highly recommended. Work is intimately shared and interdependent with the work of others, so all efforts must be made to cooperate and get along with coworkers, who also need to realize the need for harmonious interaction on the job. The querent's health seems excellent, a good union of healthy mind and body.

The Seventh House of marriage and partners has Pisces, ruled by Neptune on the cusp, and the symbol Puer (Male), indicating there will be opportunities for forming an intimate relationship based on love this coming year, as ruler Neptune is in the Fifth House of love. However, financial pressures may interfere with the relationship, as Neptune is the focus of a T-Square of dynamic energy and tension. Legal disputes are to be avoided if possible this year.

The Eighth House of sex, death, the occult and joint finances has aggressive Aries on the cusp, ruler Mars retrograde herein, and the Male symbol, Puer, herein, suggesting that the querent will see her share of violence and death, in connection with work in the health field. On a more personal level, there will also be sexual tensions or disputes with men who make themselves obnoxious. Credit spending is to be avoided, as Mars opposes Sun and Mercury in the Second House of money; the querent should also avoid lending or borrowing money, for the time being. Occult activities may generate psychic manifestations, so the querent should exert careful control.

The Ninth House of long-distance travel, higher education, religion and philosophy has Taurus on the cusp, indicating that the querent has deeply fixed and rooted philosophical beliefs. Ruler Venus is in Virgo, generating some self-criticism, as well as a demand for perfection in behavior of others. The symbol Carcer (Bondage) indicates a strong sense of duty and a somewhat pessimistic attitude toward life. However, Carcer is ruled by Saturn and gives ability to make long-range plans, while Venus in Virgo enables the querent to finalize the details of plans, and thus carry them out to successful completion. There is no strong desire to travel, as the querent enjoys the comforts and familiarity of home. As the querent is now a student as well as a worker, Carcer indicates the burden of carrying on both activities successfully.

The Tenth House of career, status, reputation, dealings with government and authority figures, and business of one's own, has intellectual, alert, curious communicative Gemini on the cusp, ruler Mercury in the house of money, and Jupiter herein, making this a year of career success and financial gain; although the symbol Cauda Draconis (Tail of the Dragon) indicates some negative influences and dealings with the lower kingdom—on the material plane, in a health career, there are always the ill and their problems to treat. Note that this symbol combined with Jupiter, a positive planet, is more easily explained or interpreted with a knowledge of the querent's career.

The Eleventh House of friends, social life, groups, has Cancer on the cusp, ruler Moon in Virgo and rising, and the symbol Cauda Draconis (Tail of the Dragon), indicating that a pleasant social life is desired. The querent has many friends, but there are influences operating which limit social life—the combined role of student and worker is the most obvious cause for the symbol Cauda Draconis. There are also casual friends who are more of a burden and take up more time and energy than the querent should be expending on them.

The Twelfth House of illness, secrets, sorrows, the unconscious mind, dreams, sleep, has Leo on the cusp, ruler Sun in Libra with Mercury, and the symbol Conjunctio (Union) herein, the same symbol that appeared in the Sixth House of health and work, again suggesting good mental and physical health. Sun ruling gives much vitality, but, opposed to Mars, warns of accident potential or inner frustrations. Conjunctio suggests the union of the querent with spiritual forces in sleep, and thus psychic messages through dreams.

In effect, this is an interesting chart with strong lunar dominance; Moon rises in the chart, and, in Virgo, indicates a quest for perfection in all areas of personal life.

We will now consider the question, "When will I feel deeper, dramatic psychic experiences?"

• • • • • • • • • •	10	○ ○
• • • • • • • • • • • • •	13	○
• • • • • • • • • •	10	○ ○
• • • • • • • • • •	10	○ ○
		—
• • • • • • • •	8	○ ○
• • • • • • • •	8	○ ○
• • • • • • • • •	9	○
• • • • • • • •	8	○ ○
		—
• • • • • • • • • • •	11	○
• • • • •	5	○
• • • • • • •	7	○
• • • •	4	○ ○
		—
• • • • •	5	○
• • • • •	5	○
• • • • • •	6	○ ○
• • • • •	5	○

Here we have the 16 lines of dots with the first four symbols:

I		II		III		IV	
	○ ○		○ ○		○		○
	○		○ ○		○		○
	○ ○		○		○		○ ○
	○ ○		○ ○		○ ○		○
Rubeus		**Albus**		**Cauda Draconis**		**Puer**	

The next four symbols are derived from the heads, necks, bodies and feet of the first four symbols:

Heads: o o, o o, o, o, placed in order:

V	o o
	o o
	o
	o
	Fortuna Major

Necks: o, o o, o, o, placed in order:

VI	o
	o o
	o
	o
	Puella

Bodies: o o, o, o, o o, placed in order:

VII	o o
	o
	o
	o o
	Conjunctio

Feet: o o, o o, o o, o, placed in order.:

VIII	o o
	o o
	o o
	o
	Tristitia

The next four symbols are derived from combining Symbols I and II, III and IV, V and VI, and VII and VIII, as follows:

I		II		4		IX	
	o o		o o	4			o o
	o		o o	3			o
	o o		o	3			o
	o o		o o	4			o o
	Rubeus		**Albus**				**Conjunctio**

III		IV				X	
	o		o	2			o o
	o		o	2			o o
	o		o o	3			o
	o o		o	3			o
	Cauda Draconis		**Puer**				**Fortuna Major**

V		VI			XI	
	o o		o	3		o
	o o		o o	4		o o
	o		o	2		o o
	o		o	2		o o
Fortuna Major		Puella			Laetitia	

VII		VIII			XII	
	o o		o o	4		o o
	o		o o	3		o
	o		o o	3		o
	o o		o	3		o
Conjunctio		Tristitia			Caput Draconis	

From the last four symbols, IX and X, and XI and XII, we derive the two Witnesses, thus:

IX		X			Witness I	
	o o		o o	4		o o
	o		o o	3		o
	o		o	2		o o
	o o		o	3		o
Conjunctio		Fortuna Major			Acquisitio	

XI		XII			Witness II	
	o		o o	3		o
	o o		o	3		o
	o o		o	3		o
	o o		o	3		o
Laetitia		Caput Draconis			Via	

From the two Witnesses, we derive the Judge:

Witness I	Witness II		Judge
o o	o	3	o
o	o	2	o o
o o	o	3	o
o	o	2	o o
Acquisitio	Via		Amissio

The completed chart is shown on page 74.

Astrological Geomancy

Name: _____Querent F_____   **Date:**_____November 12, 1988_____

Mothers

I	1	II	10	III	7	IV	4
Rubeus		Albus		Cauda Draconis		Puer	

Daughters

V	2	VI	11	VII	8	VIII	5
Fortuna Major		Puella		Conjunctio		Tristitia	

Nephews

IX	9	X	6	XI	3	XII	12
Conjunctio		Fortuna Major		Laetitia		Caput Draconis	

Witnesses

I	II
Acquistio	Via

Judge

Amissio

INTERPRETATION OF THE CHART
FOR QUERENT F

Let us recap the question, "When will I feel deeper, dramatic psychic experiences?"

The final Judge of the question is Amissio (Loss), made up of the symbols or Witnesses, Acquisitio (Success) and Via (Pathway). Intuitively I read this as Success in following the correct methods (Via) of psychic development that will bring the experiences the querent desires when there is a need; in other words, a period of problems and losses will result in ability to draw more strongly on psychic powers, for self-preservation. The same may be true in professional psychic work—only those in need of such help will find successful help from the querent. There will be no manifestations purely for pleasure or personal satisfaction. Traditionally this combination of Witnesses and Judge is mildly favorable for all questions except love, lawsuits, and similar pursuits. In this case, the answer is a mildly favorable one, but timing, in answer to the *when* of this querent, will be determined by astrological factors in the chart.

Psychic abilities are generally ruled by Neptune. Neptune is in the Eighth House of the occult in the chart, with Saturn and Uranus, indicating that much power and many experiences are available to the querent on the psychic level—but Capricorn is on the cusp indicating that necessity will rule in determining how much psychic success the querent has. Experiences should become more vivid in the near future, as Saturn and Uranus approach their conjunctions to Neptune. The symbol here is Conjunctio (Union), and this suggests that the cooperation of a spirit guide is necessary. Conjunctio is Mercury-ruled, and Mercury conjoins both Pluto and the Sun in Scorpio, the natural Eighth House sign, in the Sixth House of health, work and basic necessities. A great deal of psychic ability is present, but the querent must exercise self-control, will power and persistence in following a careful method to stimulate psychic responsiveness.

Turning to the general life reading, the First House of self-expression, new projects and contacts has the symbol Rubeus (Anger and Frustration), with its related sign, Gemini, rising, ruler Mercury in intense Scorpio, and Jupiter, the Greater Benefic herein. Unfortunately, Jupiter's influence may simply exaggerate the irritability and impatience of Rubeus, inducing the querent to leap into situations without examining possible hazards. Jupiter opposes the Moon in the seventh, suggesting that those closest to the querent stimulate this impatience and frustration.

The Second House of money, possessions, income, and resources has Cancer on the cusp, ruler Moon in Sagittarius, and Fortuna Major (Greater Fortune) herein, auguring well for good income, financial security, and accumulation of desired possessions. Financial success may come through a profitable partnership or a wealthy marriage. Travel, teaching, publishing, and public contacts are favored.

The Third House of short trips and messages, neighbors and relatives, and immediate environment, has Leo on the cusp, ruler Sun in Scorpio, and Laetitia (Joy and Happiness) herein, suggesting love of travel, local recognition and attention, good relations with neighbors, and success as a professional in local occult practices. Development of psychometry and other psychic abilities involving those in immediate contact is favored.

The Fourth House of home, family, real estate, security and the second half of life, has Virgo on the cusp, ruler Mercury in the Sixth and the male symbol, Puer, herein, indicating that the man dominates in domestic situations (the querent moved to be near this man), and there are still some of the doubts and hesitations concerning domestic life and possibilities of a move to a new locale. The wishes of the man in the querent's life will be the prime factor in any decision. Conversely, the querent may be more in the mood for a new beginning.

The Fifth House of love, children, creativity, speculation and recreation has artistic, harmonious, balanced Libra on the cusp, ruler Venus herein, and the symbol Tristitia, which suggests some problems in romance, losses in gambling, and creative successes borne of emotional upsets, as a release for strong feelings. Venus opposes Mars, emphasizing romantic difficulties; but the opposition is a creative aspect, so success in the arts is favored. This is not a good time to make decisions that affect the futures of children as judgment is clouded. Venus trines Jupiter, suggesting that a light-hearted attitude should be encouraged through relaxing recreation, and more serious emotional situations put aside for later consideration.

The Sixth House of health and work has Scorpio on the cusp, ruler Pluto herein with Mercury and Pluto, and Fortuna Major (Greater Fortune), favoring success on the job, and good opportunities for advancement, in research, occult professions, insurance, tax work, investigations, psychology and counseling. Health also benefits and recuperative powers are excellent now. Good health habits formed now will be retained, as all three planets favor Saturn in the Eighth. Cooperative work ventures are profitable.

The Seventh House of marriage and partners has Sagittarius, the bachelor sign, on the cusp, ruler Jupiter opposite in Gemini, the Moon herein, and the symbol Cauda Draconis (Tail of the Dragon), indicating that the querent is enthusiastic and optimistic about marriage, but inclined to be too trusting, especially in partnership business matters. You are under a little stress in close relationships, particularly when loved ones take a more realistic or practical attitude that simply seems to you, the querent, the most pessimistic of views, since you are so optimistic yourself.

The Eighth House of sex, death, the occult and joint funds has reserved, ambitious Capricorn on the cusp, ruler Saturn herein with Uranus and Neptune, and the symbol Conjunctio (Union), indicating a very intense, intimate sexual relationship; but also favoring union with the spiritual world in your occult studies and interests. You may unite with an occult study group, or find a master on the spirit plane to guide your steps to success. It is certain that you will be feeling more intense psychic experiences soon, as three heavy planets occupy this house.

The Ninth House of higher education, religion, philosophy and long-distance travel has independent Aquarius on the cusp, ruler Uranus in the Eighth, and Conjunctio herein, suggesting shared psychic and educational experiences, and union with higher spiritual forces that contributes to a sense of immortality and power of the soul. Travel with a group or friend is highly favored, as shared experiences, discussed from all points of view, attain greater value and are more memorable.

The Tenth House of career, status, reputation, business of one's own, dealings with supervisors and government, has intuitive Pisces on the cusp, ruler Neptune in the Eighth, and Albus (Wisdom) herein, indicating that you can make excellent progress in either teaching your skills to others, or studying with an authority figure to improve your own skills, possibly as a private student, or working in a charitable, spiritual, or occult profession. Pisces stresses divination through cards, psychometry, and similar forms, rather than through direct psychic rapport with clients, as direct contacts create too many stresses due to the conjunction of Neptune to Saturn and Uranus. The querent needs to maintain some distance from the situation, and exert the controls indicated by the form of divination used.

The Eleventh House of friends, groups, social life, has Aries on the cusp, Mars powerful herein, and the symbol Puella (Female), indicating that the querent should take the initiative to make new friends, particularly other women, or exert her charms to socialize in business matters. The emphasis is on building up a more dynamic image in social relationships. With Mars opposing Venus, there are some difficulties and disappointments involved, but the effort should be made in the right circumstances.

The Twelfth House of illness, secrets, sorrows, the unconscious mind, dreams and sleep has placid, calm Taurus on the cusp, ruler Venus powerful in its other sign, Libra, and the symbol Caput Draconis (Head of the Dragon), signifying the upper spiritual kingdom and new beginnings, and bringing favorable spiritual influences into the querent's life. Health is excellent. Dreams are mainly wish fulfillments now, and not indicative of psychic perceptions—a private time for the inner consciousness to balance the workings of the psychic forces during waking hours.

In conclusion, this chart indicates romantic problems and stress in relationships, but is excellent for the psychic progress desired by the querent.

9

Symbol and Planet Interpretation

In the following pages, you will find interpretations for each of the 16 geomancy symbols, in each of the 12 houses of the chart, alone or with each of the ten planets (including the Sun and Moon). Because this covers quite a bit of territory, and takes up a lot of space, only a very simple and basic interpretation for each individual item can be given.

Each interpretation has been designed to give the most important characteristic and function of the symbol in a house, with a given planet, or alone in a house. As you examine the rulerships section, and learn something more about the meanings of the symbols, the planets and the houses of the chart, you will be able to enrich your interpretations with much added material.

The first description of the symbol, alone with no planets, is identical for each of the twelve houses. For example, Fortuna Major alone in each of the houses is described thusly: "This is a favorable influence that remains in effect for the next few months." Subsequent statements differentiate the meaning of the symbol (i.e. Fortuna Major) in each of the 12 houses, as it relates to the individual. The interpretation proceeds with a general statement regarding the ruling planet's effect on whichever house is currently being discussed. Specific statements pertaining to the particular house that contains both the symbol (i.e. Fortuna Major) and the planet (i.e. the Sun) then follow.

In setting up the interpretations in this manner, we stress the importance of the symbol as the dominant factor, with the planetary positions and influences secondary in significance. This follows naturally from the fact that the chart itself, from the rising sign which is determined by the first symbol, is dependent on the art of geomancy for the focus of the planetary influences.

Before each set of interpretations, there is a section devoted to the meaning of the symbol, alone and in relation to each of the planets. Fortuna Major, for example, is always fortunate and always brings out the best influence of any planet in the same house, including emphasizing any good aspects to the planet, and mitigating any adverse aspects. Similarly, Rubeus is always adverse, and brings out the less favorable side of each of the planets in the same house, no matter how beneficent these planets may seem if considered only astrologically. Rubeus with Jupiter, for example, brings out the extravagance, wastefulness and overconfidence possible with a person who counts on his or her "luck" once too often.

FORTUNA MAJOR

This symbol is essentially favorable with *all* of the planets, regardless of their aspects.

Fortuna Major is ruled by the Sun, source of power and being, and the sign Aquarius, associated with humans as the completely intellectual beings, lifted above their animal desires to a status near the angels. It is the Water of Life that Aquarius brings in its association with Fortuna Major; both physical and spiritual life.

Fortuna Major in a chart always indicates a point of special luck or grace, a blessing given freely whether or not the querent has "earned" it or "deserves" it. The affairs of the house which holds Fortuna Major will prove to be the most beneficial part of the querent's life. Fortuna Major brings all the good possibilities inherent in a situation, and removes all potential difficulties.

Fortuna Major
In 1st House
Alone, no planets: This is a favorable influence that remains in effect for the next few months. Your health and vitality are excellent, and you will be successful in personal projects. You draw honors and attention for your personal qualities and achievements.

With Sun: Your personality and individuality, your qualities of leadership and courage, are your keys to great success and happiness in the near future. Honors, success and achievement of a special personal goal are yours in the coming months. You radiate confidence and leadership.

With Moon: Your popularity with the crowds and ability to deal with people are your keys to great success in the near future. Your ability to instill confidence in others and gain their support will help you achieve a special personal goal. By all means go out and meet new people.

With Mercury: Your communicative abilities, grasp of new ideas, and flexibility are your keys to success in the near future. Now is the time to express your ideas, attempt to publish writings, and speak in public when possible. Plan new projects that are dear to your heart, for all will go well.

With Venus: Your personal charm, persuasive abilities, and many friends are your keys to success in the near future. Display your artistic and creative products, and enter contests, as you may be honored for your talents. You could receive a gift from someone you admire.

With Mars: A competitive spirit and daring initiative help you achieve all your objectives. Your energy level is high, and you enjoy physical competition. You may win a contest. Your leadership qualities may also bring a position of authority and resulting honors.

With Jupiter: You can achieve your highest ambitions with ease in coming months. You have a youthful attitude, confidence in your own abilities, and faith in the projects you start now. All this is well justified, and you succeed almost without trying. Health is protected.

With Saturn: Determination and persistence will ultimately lead to success in your chosen goal. You are respected and may take on additional responsibilities that bring greater trust and rewards from those you serve or teach. Your endurance is excellent. You may diet successfully now.

With Uranus: Many beneficial changes are going on in your life in the next few months. Shape your future by grasping sudden new opportunities. You are innovative and original in your approach to new projects, and can remake your appearance successfully now.

With Neptune: Mastery in the psychic realm and a hidden treasure on the material plane are within your grasp in coming months. If you have a special personal dream, now is the time to act to fulfill it.

With Pluto: You have the promise of physical and spiritual rejuvenation in coming months. Projects you start now may take another shape, but the results will please you. A good time to diet or try to change past habits.

Fortuna Major
In 2nd House
Alone, no planets: This is a favorable influence that remains in effect for the next few months. You prosper financially, and may invest successfully. Keep your financial affairs in your own hands.

With Sun: Your personality and individuality, your qualities of leadership and courage, are your keys to great success and happiness in the near future. Investments in gold and jewelry are favored, as is a business venture of your own. Your income is steady and plentiful.

With Moon: Your popularity with crowds and ability to deal with people are your keys to great success in the near future. You profit from investments in foods, agricultural commodities, silver and antiques. Your income may be seasonal or fluctuating, but it will be excellent.

With Mercury: Your communicative abilities, grasp of new ideas and flexibility are your keys to success in the near future. Investments in communications, transportation, and information industries are favored. You profit from advertising and sales now. Study general economics and turn your knowledge into personal profit.

With Venus: Your personal charm, persuasive abilities and many friends are your keys to success in the near future. Investments in the arts and luxury items are favored. You may receive gifts or special material favors now. Your income is satisfactory.

With Mars: A competitive spirit and daring initiative help you achieve all your objectives. You profit from investments in heavy industry and from your own physical efforts. Enter contests, as you are likely to be successful.

With Jupiter: You can achieve your highest ambitions with ease in coming months. You may be lucky in some form of gambling, and almost any kind of investment is favored. You are generous with your resources to the less fortunate.

With Saturn: Determination and persistence will ultimately lead to success in your chosen goal. Investments in banking notes and securities are favored. Your income is reliable, and you are able to increase it through careful investments. Purchase of antiques and other artifacts is favored.

With Uranus: Many beneficial changes are going on in your life in the next few months. Shape your future by grasping sudden new opportunities. Investments in the aerospace, computer and electronic industries are highly favored. You may be lucky in a lottery or become financially independent in some other way.

With Neptune: Mastery in the psychic realm and a hidden treasure on the material plane are within your grasp in coming months. Investments in shipping, sea food and oil are favored now. Your intuitions are excellent, and you may be lucky in a lottery or sweepstakes now.

With Pluto: You have the promise of physical and spiritual rejuvenation in coming months. Investments in reconstruction, renewal projects are favored. You also profit from cooperative adventures. You may be lucky in a lottery or sweepstakes.

In 3rd House
Alone, no planets: This is a favorable influence that remains in effect for the next few months. You get along well with neighbors and relatives. A short trip may be profitable as well as pleasurable. You will hear good news in the near future.

With Sun: Your personaliity and individuality, your qualities of leadership and courage, are your keys to great success and happiness in the near future. You may assume a position of leadership in local government. Publicize yourself and your products now. Vacation travel is also favored.

With Moon: Your popularity with the crowds and ability to deal with people are your keys to great success in the near future. Advertising and sales are especially favored. Travel with a group and group studies would be entertaining.

With Mercury: Your communicative abilities, grasp of new ideas and flexibility are your keys to success in the near future. Highly favorable for short writings. You may hear good news now. Educational travel and discussions are favored.

With Venus: Your personal charm, persuasive abilities, and many friends are your keys to success in the near future. Excellent for better relations with neighbors and relatives, and for enjoyment of local entertainment and travel.

With Mars: A competitive spirit and daring initiative help you achieve all your objectives. Purchase a car or other means of transportation now, and prepare to travel a great deal. Enjoy local sports or take up an active hobby.

With Jupiter: You can achieve your highest ambitions with ease in coming months. Excellent for the writer or publisher of periodicals. Travel is pleasurable and profitable. You may hear some excellent news now.

With Saturn: Determination and persistence will ultimately lead to success in your chosen goal. Involve yourself in local politics and government, or a conservation movement designed to preserve nature or historical buildings. You gain the respect and trust of neighbors.

With Uranus: Many beneficial changes are going on in your life in the next few months. Shape your future by grasping sudden new opportunities. Be sure to take advantage of travel and study opportunities, as you are open to new ideas and your own thinking is original.

With Neptune: Mastery in the psychic realm and a hidden treasure on the material plane are within your grasp in coming months. You enjoy peace and serenity in your surroundings, although you opt for private studies and travel rather than community involvement. You may receive a spirit message.

With Pluto: You have the promise of physical and spiritual rejuvenation in coming months. Renew ties with neighbors and relatives, and sponsor programs to beautify your community. You may receive a message from the spirit world. Occult studies are highly favoored.

Fortuna Major
In 4th House
Alone, no planets: This is a favorable influence that remains in effect for the next few months. Family relationships are excellent, and you can profit from real estate or agricultural investments. Your home is your greatest source of pleasure now.

With Sun: Your personality and individuality, your qualities of leadership and courage, are your keys to great success and happiness in the near future. Exert your authority in the family in beneficial ways. You may enjoy creatively redecorating or renovating your home. Entertain at home and bask in the affection of good friends.

With Moon: Your popularity with the crowds and ability to deal with people are your keys to great success in the near future. Show your home to the public now if you wish to sell it. Agricultural investments are profitable; or you may simply decide to landscape or grow something special now. Invest in antiques.

With Mercury: Your communicative abilities, grasp of new ideas, and flexibility are your keys to success in the near future. Hold a family reunion or at least contact family members to get all the news. Purchase communications and convenience items for your home.

With Venus: Your personal charm, persuasive abilities, and many friends are your keys to success in the near future. Purchase luxury items for your home and redecorate if you like. An excellent time to do more entertaining for both pleasure and business purposes.

With Mars: A competitive spirit and daring initiative help you achieve all your objectives. There is a lot of activity in the home, possibly redecorating or a lot of visitors or you may be moving now. In any case, time and energy spent on home and family are well rewarded.

With Jupiter: You can achieve your highest ambitions with ease in coming months. You may receive a legacy or a gift from a family member; or you may be purchasing a new home. Real estate and agricultural investments are especially profitable now.

With Saturn: Determination and persistence will ultimately lead to success in your chosen goal. Agricultural and mining investments are favored, and you may find bargain antiques for your home. A good time to act to preserve your home and buy major appliances. Keep in touch with older family members.

With Uranus: Many beneficial changes are going on in your life in the next few months. Shape your future by grasping sudden new opportunities. You may decide to move suddenly for a job or other reasons. Purchase modern conveniences for your home.

With Neptune: Mastery in the psychic realm and a hidden treasure on the material plane are within your grasp in coming months. Enjoy peace and privacy in your home. You may receive a psychic message from a family member.

With Pluto: You have the promise of physical and spiritual rejuvenation in coming months. Home renovation is highly favored. Invest in renewable real estate. Time spent at home builds you up physically and emotionally.

Fortuna Major
In 5th House
Alone, no planets: This is a favorable influence that remains in effect for the next few months. You are lucky in gambling, content in love,

blessed with happy children, and inspired with new creative ideas. A good time for a fun vacation.

With Sun: Your personality and individuality, your qualities of leadership and courage, are your keys to great success and happiness in the near future. You are lucky in gambling, but your strongest interest lies in creative productivity. You want to express your unique individuality.

With Moon: Your popularity with the crowds and ability to deal with people are your keys to great success in the near future. You are fortunate in supermarket sweepstakes and enjoy public recreation. You achieve a better rapport with women and children now. Spend brief periods on a creative project.

With Mercury: Your communicative abilities, grasp of new ideas, and flexibility are your keys to success in the near future. Creative writing is highly favored. Establish better communications with children and loved ones. You may be lucky in a lottery.

With Venus: Your personal charm, persuasive abilities, and many friends are your keys to success in the near future. Your romantic urges are completely satisfied. You also enjoy a variety of artistic projects. You may also be mildly lucky in gambling of all sorts.

With Mars: A competitive spirit and daring initiatives help you achieve all your objectives. You may win honors in sports or expend energy successfully on a creative project. You have great luck in love also.

With Jupiter: You can achieve your highest ambitions with ease in coming months. You are especially lucky in gambling and speculative ventures. Your generosity toward loved ones is reciprocated. You take great pleasure in recreation now. A good time to start a family.

With Saturn: Determination and persistence will ultimately lead to success in your chosen goal. Your greatest pleasure now is your work or creative efforts connected with your career. You gamble on a "sure thing" and are the winner. An old romance may come back into your life.

With Uranus: Many beneficial changes are going on in your life in the next few months. Shape your future by grasping sudden new opportunities. You are lucky in lotteries. Pursue an original creative conception. Romance is fleeting but exciting, so enjoy yourself.

With Neptune: Mastery in the psychic realm and a hidden treasure on the material plane are within your grasp in coming months. Creative efforts in music, painting, photography and the dance are favored. Your romantic illusions briefly come to life. The relationship won't last, but enjoy it.

With Pluto: You have the promise of physical and spiritual rejuvenation in coming months. You are lucky in lotteries and sweepstakes. You enjoy group recreation. You may be attracted to someone you knew in a past lifetime.

Fortuna Major
In 6th House
Alone, no planets: this is a favorable influence that remains in effect for the next few months. Your health is exceptionally good, and you make excellent progress on the job. Seek promotion and recognition, or a better job.

With Sun: Your personality and individuality, your qualities of leadership and courage, are your keys to great success and happiness in the near future. Your health and vitality are excellent. You may be promoted to a higher position at work.

With Moon: Your popularity with the crowds and ability to deal with people are your keys to great success in the near future. Work with the public is especially favored and profitable now. Join a fitness group to keep your health up to par.

With Mercury: Your communicative abilities, grasp of new ideas, and flexibility are your keys to great success in the near future. You may be chosen spokesperson for coworkers, or take a job-related training course successfully. Any work in communications or transportation is favored.

With Venus: Your personal charm, persuasive abilities, and many friends are your keys to success in the near future. Your health is excellent. You advance on the job through cooperation and the favors of those who appreciate your ability to keep people working together happily.

With Mars: A competitive spirit and daring initiative help you achieve all your objectives. Seek a raise or a better-paying job and expect to be very busy in your work in the near future. Your energy level is high, and your health excellent.

With Jupiter: You can achieve your highest ambitions with ease in coming months. Your health is excellent, though you may gain a little weight. Work in publishing, banking and transportation is favored. Advancement may be offered to you now—seize the opportunity.

With Saturn: Determination and persistence will ultimately lead to success in your chosen goal. Your job is stable, but you may be saddled with extra responsibilities. Seek a management position. Your endurance and general health are excellent.

With Uranus: Many beneficial changes are going on in your life in the next few months. Shape your future by grasping sudden new opportunities. You may suddenly leave your job for a better one, or to work independently. Computer and scientific jobs are especially favored. Your health benefits from greater mental freedom.

With Neptune: Mastery in the psychic realm and a hidden treasure on the material plane are within your grasp in coming months. Your health responds favorably to harmony on the job. You have opportunities to use your imagination in your work. Jobs in the arts, music and the oil industry are favored.

With Pluto: You have the promise of physical and spiritual rejuvenation in coming months. Jobs in credit and insurance are especially favored. Your recuperative abilities are excellent now. You adjust easily to beneficial transitions on the job.

Fortuna Major
In 7th House
Alone, no planets: This is a favorable influence that remains in effect for the next few months. This is an excellent time to marry. If married already, you and your spouse have an almost ideal relationship. Legal disputes are settled in your favor. You are successful in competition.

With Sun: Your personality and individuality, your qualities of leadership and courage, are your keys to great success and happiness in the near future. If single, you may meet the person of your dreams. The man dominates in the relationship, but his strength is reliable.

With Moon: Your popularity with the crowds and ability to deal with people are your keys to great success in the near future. The emphasis is on the women in your life; if you are a woman, you will dominate or support any close relationship with a man.

With Mercury: Your communicative abilities, grasp of new ideas, and flexibility are your keys to success in the near future. A meeting of the minds is the basis for an important close relationship now. Shared ideas benefit both of you.

With Venus: Your personal charm, persuasive abilities, and many friends are your keys to success in the near future. Love and affection are especially marked in a close relationship. This is good time to marry.

With Mars: A competitive spirit and daring initiative help you achieve all your objectives. Sexual ardor is the predominant factor in a close relationship. There may be competition for the same love object; if so, you are successful.

With Jupiter: You can achieve your highest ambitions with ease in coming months. A friendly relationship with a youthful person lifts your spirits. A profitable business partnership can be formed now. Settle legal disputes amicably.

With Saturn: Determination and persistence will ultimately lead to success in your chosen goal. An older person is a source of comfort, inspiration and tangible support. A protracted legal dispute may be settled. Avoid competition.

With Uranus: Many beneficial changes are going on in your life in the next few months. Shape your future by grasping sudden new opportunities. A sudden attraction may develop, or a relationship may be broken off. In any case you are stimulated by novelty or freedom.

With Neptune: Mastery in the psychic realm and a hidden treasure on the material plane are within your grasp in coming months. A love object may prove elusive or difficult to understand; use your intuition. Avoid legal affairs which may expand beyond your original thought; it will be favorable, but time-consuming.

With Pluto: You have the promise of physical and spiritual rejuvenation in coming months. You may meet your soul mate or form a close relationship with someone you knew in a past lifetime. Abide by the terms of legal settlements. Join a cooperative rather than limit yourself to one business partner.

Fortuna Major
In 8th House
Alone, no planets: This is a favorable influence that remains in effect for the next few months. You may receive a legacy or settlement of a legal dispute; joint finances in general improve. Occult studies bring spiritual benefits. Relationships with the opposite sex are fortunate.

With Sun: Your personality and individuality, your qualities of leadership and courage, are your keys to great success and happiness in the near future. Seek financial backing for business. You may receive a gift or legacy from a man. A psychic reading is favored to resolve your problems.

With Moon: Your popularity with the crowds and ability to deal with people are your keys to great success in the near future. You profit from public investments. You may receive a gift or legacy from a woman. A psychic card reading is favored to resolve any questions or problems.

With Mercury: Your communicative abilities, grasp of new ideas, and flexibility are your keys to success in the near future. Consult with a palmist to answer questions or resolve problems. You profit from cooperative financial ventures. Expand your psychic understanding; you may receive a message.

With Venus: Your personal charm, persuasive abilities, and many friends are your keys to success in the near future. A psychometric reading of a personal object may give you much needed information. You may receive a gift from a woman. Romance with a loved one is favored.

With Mars: A competitive spirit and daring initiative help you achieve all your objectives. Your sexual ardor is reciprocated, so enjoy an intimate relationship. You may receive a prize from a competition. Your spiritual energy level is high.

With Jupiter: You can achieve your highest ambitions with ease in coming months. Karmic blessings are coming your way. You may receive a legacy or settlement of a legal dispute. Relations with the opposite sex are friendly. You profit from joint financial ventures.

With Saturn: Determination and persistence will ultimately lead to success in your chosen goal. Your sexual ardor is cooled, but your affections remain stable. Watch for karmic debts which you will be happy to repay. You may receive government benefits (tax refund, for example).

With Uranus: Many beneficial changes are going on in your life in the next few months. Shape your future by grasping sudden new opportunities. You may receive a sudden legacy or unexpected financial windfall. Relations with the opposite sex are friendly. An astrological reading could help you resolve problems.

With Neptune: Mastery in the psychic realm and a hidden treasure on the material plane are within your grasp in coming months. You may consult a medium or develop your own psychic talents successfully now. Investments from the past may suddenly pay off.

With Pluto: You have the promise of physical and spiritual rejuvenation in coming months. Delve into the occult arts to gain the understanding you need. Your relationship with a loved one is spiritual as well as sexual. You profit from a cooperative financial venture.

Fortuna Major
In 9th House

Alone, no planets: This is a favorable influence that remains in effect for the next few months. An excellent time to relocate, travel for pleasure and profit, get a book published, involve yourself in religious observances, and make plans for the future.

With Sun: Your personality and individuality, your qualities of leadership and courage, are your keys to great success and happiness in the near future. You are happiest traveling, making contacts with foreign cultures, exploring religious ideas, and publishing lengthy writings, if you are so inclined.

With Moon: Your popularity with the crowds and ability to deal with people are your keys to great success in the near future. If a writer, your published works will attain popularity. Popular religious observances appeal to you. You enjoy traveling frequently, for profit and pleasure.

With Mercury: Your communicative abilities, grasp of new ideas, and flexibility are your keys to success in the near future. Any course of study you undertake now will be learned easily and prove useful and profitable. Publishing of writings, teaching and speaking to foreign groups are especially favored.

With Venus: Your personal charm, persuasive abilities, and many friends are your keys to success in the near future. You may find romance in a distant place. Study foreign arts to expand your own techniques and ideas. Religious observances give you great emotional satisfaction.

With Mars: A competitive spirit and daring initiative help you achieve all your objectives. You enjoy traveling and exploring places and ideas. A literary competition might interest you. You are active in religious observances. Mechanical and engineering studies are favored.

With Jupiter: You can achieve your highest ambitions with ease in coming months. All Ninth House matters prosper exceptionally well. Publishing, travel, and studies of all sorts are favored. You are absorbed in religion and philosophy now.

With Saturn: Determination and persistence will ultimately lead to success in your chosen goal. You travel strictly for business profits and study practical subjects. Political interests and factual writings are favored. You enjoy the Stoic philosophers now.

With Uranus: Many beneficial changes are going on in your life in the next few months. Shape your future by grasping sudden new opportunities. Study of the sciences, social science and astrology is highly favored. You are open to new ideas that will prove useful in the future.

With Neptune: Mastery in the psychic realm and a hidden treasure on the material plane are within your grasp in coming months. Sea travel is highly favored. Studies of the arts, music and mathematics are successfully pursued now. Your intuition is the best guide to future planning.

With Pluto: You have the promise of physical and spiritual rejuvenation in coming months. Economic and occult studies are favored. You enjoy delving into the mystery religions, karma and fate. Underground and underwater exploration appeal to you.

Fortuna Major
In 10th House
Alone, no planets: This is a favorable influence that remains in effect for the next few months. Career and business success is assured now. You may confidently run for public office or seek a supervisory position on the job or in government.

With Sun: Your personality and individuality, your qualities of leadership and courage, are your keys to great success and happiness in the near future. Your personal leadership on the job and in government or public affairs brings both profit and satisfaction. You may be honored for your efforts.

With Moon: Your popularity with the crowds and ability to deal with people are your keys to great success in the near future. Seek elective office now if you wish. Any business devoted to direct public contact and service is sure to succeed.

With Mercury: Your personal charm, persuasive abilities, and many friends are your keys to success in the near future. Bring your ideas to the attention of the public, government officials and employers. Work in the communications and transportation industries, along with teaching, is highly favored.

With Venus: Your personal charm, persuasive abilities, and many friends are your keys to success in the near future. Careers in the arts, decorating, luxury items and entertainment are all highly favored. Attend public social events for business and for pleasure.

With Mars: A competitive spirit and daring initiative help you achieve all your objectives. Careers in the military, the police force, engineering and mechanics are highly favored. Compete now for the job of your choice, as you will come out the winner.

With Jupiter: You can achieve your highest ambitions with ease in coming months. Seek elective office now, or participate in legislative and judicial activities in your community. Your judgment and honesty are highly respected. Any business venture is successful now.

With Saturn: Determination and persistence will ultimately lead to success in your chosen goal. Seek a management position in industry or government now. Your experience and integrity are valued highly. Any business in basic industry is favored.

With Uranus: Many beneficial changes are going on in your life in the next few months. Shape your future by grasping sudden new opportunities. Start an independent business or consulting service of your own. Any business in astrology, computers, electronics and the aviation industry is favored.

With Neptune: Mastery in the psychic realm and a hidden treasure on the material plane are within your grasp in coming months. Participate in social improvement projects and public charity. Perform or display your creative projects in public now, as you will be well-received.

With Pluto: You have the promise of physical and spiritual rejuvenation in coming months. Public reform efforts benefit from your support. Make a transition in your career now if you wish, as you will be successful.

Fortuna Major
In 11th House
Alone, no planets: This is a favorable influence that remains in effect for the next few months. Your greatest asset is your ability to make friends with people who benefit you in career or financial areas, as well as personally and socially. Join a new group now.

With Sun: Your personality and individuality, your qualities of leadership and courage, are your keys to great success and happiness in the near future. Join groups that help you develop as an individual. You may meet someone who helps you achieve more in life.

With Moon: Your popularity with the crowds and ability to deal with people are your keys to great success in the near future. You benefit from the public groups you join, supporting various causes beneficial to your community. You may become spokesperson for such a group.

With Mercury: Your communicative abilities, grasp of new ideas, and flexibility are your keys to success in the near future. An intellectually stimulating discussion or study group can be most helpful. You may become spokesperson for a public group.

With Venus: Your personal charm, persuasive abilities, and many friends are your keys to success in the near future. Your interests in group activities are purely social, and you are welcome as an organizer and mediator in any group you choose.

With Mars: A competitive spirit and daring initiative help you achieve all your objectives. Active sports, physical fitness and out of doors exploration appeal to you most now. You are a natural leader in all group activities.

With Jupiter: You can achieve your highest ambitions with ease in coming months. You set a good example for younger people, and may join groups which support programs for youth. You manage to bridge the gap between child and adult exceptionally well.

With Saturn: Determination and persistence will ultimately lead to success in your chosen goal. Your local historical museum or conservation society would welcome your presence now. You may also search into the past for old friends and acquaintances successfully.

With Uranus: Many beneficial changes are going on in your life in the next few months. Shape your future by grasping sudden new opportunities. You would enjoy a New Age astrological and occult group now, as well as political independents. Scientific groups also appeal to you.

With Neptune: Mastery in the psychic realm and a hidden treasure on the material plane are within your grasp in coming months. You would appreciate the local opera, musical and artistic groups now; you might also examine a spiritualist group.

With Pluto: You have the promise of physical and spiritual rejuvenation in coming months. You would enjoy an occult society or a social reform group now. You may meet someone whom you knew in a past lifetime among your casual acquaintances.

Fortuna Major
In 12th House
Alone, no planets: This is a favorable influence that remains in effect for the next few months. Your health is good, you sleep well, you harbor no grudges or disappointments, and you may have intuitive dreams now.

With Sun: Your personality and individuality, your qualities of leadership and courage, are your keys to great success and happiness in the near future. Your health and vitality are excellent. This combination favors greater self-understanding through meditation. Strengthen your inner as well as your physical self.

With Moon: Your popularity with the crowds and ability to deal with people are your keys to great success in the near future. You may have intuitive dreams and inner tensions with the waxing and waning of the Moon; however, none of these are serious ailments, simply stresses that expand your inner self.

With Mercury: Your communicative abilities, grasp of new ideas, and flexibility are your keys to success in the near future. Your best ideas for the future come in your dreams, as well as answers to questions and problems. Delve into your inner motivations and interests now. Self-analysis is favored.

With Venus: Your personal charm, persuasive abilities, and many friends are your keys to success in the near future. You are happy in solitude; but may be sharing a romantic interlude in private that is as important to your emotions as food and drink to your body.

With Mars: A competitive spirit and daring initiative help you achieve all your objectives. Your vitality is excellent and your energy level high. You may be restless at night, as there aren't enough hours in the day to accomplish everything you plan.

With Jupiter: You can achieve your highest ambitions with ease in coming months. Your health is excellent. You may have prophetic dreams and certainly benefit spiritually, as well as physically, from periods of meditation.

With Saturn: Determination and persistence will ultimately lead to success in your chosen goal. You sleep more and take better care of your health. Your endurance is excellent, and you can establish good control over your habits.

With Uranus: Many beneficial changes are going on in your life in the next few months. Shape your future by grasping sudden new opportunities. Use periods of sleeplessness to note the original ideas that come to you. You may have surprising clairvoyant visions in solitude.

With Neptune: Mastery in the psychic realm and a hidden treasure on the material plane are within your grasp in coming months. Your psychic abilities are heightened in privacy and in sleep. Keep track of your dreams. Your health is excellent, as your spirits are positive.

With Pluto: You have the promise of physical and spiritual rejuvenation in coming months. Now is the time to remedy any ailment or bad health habits of the past. Your recuperative abilities are excellent. Delve into past lives for valuable information.

FORTUNA MINOR

This mildly adverse symbol is mitigated by the Sun, Venus and Jupiter; made somewhat more adverse by Saturn, Uranus, Mars, Neptune and Pluto; and dissipated to some extent by Mercury and the Moon.

Fortuna Minor is ruled by the Sun and is associated with the material sign Taurus, denoting physical well-being and life of the body on the material plane. As such, Fortuna Minor can be mildly adverse, as it ties the individual to the material plane, where he or she is well-protected, but limits spiritual expansion.

Fortuna Minor in a chart always represents a point of self-preservation, to the extent of selfish disregard for the rights of others. This sometimes generates a form of cowardice in the face of physical threats which ought to be dealt with, for moral or spiritual principles. Fortuna Minor dictates that the querent will opt for safety of the physical self and continuity of the material life span. However, when this protection is extended to include others as well, Fortuna Minor can be a constructive force in molding a secure society. Excellent for nurses, doctors, firefighters, police officers, health inspectors, and crossing guards—all the people who look after the physical welfare of others.

Fortuna Minor
In the 1st House
Alone, no planets: This influence protects you against your own impulses as well as external enemies, helpful but not entirely favorable. Try to complete the projects you have already started, rather than initiating new ones. New people can be helpful at the moment, but are not always congenial on a long-term basis.

With Sun: You can take advantage of opportunities with greater energy and confidence. Take better control of your personal life, but don't ignore the help and advice of an experienced authority figure. Channel creative impulses into a definite project.

With Moon: Fortune is fickle, sometimes favorable and sometimes adverse, with frequent fluctuations. You meet many new people, adding to your experience in dealing with the public. Pick and choose among them for closer ties. Take up a hobby that is popular at the moment.

With Mercury: You are quick to grasp opportunity and adapt to changing circumstances. Much wheat mixed with even more chaff will come your way in conversations with new contacts. Express your own ideas carefully in the right ears, or through a worthwhile creative channel.

With Venus: Fortune smiles on you in small ways, making life more pleasurable and profitable. Stick to an artistic project you have in mind, or any improvements in your appearance. The results will be agreeable, if not all that you hoped for.

With Mars: Your physical strength and agility are called into play more frequently in coming months. Enjoy physical activities, but aim for productive action. Introduce yourself to new people, but scrutinize them first. Calculate the demands of new projects before starting them.

With Jupiter: Fortune smiles on you and brings success in all your efforts in coming months. You may gain a little weight now. Try to indulge yourself in other ways, with a new wardrobe and general physical shape-up for example. Pick and choose among projects for the most profitable.

With Saturn: An influential person or authority figure is supportive in coming months. Your conservatism now is a good shield against opportunists and personal mistakes, but your options for self-expression and new projects are somewhat limited. Complete what you are working on now.

With Uranus: Changes in your circumstances are helpful in the next few months. Improve your appearance and exchange bad habits for new, beneficial ones. You'll widen your circle of acquaintances and find new ways to express yourself as a result.

With Neptune: You can rely on the sympathy and understanding of others in coming months. Your sensitivity to new people and situations is a plus, for you can take up the projects you desire and reject the undesirable with far less effort now. Your imagination produces realizable visions.

With Pluto: Fate steps in to help you out of an apparently insoluble situation in the near future. You are reaping karmic benefits from past good deeds. The people you meet now may have been part of one of your past lives, and their presence now is helpful to you.

Fortuna Minor
In the 2nd House
Alone, no planet: this influence protects you against your own impulses as well as external enemies, helpful but not entirely favorable. You won't see much of a financial increase, but what you now own and earn are secure. Stick to safe investments.

With Sun: You can take better advantage of opportunities with greater energy and confidence. Some financial improvement could take place if you keep control of your financial affairs, and invest under the guidance of an experienced authority.

With Moon: Fortune is fickle, sometimes favorable and sometimes adverse, with frequent fluctuations. Your inclination to follow the popular lead in investments is inadvisable, although your basic income is secure. Avoid emotional spending and fad purchases.

With Mercury: You are quick to grasp opportunity and adapt to changing circumstances. An economic learning experience will not put much extra cash in your pocket, but you will not lose either. Investments in the communications and transportation industries are your best bets.

With Venus: Fortune smiles on you in small ways, making life more pleasurable and profitable. You tend to spend and invest on an emotional basis, for pleasure. Stick to luxury items and the cosmetics and fashion industries for investments.

With Mars: Your physical strength and agility are called into place more frequently in coming months. You tend to invest in a lot of areas, keeping your money in play. Profits will not be high. Stick to the recreational and sporting goods industries for investments. Avoid making hasty purchases.

With Jupiter: Fortune smiles on you and brings success in all your efforts in coming months. You can make definite small gains by investing now. Almost any business that has an expanding economy will be profitable now.

With Saturn: An influential person or authority figure is supportive in coming months. Investments in securities, heavy industries and appliances are your best sources for profit. Although returns may be small, they will be reliable. The payoff will take time.

With Uranus: Changes in your circumstances are helpful in the next few months. Investments in the computer, electronics and aerospace industries are favored, although profits will not be large. Expect somewhat sporadic returns on your outlay.

With Neptune: You can rely on the sympathy and understanding of others in coming months. Investments in shipping, sea food and oil may bring a small profit. You may be lucky in a lottery or sweepstakes now. Avoid emotional spending.

With Pluto: Fate steps in to help you out of an apparently insoluble situation in the near future. You may win a small lottery or sweepstakes now. Investments in cooperative ventures are favored for small profits also. Economic changes are mildly beneficial.

Fortuna Minor
In the 3rd House
Alone, no planets: This influence protects you against your own impulses as well as external enemies, helpful but not entirely favorable. You are relatively safe in travel, and should take advantage of local educational opportunities. Relations with those around you are good.

With Sun: You can take advantage of opportunities with greater energy and confidence. You may assume a position of minor authority in local government. Advertising your skills and wares brings attention and profits now.

With Moon: Fortune is fickle, sometimes favorable and sometimes adverse, with frequent fluctuations. Advertising and sales are profitable. Enjoy local group and public entertainment and lectures. Group travel is most favored, You get along better with women acquaintances now.

With Mercury: You are quick to grasp opportunity and adapt to changing circumstances. Advertising and sales are favored, as is purchase of a car or other means of transportation. Short study courses of practical nature are valuable. Join a local travel or discussion group.

With Venus: Fortune smiles on you in small ways, making life more pleasurable and profitable. You receive small favors and attention from those around you. Smooth relations with neighbors and relatives, and take pleasure trips now.

With Mars: Your physical strength and agility are called into play more frequently in coming months. You take trips more often and are busy with shared activities in your community. Enjoy local sports and competition, nature study and other sporting excursions.

With Jupiter: Fortune smiles on you and brings success in all your efforts in coming months. You may hear some favorable news. Travel is highly favored, as is advertising. A study course could change your life for the better now.

With Saturn: An influential person or authority figure is supportive in coming months. Travel and news are delayed and your daily routine is more organized and restrictive. Government work and political activities are highly favorable.

With Uranus: Changes in your circumstances are helpful in the next few months. Impulsiveness characterizes your daily activities, and independence your relations with those around you. Seek out stimulating lectures and new local entertainment, as well as new places to visit.

With Neptune: You can rely on the sympathy and understanding of others in coming months. Excellent for short term musical and artistic studies, and involvement in meditation and psychic development classes. You are fortunate in your relations with neighbors and relatives.

With Pluto: Fate steps in to help you out of an apparently insoluble situation in the near future. Occult studies and past-life regressions are favored. Take advantage of books and classes to approve your life and transform your habits.

Fortuna Minor
In the 4th House
Alone, no planets: This influence protects you against your own impulses as well as external enemies, helpful but not entirely favorable. Small profits are possible from real estate investments. Family relationships are excellent, so entertain more at home, Your future is secure.

With Sun: You can take advantage of opportunities with greater energy and confidence. This is a good time to purchase a new home, put aside funds for retirement years, and profit from real estate and agricultural investments. Your father is prominent in your life now.

With Moon: Fortune is fickle, sometimes favorable and sometimes adverse, with frequent fluctuations. You enjoy inviting groups to your home, and basking in public attention. You profit from agricultural investments. Landscaping and home decorating are favored.

With Mercury: You are quick to grasp opportunity and adapt to changing circumstances. Communications with family members increase, and you travel more to visit family members. You give productive thought to retirement planning.

With Venus: Fortune smiles on you in small ways, making life more pleasurable and profitable. You greatly enjoy entertaining at home, and may redecorate now. Family ties are strengthened and affections deepen.

With Mars: Your physical strength and agility are called into play more frequently in coming months. Home remodeling or a business in your home occupies much time and generates activity on the premises. You may be spending a lot of time on gardening.

With Jupiter: Fortune smiles on you and brings success in all your efforts in coming months. This is a good year to try growing plants you haven't had luck with before—you should have a bountiful harvest. Real estate can be very profitable now. Family relations are excellent.

With Saturn: An influential person or authority figure is supportive in coming months. A strong parent absorbs your attention now. You can learn a great deal. Investments from real estate are slow. Plant a long-term garden, with trees and shrubs—it will prosper.

With Uranus: Changes in your circumstances are helpful in the next few months. You may move suddenly, due to desire for a new home or an irresistible offer for your present home. A good time to modernize your home with the latest conveniences.

With Neptune: You can rely on the sympathy and understanding of others in coming months. Your grandparents are the focus of your attention. You seek more peace and privacy. Real estate investments offer only elusive profits.

With Pluto: Fate steps in to help you out of an apparently insoluble situation in the near future. Hold a family reunion and renew family ties in other ways. You may also consider renovating your home or investing in real estate to renovate and sell.

Fortuna Minor
In the 5th House
Alone, no planets: This influence protects you against your own impulses as well as external enemies, helpful but not entirely favorable. Small winnings in gambling, bursts of creative enthusiasm, and pleasure in group recreation are yours. You are successful in sporting competitions, and enjoy time spent with children and loved ones.

With Sun: You can take advantage of opportunities with greater energy and confidence. You devote special attention to creative self-expression, and take the lead in love. Children look up to you and respect your wishes. You are also lucky in speculation.

With Moon: Fortune is fickle, sometimes favorable and sometimes adverse, with frequent fluctuations. Take up a popular craft, as you will be successful in your efforts. Young children are especially interesting to you now. You are more moody in love, but a supermarket sweepstakes may make you a winner.

With Mercury: You are quick to grasp opportunity and adapt to changing circumstances, Communications with children and loved ones improve, and you may try your hand at creative writing. You may be lucky at games of chance. Contests of skill and wit bring pleasure now.

With Venus: Fortune smiles on you in small ways, making life more pleasurable annd profitable. This is a romantic time, though you may not take it too seriously. You are in pursuit of affection and pleasure. You do exceptionally well in artistic projects and get along well with children.

With Mars: Your physical strength and agility are called into play more frequently in coming months. Your sexual ardor is reciprocated. You are successful in sports and competition, and enjoy active recreation. You also approach creative projects energetically.

With Jupiter: Fortune smiles on you and brings success in all your efforts in coming months. You are lucky in gambling, successful in love, popular with children, and happy in your choices of recreation. You develop new creative talents successfully.

With Saturn: An influential person or authority figure is supportive in coming months. Romantic reminiscence is your mood; old loves are preferred to new ones. Creative opportunities are limited and speculation yields only small, slow profits. You tend to be authoritative with children, but this is propitious.

With Uranus: Changes in your circumstances are helpful in the next few months. Unexpected speculative opportunities yield modest profits; games of chance and casino gambling also show a gain, rather than a loss. Romance is exciting, but unpredictable. You maintain an attitude of detachment toward children.

With Neptune: You can rely on the sympathy and understanding of others in coming months. You are in the mood for romantic illusions, and may enjoy an infatuation. Your creative imagination is stimulated. You may be mildly lucky in a lottery or sweepstakes. You are not on the same wavelength as children, although you are kind to them.

With Pluto: Fate steps in to help you out of an apparently insoluble situation in the near future. A romantic encounter with someone you knew in a past life is possible. You are mildly fortunate in gambling, specially lotteries and sweepstakes. Children make you feel young again.

Fortuna Minor
In the 6th House
Alone, no planets: This influence protects you against your own impulses as well as external enemies, helpful but not entirely favorable. Both your health and your job are protected. You will not make much extra progress,but you will not lose ground either.

With Sun: You can take advantage of opportunities with greater energy and confidence. Your health and vitality are improving steadily. Seek advancement on the job, as you stand well with supervisors.

With Moon: Fortune is fickle, sometimes favorable and sometimes adverse, with frequent fluctuations. If your work depends on contacts with the public, or dealing with people as individuals, you can make progress now. Your vitality and energy level are not always consistent.

With Mercury: You are quick to grasp opportunity and adapt to changing circumstances. Job-related studies and travel, and interest in the transportation and communications industries are favored. Become more informed about general health needs and physical fitness.

With Venus: Fortune smiles on you in small ways, making life more pleasurable and profitable. You receive approval and cooperation on the job, and profit from work in the arts and luxury items. Your health is good, but avoid self-indulgence or physical laziness.

With Mars: Your physical strength and agility are called into play more frequently in coming months. You are faced with much activity on the job, where you shine in competition. Your energy level is high, and you are productive.

With Jupiter: Fortune smiles on you and brings success in all your efforts in coming months. You have the opportunity to get a highly desirable job, with better pay. Make the effort. Your health is good, but you tend to overeat and take your health for granted.

With Saturn: An influential person or authority figure is supportive in coming months. Your endurance is good, and it needs to be, as you can expect an extra load of work and more responsibilities which may lead to advancement later on.

With Uranus: Changes in your circumstances are helpful in the next few months. You suffer from nervous tension or insomnia, but may have some original ideas that lead to greater job independence. Freelance work is favored now, as is a change of job interests.

With Neptune: You can rely on the sympathy and understanding of others in coming months. Allergies and other physical sensitivities, as to drugs or alcohol, may surface now. Change your habit patterns as necessary. Your feelings are your best guide on the job.

With Pluto: Fate steps in to help you out of an apparently insoluble situation in the near future. You can improve your health and vitality with vitamins and diet now. You can also make successful job transitions.

Fortuna Minor
In the 7th House
Alone, no planets: This influence protects you against your own

impulses as well as external enemies, helpful but not positively favorable. Your marriage and business partnerships are secure, and you succeed in competition and legal disputes. Stick to the people who are already close to you.

With Sun: You can take advantage of opportunities with greater energy and confidence. Strengthen close relationships by exerting your power and personal influence. You are successful in competition and legal disputes.

With Moon: Fortune is fickle, sometimes favorable and sometimes adverse, with frequent fluctuations. You face some ups and downs in marriage or business partnerships, but succeed by using your intuition and sensitivity to the needs and moods of others. Avoid competition and legal disputes.

With Mercury: You are quick to grasp opportunity and adapt to changing circumstances. Establish better communications with loved ones and business partners. This is a good time to sign agreements. Shared travel is favored but avoid litigation and competition.

With Venus: Fortune smiles on you in small ways, making life more pleasurable and profitable. Marriage and business partnerships are highly favorable. You succeed in legal disputes, but seek cooperation rather than competing for your desires.

With Mars: Your physical strength and agility are called into play more frequently in coming months. You enjoy competition with your equals, but avoid litigation now. You and a special loved one share heightened romantic ardor.

With Jupiter: Fortune smiles on you and brings success in all your efforts in coming months. A business partnership is profitable and your marital relationship excellent. Expand your circle of close friends. You are succcessful in competition and litigation.

With Saturn: An influential person or authority figure is supportive in coming months. You're more comfortable with close, longtime friends. You can count on the security of your marriage even with added responsibilities or joint ambitions. Avoid litigation and competition.

With Uranus: Changes in your circumstances are helpful in the next few months. Changes and surprises in your marital relationship lead to greater excitement and stimulation. You may make an individualistic new friend. Competition is unpredictable, as is litigation.

With Neptune: You can rely on the sympathy and understanding of others in coming months. Your heightened sensitivity and intuition enable you to ease any friction in your marriage, and take uncanny advantage of joint business opportunities, avoid litigation, which may be confusing; and competition which may be deceptive.

With Pluto: Fate steps in to help you out of an apparently insoluble situation in the near future. Your marriage and close relationships reflect the karmic benefits coming to you from past life efforts. Avoid litigation and competition, as unforeseen factors crop up and prolong the situations.

Fortuna Minor
In the 8th House

Alone, no planets: This influence protects you against your own impulses as well as external enemies, helpful but not entirely favorable. Present joint ventures are profitable, but avoid further ventures. Keep track of credit spending. Relations with the opposite sex are smooth, but not exciting. Occult studies are favored, but you will have to work for results.

With Sun: You can take advantage of opportunities with greater energy and confidence. Joint finances are favored, and credit is easy to obtain. Old debts may be paid to you soon. Occult studies are highly favored also. Take the initiative in romance.

With Moon: Fortune is fickle, sometimes favorable and sometimes adverse, with frequent fluctuations. Avoid being moody in a romantic relationship. A card reading or studies of the Tarot are favored. You get along better with women than with men now. Seek cooperative ventures for investments.

With Mercury: You are quick to grasp opportunity and adapt to changing circumstances. Sign joint finiancial papers and send in credit applications now. Financial news is good, and money owed you will be paid soon. Mental rapport is stronger with the opposite sex.

With Venus: Fortune smiles on you in small ways, making life more pleasurable and profitable. You are sexually more attractive and get along well with the opposite sex. Cooperative financial ventures are favored, and credit easy to obtain. You may receive a gift now. Occult entertainment is favored.

With Mars: Your physical strength and agility are called into play more frequently in coming months. You are intensely physical now in your sexual relationship. Avoid excess credit spending, but take advantage of joint investment opportunities. Occult interests may lead to interesting phenomena.

With Jupiter: Fortune smiles on you and brings success in all your efforts in coming months. Occult interests bring greater beneficial results and add to your spiritual energy. Relations with the opposite sex are friendly. Joint financial ventures are profitable.

With Saturn: An influential person or authority figure is supportive in coming months. Sexual relations cool as you look for security rather than expression. High magic ceremonies are favored. Credit dealings are slow, debts climb somewhat and joint ventures yield only gradual profits.

With Uranus: Changes jn your circumstances are helpful in the next few months. Studies in astrology and clairvoyance are favored. Sexual excitement prevails. A joint financial venture may lead to greater financial independence.

With Neptune: You can rely on the sympathy and understanding of others in coming months. Cooperative financial ventures prosper. Any interest in the occult could resurrect a buried psychic talent, such as psychometry or mediumship. Sex reaches an elevated spiritual plane.

With Pluto: Fate steps in to help you out of an apparently insoluble situation in the near future. Occult interests bring past talents to light;

past life regression is especially favored. Relations with the opposite sex become more intense.

Fortuna Minor
In the 9th House
Alone, no planets: This influence protects you against your own impulses as well as external enemies, helpful but not entirely favorable. Both travel and studies bring spiritual as well as material benefits. You seek reassurance and strength from religious observances, and develop a more confident philosophy of life.

With Sun: You can take advantage of opportunities with greater energy and confidence. Religious observances greatly increase your self-confidence and inner strength. Travel to build up your physical vitality. Focus on creativity and self-expression in your studies.

With Moon: Fortune is fickle, sometimes favorable and sometimes adverse, with frequent fluctuations. Public religious observances give you an emotional lift now. You feel more comfortable as part of a crowd in both travel and studies. Avoid making long-range plans, as your desires shift a lot now.

With Mercury: You are quick to grasp opportunity and adapt to changing circumstances. You can easily comprehend whatever you decide to study. Focus on communicating your ideas to others through speech and the printed word. You search for the ideas behind religious practices.

With Venus: Fortune smiles on you in small ways, making life more pleasurable and profitable. Religious observances bring contentment and satisfy your love of beauty and pageantry, Studies in the arts, various cultures, and social sciences are favored. Travel with friends to places that bring pleasure.

With Mars: Your physical strength and agility are called into play more frequently in coming months. Active travel suits you now, especially trips of exploration. You are dynamic in support of your religious affiliation, and your philosophy of life is more competitive. Hands-on studies are favored.

With Jupiter: Fortune smiles on you and brings success in all your efforts in coming months. You feel a strong rapport with higher spiritual forces as a result of religious observances. Your philosophy of life becomes more charitable and optimistic. Any studies or travel provide the mental and physical expansion you desire.

With Saturn: An influential person or authority figure is supportive in coming months. Travel for business purposes is favored, as is realistic planning for the future. You are more conscious of your duties to others and to your religious affiliation. Practical studies are also favored.

With Uranus: Changes in your circumstances are helpful in the next few months. Air travel, a change in your religious affiliation, and scientific studies are favored. You develop a more independent philosophy of life, focusing on free will.

With Neptune: You can rely on the sympathy and understanding of others in coming months. You become more mystical and emotional in your religious observances. You prefer solitary travel, or travel by sea. You are more concerned with universal peace now. Artistic, musical and psychic studies are favored.

With Pluto: Fate steps in to help you out of an apparently insoluble situation in the near future. You develop a strong interest and even belief in reincarnation and the principles of karma. Group travel is favored along with occult studies and greater interest in psychology and hypnosis.

Fortuna Minor
In the 10th House
Alone, no planets: This influence protects you against your own impulses as well as external enemies, helpful but not entirely favorable. Your career is secure, but it will take a major effort to gain advancement. You do receive minor favors and attention from authority figures.

With Sun: You can take advantage of opportunities with greater energy and confidence. You may seek advancement with the support of an important person in your line of work. Take a more prominent role in public affairs.

With Moon: Fortune is fickle, sometimes favorable and sometimes adverse, with frequent fluctuations. You deal better on the job with women and the public, and may seek election for a public or organizational position now.

With Mercury: You are quick to grasp opportunity and adapt to changing circumstances. Job planning, discussions, meetings, training, studies and travel are highly favored. You may assume an authoritative position as spokesperson now.

With Venus: Fortune smiles on you in small ways, making life more pleasurable and profitable. You receive greater cooperation and some favors on the job, particularly from women. A good time to appear at public social events.

With Mars: Your physical strength and agility are called into play more frequently in coming months. You are much more active and competitive on the job, and in dealings with government and authority figures. Take your ideas to people with influence.

With Jupiter: Fortune smiles on you and brings success in all your efforts in coming months. A good time to start a modest business of your own, or seek advancement in your career. Feel free to relocate for a new and better job.

With Saturn: An influential person or authority figure is supportive in coming months. Expect a slowdown on the job and use the time to consolidate your position by taking on little extra responsibilities. Good for seeking political patronage or a government job.

With Uranus: Changes in your circumstances are helpful in the next few montns. You may go into an entirely new line of work now. Be confident, no matter how suddenly the opportunity arises. Be careful in dealings with government, however.

With Neptune: You can rely on the sympathy and understanding of others in coming months. Seek professional guidance and consult superiors on any job confusion or necessary decisions. Your intuition on the job can also be helpful.

With Pluto: Fate steps in to help you out of an apparently insoluble situation in the near future. You may be faced with the need to retrain or rethink your job goals. Be open to new ideas and consult the experts.

Fortuna Minor
In the 11th House

Alone, no planets: This influence protects you against your own impulses as well as external enemies. Helpful but not entirely favorable. Stick to regular social activities and familiar friends now, rather than trying to experiment with new social goals. You are better off as the big frog in a small pond, where you are secure.

With Sun: You can take advantage of opportunities wth greater energy and confidence. You may be asked to assume a position of leadership in a group to which you belong. Part of your strength now is the support you garner for your goals and interests.

With Moon: Fortune is fickle, sometimes favorable and sometimes adverse, with frequent fluctuations. You are more popular with the crowds than with individuals in your social circle, so stick to attending large social events where you can circulate and make new acquaintances.

With Mercury: You are quick to grasp opportunity and adapt to changing circumstances. Your best ideas come from discussions with friends, or group lectures you attend. Speak up on issues of importance to you now.

With Venus: Fortune smiles on you in small ways making life more pleasurable and profitable. Your purpose in social activities is purely people-oriented, so make your feelings the basis of your participation in group plans.

With Mars: Your physical strength and agility are called into play more frequently in coming months. You are very active in the groups to which you belong, and plan many interesting outings and events.

Your initiatives are appreciated and followed. Sports are favored.

With Jupiter: Fortune smiles on you and brings success in all your efforts in coming months. An excellent time to expand your social life under the beneficence of Jupiter, but remember to stick to conventional groups.

With Saturn: An influential person or authority figure is supportive in coming months. Political activism as part of a group is favored now. You prefer old friends who give you a sense of security and continuity.

With Uranus: Changes in your circumstances are helpful in the next few months. You will be meeting many new people, possibly joining a new social or business group. Maintain your independence until you are more familiar with their aims.

With Neptune: You can rely on the sympathy and understanding of others in coming months. You may join a charitable group, or spend more time in the company of artists, musicians and pacifists. Give your support to talent when you find it.

With Pluto: Fate steps in to help you out of an apparently insoluble situation in the near future. Among the groups you join will be people you knew in past lifetimes. You are coming together for a specific social purpose.

Fortuna Minor
In the 12th House
Alone, no planets: This influence protects you against your own impulses as well as external enemies, helpful but not entirely favorable. You can find a cure for ailments now, and ways to relieve inner tensions or sorrows. Meditation brings inner strength.

With Sun: You can take advantage of opportunities with greater energy and confidence. Your health and vitality benefit from a little more attention. You can cultivate inner strength through meditation and better self-understanding. Frustrations pass.

With Moon: Fortune is fickle, sometimes favorable and sometimes adverse, with frequent fluctuations. A minor ailment or your inner ups and downs, can make life difficult, keeping you too private or self-absorbed. Share a weight problem or similar difficulties with a group.

With Mercury: You are quick to grasp opportunity and adapt to changing circumstances. Nervous strain is your problem at the moment. Practice meditative techniques for relaxation, and if study is necessary, do it privately, to avoid distraction. You may receive spiritual messages or solutions to problems in your dreams.

With Venus: Fortune smiles on you in small ways, making life more pleasurable and profitable. You are in the mood to pamper yourself and take better care of yourself. Avoid self-indulgent food or other binges, and you will continue to feel in good shape.

With Mars: Your physical strength and agility are called into play more frequently in coming months. You are filled with abundant energy, but frustrated in trying to use it to pursue your ambitions. Physical exercise helps alleviate tensions. Build up physical skills now.

With Jupiter: Fortune smiles on you and brings success in all your efforts in coming months. Your health is excellent, and you feel on top of the world. You may have prophetic dreams, and enjoy solitude now.

With Saturn: An influential person or authority figure is supportive in coming months. Pay attention to your teeth and bones now, and watch for any vitamin deficiencies. Saturn gives a realistic approach to maintaining good health, but you also need more sleep and possibly laxatives (natural) for sluggishness.

With Uranus: Changes in your circumstances are helpful in the next few months. You may suffer from insomnia or nervous tension now. Establish good, relaxing routines prior to bedtime in order to get more regular rest. You may have clairvoyant visions of the future in your dreams.

With Neptune: You can rely on the sympathy and understanding of others in coming months. Your psychic abilities are stimulated and reveal themselves mainly in dreams, although meditation and solitude may lead to visions.

With Pluto: Fate steps in to help you out of an apparently insoluble situation in the near future. You are more active in the hours of darkness than in daytime, and are physically rejuvenated by spiritual forces.

VIA

This symbol is strengthened and given direction by *all* of the planets, regardless of their aspects.

Via is ruled by the Moon and associated with the sign Leo, where the Sun which illuminates the Moon is the most powerful, providing light for travel by day and by night.

This symbol always represents a point of conscious thought and planning in the querent's chart. Via represents all forms of planning, maps, directions and instructions on how to perform activities, and thus textbooks and medical prescriptions. Via represents all forms of organized behavior designed to produce a given result. Thus Via is involved in life planning, architectural designs, city planning, and landscaping. Always it is the pathway to a certain destination, be it a city, a state of health or mind, or the attainment of a goal or object. Forethought and preparedness for travel and action are involved in the house which holds Via.

Via
In the 1st House
Alone, no planets: This is a fluctuating influence, sometimes mildly favorable, sometimes mildly adverse. The pathway to your desires seems clear, but you must be more persistent and self-interested to achieve them. Dictate your own terms in running your personal life.

With Sun: You have the strength and confidence to plan your course in life and stick to it in coming nonths. Your inner strength and courage enable you to take advantage of opportunity and put aside obstacles with fortitude and confidence. Your personality dominates in contacts with others.

With Moon: You are very vulnerable to changes in your mood and circumstances which affect your course in life. You are wise to stick to courses of action demonstrated by the experiences of others, than to go off on your own. Enjoy new people, but be cautious.

With Mercury: You are flexible and quick to adapt to opportunities which you work into your general life plan. This is the time to introduce your ideas to the public, to express your personal goals, and to seek out others who share your beliefs. You then benefit from the knowledge of many people in dealing with personal affairs.

With Venus: You count on the cooperation and support of others in planning your life strategy. Respond to the affection others display, and enjoy the arts and music, beauty and pleasure, important parts of your personal life now.

With Mars: Organize activities to make the most of short bursts of energy. A regimen of exercise and sports benefits your health. Enjoy competitive games, and set your sights on a new personal goal toward which you can strive while your energy level is so high.

With Jupiter: Your course in life is smooth and rewarding in coming months. You are lucky in your personal life, partly from your openness to new ideas and the ability to see the chances that will aid your well-developed personal goals.

With Saturn: In coming months, adhere strictly to the course of action you have already set up. You have very high personal ambitions; do not let delays or distractions keep you from striving for your goals.

With Uranus: Ongoing changes create tension or indecision in the next few months. Be flexible within the limits of the goals you set for yourself, and be prepared to take advantage of new contacts and opportunities for self-development.

With Neptune: Intuition and imagination can point you in the right direction in coming months. Don't be afraid to turn aside from your regular personal activities to listen to unseen spiritual guides on higher plateaus of self-development.

With Pluto: Be receptive to higher spiritual guidance in planning for the coming months. Past life experiences coming to the surface now should be used when positive and resolved when difficult. You feel a resurgence of inner confidence.

Via
In the 2nd House

Alone, no planets: This is a fluctuating influence, sometimes mildly favorable, sometimes mildly adverse. You have income from several sources, some productive, and some minimal. Watch a tendency to spend emotionally on the spur of the moment.

With Sun: You have the strength and confidence to plan your course in life and stick to it in coming months. You will be taking up several projects to increase your income in the near future. Your personal energy makes them a success.

With Moon: You are very vulnerable to changes in your mood and circumstances which affect your course in life. Watch impulsive emotional spending, and following the crowd in investments. Keep your nesteggs in different baskets to avoid loss.

With Mercury: You are flexible and quick to adapt to opportunities which you work into your general life plan. You profit from various ventures into sales and advertising. Watch your timing so that you move from one project to another when you can reap the greatest profits.

With Venus: You count on the cooperation and support of others in planning your life strategy. You may receive some gifts or added benefits from investments. Set aside a certain amount for luxury spending, and reinvest the remainder while you are fortunate in your choices.

With Mars: Organize activities to make the most of short bursts of energy. you may take on several part-time jobs or projects to increase funds. You are successful, but watch the tendency to spend in haste because your time is limited.

With Jupiter: Your course in life is smooth and rewarding in coming months. You profit from sales and advertising now; everything you touch prospers. Excellent for short-term speculative ventures. Watch your tendency to spend on extravagant luxury items.

With Saturn: In coming months, adhere strictly to the course of action you have already set up. Financial returns are slow and small; stick to securities. Watch for sales to find what you want at bargain prices.

With Uranus: Ongoing changes create tension or indecision the next few months. Your sources of income are interrupted at times, at other times offer real windfalls. Avoid impulse spending or fad items. You can profit from electronic and computer areas now.

With Neptune: Intuition and imagination can point you in the right direction in coming months. You may hit on a winning formula in gambling, such as lotteries, or in your investments. Follow your hunches, but know when to cash in.

With Pluto: Be receptive to higher spiritual guidance in planning for the coming months. Cooperative ventures and municipal bonds are good investments, as are renewal projects, such as real estate. Invest in an annuity if possible.

Via
In the 3rd House
Alone, no planets: This is a fluctuating influence, sometimes mildly favorable, sometimes mildly adverse. Your opinions and viewpoints change frequently, because you eagerly keep up with the news. You may be doing a great deal of local traveling now.

With Sun: You have the strength and confidence to plan your course in life and stick to it in coming months. You may wind up teaching a skill or ideas to another person or a group, because you are regarded as an authority in some field of knowledge. Go after a special goal, for your motto now is "where there's a will, there's a way."

With Moon: You are very vulnerable to changes in your mood and circumstances which affect your course in life. Involve yourself in public projects, attend lectures, and travel with tours and other groups. You learn as much from the observations of others as you do from your own.

With Mercury: You are flexible and quick to adapt to opportunities which you work into your general life plan. Your mind is especially quick in picking up difficult manual skills and mental techniques. Now is the time to successfully study a sometimes difficult subject.

With Venus: You count on the cooperation and support of others in planning your life strategy. You can develop any artistic or musical talents more easily now, as the techniques that attract you are ideal. You may also take up design or interior decorating.

With Mars: Organize activities to make the most of short bursts of energy. You can learn new physical skills easily now, particularly martial arts and body building, along with engineering and other technical skills, if these are of interest to you.

With Jupiter: Your course in life is smooth and rewarding in coming months. You can undertake any type of study, or put your own ideas into a book or article, with great ease. Travel is also highly favored for learning purposes.

With Saturn: In coming months, adhere strictly to the course of action you have already set up. You can stay the course in difficult studies that require much concentration and absorption of factual material. Take guided tours to make the most of any travel time.

With Uranus: Ongoing changes create tension or indecision the next few months. Take an independent trip of exploration to learn, as you travel and absorb more quickly on your own. Studies of astrology and the sciences are especially favored now.

With Neptune: Intuition and imagination can point you in the right direction in coming months. You can harness your imagination with writing now if you choose. Studies of religion, philosophy, mysticism and the psychic arts are easier to comprehend and practice now.

With Pluto: Be receptive to higher spiritual guidance in planning for the coming months. You are adept in applying the techniques of psychology and hypnotism if you study such topics now. You are especially interested in group interactions.

Via
In the 4th House
Alone, no planets: This is a fluctuating influence, sometimes mildly favorable, sometimes mildly adverse. This is a good time to design a home of your own, develop new household routines and arrangements, make plans for shared family activities. Details seem to fall into place easily.

With Sun: You have the strength and confidence to plan your course in life and stick to it in coming months. You assume a dominant role in the course your family takes in the near future, including the running of your home, and family activites. You profit from dealings in real estate.

With Moon: You are very vulnerable to changes in your mood and circumstances which affect your course in life. Your mother, the woman of the family, or some dominant female figure is the center of family attention. Attend a public auction of household items which you might need or want for your own home.

With Mercury: You are flexible and quick to adapt to opportunities which you work into your general life plan. You spend more time thinking about and communicating with family members, and may take a trip to visit a family member in the near future.

With Venus: You count on the cooperation and support of others in planning your life strategy. You enjoy entertaining at home and also directing your artistic talents into home decorating.

With Mars: Organize activities to make the most of short bursts of energy. Home repairs and family activities absorb your energy and attention now. You may be in the arduous process of moving or remodeling.

With Jupiter: Your course in life is smooth and rewarding in coming months. An excellent time to invest in real estate or agriculture for both pleasure and profit. Family relations are very harmonious, particularly relations with the women in the family.

With Saturn: In coming months, adhere strictly to the course of action you have already set up. This is a good time to make concrete plans for your retirement years, such as setting funds aside and considering where and how you would like to live. You might enjoy researching the family tree.

With Uranus: Ongoing changes create tension or indecision the next few months. A sudden move, or a visit from a family member could upset your household routine somewhat. Be flexible, but firm on keeping things running for your immediate family.

With Neptune: Intuition and imagination can point you in the right direction in coming months. You have the urge to escape from the house and family routine, but maybe a little more peace for your personal interests would keep you happy at home.

With Pluto: Be receptive to higher spiritual guidance in planning for the coming months. You may be busy planning to remodel or improve your home; consider mending any family emotional fences while you are at it.

Via
In the 5th House
Alone, no planets: This is a fluctuating influence, sometimes mildly favorable, sometimes mildly adverse. You are flirtatious in love, changeable with children, impulsive in recreation, and sporadic in your creative efforts. You may be lucky in a supermarket sweepstakes however. Try to organize your life a little, but not too rigidly.

With Sun: You have the strength and confidence to plan your course in life and stick to it in coming months. Your creative drives are strong, your affections deep, and your relations with children good. You are more interested in the entertainment value of gambling, but winning is fun, too.

With Moon: You are very vulnerable to changes in your mood and circumstances which affect your course in life. You enjoy popular recreation, share a good rapport with children, and tend to cater to loved ones. Your cooking is highly creative.

With Mercury: You are flexible and quick to adapt to opportunities which you work into your general life plan. Your major recreation involves talk and travel. You establish better communications with loved ones and children. Creative writing attracts you.

With Venus: You count on the cooperation and support of others in planning your life strategy. An engagement announcement may be the high point in your love life; or you may take off on a pleasure trip with your spouse. Take up a creative new hobby now. You may be mildly lucky in supermarket sweepstakes.

With Mars: Organize activities to make the most of short bursts of energy. You express your feelings toward a loved one with great ardor. You easily direct excess energy into sports and creative crafts. You are successful in competition.

With Jupiter: Your course in life is smooth and rewarding in coming months. You are lucky in gambling now, particularly horse racing and speculative investments. Your optimism and expansivenesss brighten the lives of loved ones and children.

With Saturn: In coming months, adhere strictly to the course of action you have already set up. Your devotion and loyalty toward a loved one reap a romantic harvest. You are cautious in speculation and prefer productive hobbies, where you feel you are accomplishing something useful as well as attractive.

With Uranus: Ongoing changes create tension or indecision the next few months. You are fortunate in games of chance, but watch for minor accidents in hazardous recreation. You seek excitement and stimulation in love. Your originality can be successfully applied to a new creative hobby.

With Neptune: Intuition and imagination can point you in the right direction in coming months. You seek romance and glamour in love, peace and harmony in your relations with young people. Your imagination finds an outlet in the arts and music. You may be lucky in a lottery or sweepstakes.

With Pluto: Be receptive to higher spiritual guidance in planning for the coming months. Fate may bring affection from one you knew in a past lifetime. Your understanding of young people is penetrable and useful. Group recreation is favored. You may be lucky in a sweepstakes or lottery.

Via
In the 6th House
Alone, no planets: This is a fluctuating influence, sometimes mildly favorable, sometimes mildly adverse. Your health maintains an even keel, and your job retains a predictable, if varied course. You may suffer from boredom, but you find diversion if you try for added job training or advancement.

With Sun: You have the strength and confidence to plan your course in life and stick to it in coming months. You may attain a position of authority on the job through the regular promotional scales; make the effort. Your vitality remains high as long as you stick to good health routines.

With Moon: You are very vulnerable to changes in your mood and circumstances which affect your course in life. You do best dealing with the vagaries of the public, or in seasonal work just now. If with a long-term employer, consider advancing through the ranks. You tend to retain water, so watch your diet.

With Mercury: You are flexible and quick to adapt to opportunities which you work into your general life plan. You may suffer from some nervous tension or boredom on the job; look for additional training through study courses or on-the-job activities. Your communicative abilities are excellent.

With Venus: You count on the cooperation and support of others in planning your life strategy. Your only health problem is likely to be self-indulgence of your appetite, particularly in group activities. Your love of comfort affects your work, so improve working conditions as best you can.

With Mars: Organize activities to make the most of short bursts of energy. You can accomplish a lot at work, but pace yourself; compete for advancement or a better-paying job now. Your energy level is high, but watch for minor accidents when you attempt to hurry the job along.

With Jupiter: Your course in life is smooth and rewarding in coming months. You tend to gain weight as your delight in physical life and satisfactions includes good food. You make easy progress on the job, and can easily train for a new position.

With Saturn: In coming months, adhere strictly to the course of action you have already set up. You have heavy job responsibilities, but avoid overtime in order to maintain steady progress and your general good health. A good time to attend to dental needs.

With Uranus: Ongoing changes create tension or indecision the next few months. Be flexible and receptive to changes on the job, but demand adequate training for any new responsibilities. You may suffer from some tension or insomnia. Do not accept swing shift types of work.

With Neptune: Intuition and imagination can point you in the right direction in coming months. You may be sensitized to drugs and alcohol now. You prefer to work alone or at nights now, and take on more responsibilities on your own.

With Pluto: Be receptive to higher spiritual guidance in planning for the coming months. Your health improves with your emotional uplift; try suggestion techniques to improve health routines. You find it easiest to work on the job when you join others in the activities required.

VIA
In the 7th House
Alone, no planets: This is a fluctuating influence, sometimes mildly favorable, sometimes mildly adverse. Set a reasonable length of time for an engagement, and plan the wedding carefully, so details are set. If married, make an effort to keep special time open for shared activities.

With Sun: You have the strength and confidence to plan your course in life and stick to it in coming months. You are the dominant factor in planning for a wedding, or guiding your spouse in satisfying directions. Sign partnership papers.

With Moon: You are very vulnerable to changes in your mood and circumstances which affect your course in life. You are eager to be guided by a strong person in a close relationship, and in business matters.

With Mercury: You are flexible and quick to adapt to opportunities which you work into your general life plan. Develop long-range business plans and sign legal papers now, while details are clear in your mind.

With Venus: You count on the cooperation and support of others in planning your life strategy. A romantic outing with a loved one is favored. You profit from any partnership business venture, particularly involving luxury items.

With Mars: Organize activities to make the most of short bursts of energy. You take the initiative in a close relationship, and enjoy competing with others for a prize. Avoid quarrels that could lead to legal disputes.

With Jupiter: Your course in life is smooth and rewarding in coming months. You are highly successful as part of a team in business matters, and enjoy the generosity of your spouse or special loved one. You feel protected and confident.

With Saturn: In the coming months, adhere strictly to the course of action you have already set up. You may finally decide to marry an admirer who has persisted for some time; or you may spend time at a place of happy memories with your spouse. Long-term business partnership is favored.

With Uranus: Ongoing changes create tension or indecision in the next few months. Proceed with plans to end a business partnership. A sudden excitement permeates the more romantic side of your close relationships.

With Neptune: Intuition and imagination can point you in the right direction in coming months. A close relationship seems to be fading, with few regrets on either side. This is not the time to become involved in poorly defined partnership business activities.

With Pluto: Be receptive to higher spiritual guidance in planning for the coming months. You are drawn to someone who was an important part of a past lifetime. Carry out your end of a business partnership, however you feel at the moment, as you may reap some good profits.

Via
In the 8th House
Alone, no planets: This is a fluctuating influence, sometimes mildly favorable, sometimes mildly adverse. Membership in an occult fraternity or studies on an organized basis yield spiritual and material results. Short term commodities investments, and silver purchases are favored. Your sexual moods vary with the moment; avoid being fickle.

With Sun: You have the strength and confidence to plan your course in life and stick to it in coming months. You profit when you take charge of joint financial ventures. You also develop your spirituality and self-mastery through occult interests. You are the dominant force in a sexual relationship which has its ups and downs.

With Moon: You are very vulnerable to changes in your mood and circumstances which affect your course in life. You get along better with women than with men at the moment; enhance your attractiveness to the opposite sex. The study of the cards in divination is favored. Group or cooperative financial ventures are most profitable.

With Mercury: You are flexible and quick to adapt to opportunities which you work into your general life plan. You may receive spirit messages if you make a habit of being receptive. Exchange of ideas and information transcends sexual differences. Sign joint financial papers now.

With Venus: You count on the cooperation and support of others in planning your life strategy. Your sexual charms are potent and you are happy in love. You profit from cooperative financial ventures. The artistry of occult rituals and books appeals to you.

With Mars: Organize activities to make the most of short bursts of energy. Your sexual ardor is intense but short-lived, and you enjoy quarreling and making up. Avoid credit dealings and joint ventures now; you are in too much of a hurry, and the con artists know it.

With Jupiter: Your course in life is smooth and rewarding in coming months. You may receive a legacy from a female relative, or profit from a joint venture. Occult studies bring spiritual and material benefits. Develop your gift of prophecy.

With Saturn: In coming months, adhere strictly to the course of action you have already set up. You face both spiritual and material debts now, but you have the means to settle these problems. High magic attracts you now.

With Uranus: Ongoing changes create tension or indecision the next few months. Astrology is particularly helpful now. You have the method and means to achieve greater financial independence.

With Neptune: Intuition and imagination can point you in the right direction in coming months. Develop your mediumistic and clairvoyant abilities through regular study and practice. Avoid joint financial ventures, as con artists abound.

With Pluto: Be receptive to higher spiritual guidance in planning for the coming months. You develop a sense of spiritual revitalization and purpose through occult studies. Cooperative joint ventures can be profitable. Use credit when time and convenience are more important than interest rates.

Via
In the 9th House
Alone, no planets: This is a fluctuating influence, sometimes mildly favorable, sometimes mildly adverse. You do best in planned, organized studies directed toward a specific short-term goal. Plan to travel with a

group of familiar people when you leave your home area.

With Sun: You have the strength and confidence to plan your course in life and stick to it in coming months. Your religious affiliation gives you greater self-confidence in dealing with new ideas and developments in your life. Travel to benefit your health.

With Moon: You are very vulnerable to changes in your mood and circumstances which affect your course in life. Enjoy the mental stimulation of new ideas and places, but don't expect to build anything permanent on these new experiences.

With Mercury: You are flexible and quick to adapt to opportunities which you work into your general life plan. Your communicative abilities find a new audience in print or speech. You may also teach others while learning new subjects yourself. Travel for any reason is favored.

With Venus: You count on the cooperation and support of others in planning your life strategy. Pleasure is your major objective in travel now. Studies in the arts and culture are highly favored.

With Mars: Organize activities to make the most of short bursts of energy. A trip of exploration can turn the course of your life in a new direction. Be sure you thoroughly grasp new ideas and are able to apply them before contradicting your teachers.

With Jupiter: Your course in life is smooth and rewarding in coming months. Consider teaching and thereby spreading enlightenment to others. Any publishing interests are successful, as is travel for any purpose. Your religion gives you a new sense of well-being.

With Saturn: In coming months, adhere strictly to the course of action you have already set up. This is an excellent time for making long-range business plans and trips. You have the persistence and realism to follow up on your plans for achievement. Practical business studies are favored.

With Uranus: Ongoing changes create tension or indecision the next few months. Travel may bring revelations of new ways to expand your mental horizons and change the course of your life for the better. Religious observances bring forth a new you.

With Neptune: Intuition and imagination can point you in the right direction in coming months. A mystical religious experience or an astral travel adventure can change the course of your life for the better. Travel and artistic studies are also favored.

With Pluto: Be receptive to higher spiritual guidance in planning for the coming months. Religious activities, travel and psycological studies combine to rejuvenate you both physically and spiritually. You are attracted to the concept of karma.

Via
In the 10th House
Alone, no planets: This is a fluctuating influence, sometimes mildly favorable, sometimes mildly adverse. Do not rely on the fickle applause of the crowds, but capitalize on public attention by promoting your products and skills in the right places. Special business sales are favored.

With Sun: You have the strength and confidence to plan your course in life and stick to it in coming months. An excellent time to start a business of your own or seek a position of authority in your profession. You may receive honors now.

With Moon: You are very vulnerable to changes in your mood and circumstances which affect your course in life. Start a business catering to the public, as you attract customers easily with advertising. Quick turnover products are most favored. You may also campaign for public office.

With Mercury: You are flexible and quick to adapt to opportunities which you work into your general life plan. Your writing or speaking talents may receive public attention and approval. Your ideas receive a favorable hearing from persons in authority on the job.

With Venus: You count on the cooperation and support of others in planning your life strategy. Public social affairs are the right setting for your charm and talent. You may receive favors from persons in authority. A business of your own in the arts or luxury items is favored.

With Mars: Organize activities to make the most of short bursts of energy. You may win a competition and gain public attention as a result. Your initiatives receive a favorable hearing on the job.

With Jupiter: Your course in life is smooth and rewarding in coming months. Start or expand a business of your own, or seek a position at the top of your profession. Your talents are easily recognized now.

With Saturn: In coming months, adhere strictly to the course of action you have already set up. You find it difficult to respond to the fluctuations of the public in your work, and the political upheavals in public affairs.

With Uranus: Ongoing changes create tension or indecision the next few months. You will discover new ways and places to apply your skills in the near future.

With Neptune: Intuition and imagination can point you in the right direction in coming months. You are imbued with a charitable spirit best expressed through public activities to support your favored groups.

With Pluto: Be receptive to higher spiritual guidance in planning for the coming months. A career in insurance, investigative research, or the health professions may be opening up for you now.

Via
In the 11th House
Alone, no planets: This is a fluctuating influence, sometimes mildly favorable, sometimes mildly adverse. Your social circle constantly changes, with people moving in and out of your life. Stick to established organizations so you have some social continuity. You are popular wherever you go.

With Sun: You have the strength and confidence to plan your course in life and stick to it in coming months. You can assume a position of leadership and authority in an organized social group if you choose. Others come for your advice in any case.

With Moon: You are very vulnerable to changes in your mood and circumstances which affect your course in life. You get a greater social response from women and public groups rather than more private social alliances. If economically helpful, this is a good time to publicize your work socially.

With Mercury: You are flexible and quick to adapt to opportunities which you work into your general life plan. You are likely to be chosen secretary or spokesperson for a group to which you belong. Your ideas receive a good reception from the public, and are sought in planning group action.

With Venus: You count on the cooperation and support of others in planning your life strategy. You take pleasure in the crowds, and they in turn lavish you with attention, praise and affection. Cooperative group ventures are successful now.

With Mars: Organize activities to make the most of short bursts of energy. Your initiative and sense of adventure put you in the forefront for group leadership, particularly involving any sports or competitive events. Expect to meet many new people in the near future.

With Jupiter: Your course in life is smooth and rewarding in coming months. You profit financially and spiritually from the friendships you form now. Be sure to join groups that express your religious beliefs and offer you learning experiences. Organized group travel is also favored.

With Saturn: In coming months, adhere strictly to the course of action you have already set up. You get the greatest benefit when you join job-related professional groups and political organizations that promote your beliefs and business interests.

With Uranus: Ongoing changes create tension or indecision the next few months. This is the time to hang loose and maintain your social freedom and independence, so take advantage of opportunities for group action and fun at short notice.

With Neptune: Intuition and imagination can point you in the right direction in coming months. You would enjoy joining an occult society, a group devoted to music and the arts, or simply attending a seance. Spiritual growth through group activities is your ideal goal now.

With Pluto: Be receptive to higher spiritual guidance in planning for the coming months. An occult society appeals to you but you are also interested in social reform that improves society as a whole. You may meet people with whom you share karmic ties now.

Via
In the 12th House
Alone, no planets: This is a fluctuating influence, sometimes mildly favorable, sometimes mildly adverse. While you do not have any particular health problems, you are more conscious of ailments making the rounds, and more inclined to practice good preventative medicine.

With Sun: You have the strength and confidence to plan your course in life and stick to it in coming months. Your vitality is excellent, and you are full of confidence about both physical and spiritual health. A good time to develop new beneficial health habits, as you have the will power to carry through with your goals.

With Moon: You are very vulnerable to changes in your mood and circumstances which affect your course in life. You may have intuitive dreams that reflect the state of your inner spiritual health as well as your physical well-being. Be aware that your emotions definitely affect your health, and stay positive.

With Mercury: You are flexible and quick to adapt to opportunities which you work into your general life plan. Your best ideas and hints of any health problems come in dreams and meditation. A good time for scrupulous self-examination to better understand your inner self and your physical health needs.

With Venus: You count on the cooperation and support of others in planning your life strategy. Your health is generally good, because you enjoy the activities you perform in contribution to physical well-being, such as exercise, good diet, positive meditation.

With Mars: Organize activities to make the most of short bursts of energy. Watch for feverish ailments or frustration, as your energies are confined to limited objectives in this house.

With Jupiter: Your course in life is smooth and rewarding in coming months. Your health is excellent. Make a point to keep track of your dreams, some of which will be prophetic. The details of any astral travel experiences may prove to be a guide to future action.

With Saturn: In coming months, adhere strictly to the course of action you have already set up. You rebound from illness slowly, and need more sleep, but a regular routine takes the edge off depression or fatigue. Dental and other exams are favored.

With Uranus: Ongoing changes create tension or indecision the next few months. The combination of nervous tension and insomnia creates sleep that yields clairvoyant visions or other surprises. Keep track of dreams for original and useful ideas.

With Neptune: Intuition and imagination can point you in the right direction in coming months. Intuition can be organized through meditation and careful scrutiny of dreams for psychic content. You may also have astral travel experiences. Watch for sensitivity to drugs and alcohol.

With Pluto: Be receptive to higher spiritual guidance in planning for the coming months. Your physical recuperative abilities are excellent, and you may be able to mend psychic traumas now through positive meditation and self-analysis.

POPULUS

This symbol is strengthened and given direction by *all* of the planets, regardless of their aspects.

Populus is ruled by the Moon and relates to the sign Capricorn where the Moon is in detriment; thus, Populus is a variable figure, sometimes mildly favorable, sometimes mildly adverse, swaying with the intentions and moods of the public, or people, which Populus represents. Capricorn represents the organization of people into an orderly society, a constructive side of people as a whole.

Populus represents all gatherings of the public, and, for their safety, is associated with the sign of rules and regulations of group behavior. Restaurants, mass transit, schools, all the places that people gather in groups are ordered and conducted under Saturnian rules. Where there are too many restrictions, people leave or protest. Thus, in a chart Populus represents the areas of life where the querent is an effective part of the public body, or needs the support of large numbers of people to achieve contemplated goals.

Populus
In the 1st House
Alone, no planets: This is a fluctuating influence, sometimes mildly favorable, sometimes mildly adverse. You are very conscious of public opinion and can do much to promote your interests if you take advantage of this public attention.

With Sun: Your personality dominates public gatherings, where you have a definite effect on decisions. You are regarded as a source of strength and leadership to the new contacts you make. Broaden your audience to include the general public, in sales, advertising or any personal service you perform.

With Moon: You are completely attuned with the moods of the people and make an excellent representative. Take advantage of your personal popularity to set an example in style, ideas, competition, and other public activities.

With Mercury: Public opinion is important to your interests the next few months. You excel as a public spokesperson. Your ability to sway the public can be valuable in sales, advertising and other public contact work, or in publicizing your writings or lectures.

With Venus: You excel as a mediator of public disputes, and achieve cooperation among various groups. Your charm wins you many new friends. A new wardrobe and appearance can bring other benefits, perhaps financial or personal. Display artistic creations now.

With Mars: Increased interaction with people and involvement in public affairs absorb your energy in coming months. Your initiative, daring and leadership qualities can bring you quickly to the forefront of public attention. Use this attention to promote your work and ambitions.

With Jupiter: Good fortune follows when you participate in public activities and meet new people. Enjoy public entertainment, promote your ideas and products, especially try to sell any personal items at a profit now.

With Saturn: Your contacts with people seem to add to your responsibilities and obligations in coming months. If your professional advice is sought, be sure to charge for it, regardless of friendship or acquaintance. Political activism is favored.

With Uranus: Ongoing changes create tension or indecision the next few months. You are attracted to public fads, but avoid going alone with the crowd in extremist behavior. Direct originality into creative projects which may gain instant acclaim from the public.

With Neptune: Rely on intuition in dealing with people the next few months. Your psychic sensitivity may win you public attention when your predictions are accurate—excellent for anyone working in a psychic or occult occupation.

With Pluto: Contact with the public seems to resurrect past life acquaintances in coming months. You feel the hand of fate strongly in your life; accept and grow, rather than resist because of doubts. A revamp of your appearance and health is favored.

Populus
In the 2nd House

Alone, no planets: This is a fluctuating influence, sometimes mildly favorable, sometimes mildly adverse. Your best sources of income involve public contacts, as in sales, advertising, communications. You also benefit from purchases at special sales.

With Sun: Your personality dominates public gatherings, where you have a definite effect on decisions. You may seek a better job that recognizes your inner abilities and strength, and thus increase your income. Sales of luxury items and property are favored.

With Moon: You are completely attuned with the moods of the people and make an excellent representative. You profit from any type of seasonal work and dealings with the public, and go in for the popular, trendy items in personal purchases.

With Mercury: Public opinion is important to your interests the next few months. You excel as a public spokesperson. You are on top of economic news and can profit from investments now, or from writings and lectures on popular subjects.

With Venus: You excel as a mediator of public disputes, and achieve cooperation among various groups. Your charm may bring you gifts and favors, tips about investments, and success in acquiring desired possessions.

With Mars: Increased interaction with people and involvement in public affairs absorb your energy in coming months. You have several financial irons in the fire, but avoid haste or carelessness in shopping and maintenance of your possessions.

With Jupiter: Good fortune follows when you participate in public activities and meet new people. You profit from any type of sales or publishing work, banking or investments in public stocks.

With Saturn: Your contacts with people seem to add to your responsibilities and obligations in coming months. Purchasing low and selling dear in investments and actual products can be a source of good income. Antiques and other valuable items may be found at public auctions and estate sales now.

With Uranus: Ongoing changes create tension or indecision the next few months. An invention or an original advertising approach could reap a harvest from the public. Financial independence through dealings with the public is a real possibility.

With Neptune: Rely on intuition in dealing with people the next few months. Any work in the occult or psychic professions, or in organizing charitable functions can be profitable. Follow your own hunches in investments.

With Pluto: Contact with the public seems to resurrect past life acquaintances in coming months. Work in insurance, investigations, research, occult activities, can all be profitable now. Hold a sale of reusable items now.

Populus
In the 3rd House
Alone, no planets: This is a fluctuating influence, sometimes mildly favorable, sometimes mildly adverse. You are on the receiving end of a lot of messages or information, some of it to your liking, and some not. This is the time to deal with paperwork and maintain good contacts for sales and advertising purposes.

With Sun: Your personality dominates public gatherings, where you have a definite effect on decisions. You may be elected to a local political office, or accept a local government job now, as your expertise is much remarked on.

With Moon: You are completely attuned with the moods of the people and make an excellent representative. Your contacts with those around you wax and wane with the phases of the Moon—sometimes you are active, sometimes inert—but you are always aware of what is going on. Travel is favored.

With Mercury: Public opinion is important to your interests the next few months. You excel as a public spokesperson. This is a good time to deal with paperwork, take a popular study course, express yourself in print or speech, and generally use your mind and knowledge to deal with everyday problems and activities.

With Venus: You excel as a mediator of public disputes, and achieve cooperation among various groups. Your charm and friendliness win you new friends in your daily activities. Travel for pleasure and art studies or tours of galleries and museums are favored.

With Mars: Increased interaction with people and involvement in public affairs absorb your energy in coming months. A good time to purchase a new car in a popular new model, and enter public contests and competitions. You travel a great deal and express your opinions forcefully.

With Jupiter: Good fortune follows when you participate in public activities and meet new people. Excellent for the writer, teacher, lecturer, speaker, or any type of communications or transportation worker. Your daily routine is smoothed in all ways.

With Saturn: Your contacts with people seem to add to your responsibilities and obligations in coming months. You may be elected to public office or be chosen for a government job, or asked to volunteer for some type of community service. Messages are delayed, as is travel.

With Uranus: Ongoing changes create tension or indecision the next few months. Stimulating changes in your surroundings bring you into contact with a wide variety of people. You can learn by detached observation now. Messages and travel are sudden and sporadic.

With Neptune: Rely on intuition in dealing with people the next few months. You are likely to have premonitions or visions about events that affect people around you. Develop your psychic sensitivity while you are exposed to such a variety of people.

With Pluto: Contact with the public seems to resurrect past life acquaintances in coming months. This is an excellent time to review studies, research subjects of interest, and visit museums and historical places.

Populus
In the 4th House
Alone, no planets: This is a fluctuating influence, sometimes mildly favorable, sometimes mildly adverse. You are likely to have a lot of drop-in guests, and a variety of family activities to participate in, some of them conflicting. Spread yourself around while you are popular with the family.

With Sun: Your personality dominates public gatherings, where you have a definite effect on decisions. This is an excellent time to invest in real eatate, and make major plans for your family and future security. Your home is a magnet for acquaintances and friends.

With Moon: You are completely attuned with the moods of the people and make an excellent representative. Excellent for interior decorating and any sales work connected with homes, real estate or furnishings. A good time to hold a family get-together.

With Mercury: Public opinion is important to your interests the next few months. You excel as a public spokesperson. Sign any papers connected with real estate now. You may receive an important message from a family member. Advertise your home for sale now, if desired.

With Venus: You excel as a mediator of public disputes, and achieve cooperation among various groups. Home entertaining and decorating are especially favored, and you may pursue decorating professionally now with success.

With Mars: Increased interaction with people and involvement in public affairs absorb your energy in coming months. Home repairs and remodeling are favored, as are shared family activities. You accomplish more work at home than on the job.

With Jupiter: Good fortune follows when you participate in public activities and meet new people. Sale of your home now would bring a better price than ordinarily. You may receive a gift or a legacy from a parent or relative now.

With Saturn: Your contacts with people seem to add to your responsibilities and obligations in coming months. Purchase long-term basic necessities for your home, as you will find good bargains. Invest in business property.

With Uranus: Ongoing changes create tension or indecision the next few months. You may be moving in the near future to an area where you can make more contact with people and gain greater convenience in your domestic life.

With Neptune: Rely on intuition in dealing with people the next few months. You are more sensitive to people around your home, and may prefer more peace and privacy.

With Pluto: Contact with the public seems to resurrect past life acquaintances in coming months. Home renovation increases the value of your home; or you may invest in property to renovate and resell profitably.

Populus
In the 5th House
Alone, no planets: This is a fluctuating influence, sometimes mildly favorable, sometimes mildly adverse. You are more likely to lose than to win at gambling, and find loved ones somewhat moody or fickle. However, short-term creative projects are favored.

With Sun: Your personality dominates public gatherings, where you have a definite effect on decisions. You are successful in sports and contests, and really put your heart into creative projects. A good time to show your products to the public, or perform in public. You are the one who loves, while your loved one may appear fickle.

With Moon: You are completely attuned with the moods of the people and make an excellent representative. You are drawn to children now, and somewhat moody in romance. You trust the younger generation more than adults. Your creative projects have definite popular appeal. You may be lucky in a supermarket sweepstakes.

With Mercury: Public opinion is important to your interests the next few months. You excel as a public spokesperson. Your creative instincts run to writing and any form of communication that offers new ideas. You may be mildly lucky in a lottery or other numbers-oriented game. Love expands with shared ideas.

With Venus: You excel as a mediator of public disputes, and achieve cooperation among various groups. A romantic time for an engagement announcement or a wedding. Any artistic talents should be brought to the attention of the public. Gambling brings small profits.

With Mars: Increased interaction with people and involvement in public affairs absorb your energy in coming months. You are the winner in contests and competitions. You also come out ahead when you take the initiative in love. Sports betting is entertaining, and may bring minor profits.

With Jupiter: Good fortune follows when you participate in public activities and meet new people. You are very lucky in gambling when you follow the favorites at the track, or take up the most popular form of local gambling. You may have too many loves, of both individuals and hobbies, to keep up with.

With Saturn: Your contacts with people seem to add to your responsibilities and obligations in coming months. Watch for frustrations in love and creative efforts due to the interference of other people. Avoid gambling and other speculative ventures now.

With Uranus: Ongoing changes create tension or indecision the next few months. You may meet someone new and exciting who puts old loves entirely out of mind, but this person may be fickle. Do not burn romantic bridges behind you. You may be briefly lucky in games of chance, such as casino gambling. Apply your creative originality.

With Neptune: Rely on intuition in dealing with people the next few months. You are particularly susceptible to the appeals of children now. Your creative imagination is highly stimulated, so find time to express it in arts or music. Enjoy the popular romance of the season, whether a movie, book, or a real life situation.

With Pluto: Contact with the public seems to resurrect past life acquaintances in coming months. The more people you share recreation and creative hobbies with, the more your own pleasure and talent will be stimulated. You may also be lucky in a sweepstakes or lottery.

Populus
In the 6th House
Alone, no planets: This is a fluctuating influence, sometimes mildly favorable, sometimes mildly adverse. Your job involves you with lots of people now, both coworkers and the public, or with the demands of the public. Your health can suffer from too many contacts, particularly during cold and flu season, so build yourself up.

With Sun: Your personality dominates public gatherings, where you have a definite effect on decisions. Others look to you for supervision or support on the job. Your energy peps up the less energetic and more pessimistic people around you at work. This is a good time to seek advancement.

With Moon: You are completely attuned with the moods of the people and make an excellent representative. Your powers of adaptability are tested as many fluctuations and changes occur on the job, particularly busy and slow periods, depending on the phase of the Moon. Avoid becoming emotional over the problems of others.

With Mercury: Public opinion is important to your interests the next few months. You excel as a public spokesperson. A job-training course offered by a public institution could be just what you need for advancement now.

With Venus: You excel as a mediator of public disputes, and achieve cooperation among various groups. Charm, grooming, tact, and genuine artistic talents make you popular on the job and favor advancement.

With Mars: Increased interaction with people and involvement in public affairs absorb your energy in coming months. Your energy level is high, and you manage to accomplish a great deal with the cooperation of others. However, competition for advancement on the job brings the greatest awards.

With Jupiter: Good fortune follows when you participate in public activities and meet new people. Your health is excellent and you sail ahead on the job with complete confidence, tackling tasks that may daunt others.

With Saturn: Your contacts with people seem to add to your responsibilities and obligations in coming months. Your sense of responsibility may be overextended as you carry the load for one person after another. Restrain yourself and think in terms of self-preservation.

With Uranus: Ongoing changes create tension or indecision the next few months. Your powers of flexibility are tested to the utmost on the job, as changing ideas and technology demand constant learning. Watch for insomnia and nervous tension.

With Neptune: Rely on intuition in dealing with people the next few months. Try to find outlets for imaginative abilities on the job, and avoid the emotionalism easily generated by the ups and downs of those you work with.

With Pluto: Contact with the public seems to resurrect past life acquaintances in coming months. Your health improves when you join with others in self-improvement plans. Cooperation is also the key to job success now.

Populus
In the 7th House
Alone, no planets: This is a fluctuating influence, sometimes mildly favorable, sometimes mildly adverse. An engagement or wedding may be an important part of your life shared with those close to you. If single, you are certainly exposed to many potential partners; if married, you may have to share your spouse with the public.

With Sun: Your personality dominates public gatherings where you have a definite effect on decisions. You are the strong person in your marital relationship or business partnership, and set the direction of these major relatonships. Be strong, but not domineering.

With Moon: You are completely attuned with the moods of the people and make an excellent representative. You tend to be the passive half of your marriage or business partnership. Avoid becoming moody or emotional and use your understanding of human nature to give your relationships a boost.

With Mercury: Public opinion is important to your interests the next few months. You excel as a public spokesperson. You can now share your ideas and innermost feelings with spouse or partner, as the rapport between you is strong. Sign any business agreements now.

With Venus: You excel as a mediator of public disputes, and achieve cooperation among various groups. Displays of affection and sincere warmth are the keys to success in your marriage and partnerships. Avoid flirting with casual acquaintances, however.

With Mars: Increased interaction with people and involvement in public affairs absorb your energy in coming months. Your sex drive is a strong feature of your marriage, and your initiatives direct any business partnership. Public competitions are successful.

With Jupiter: Good fortune follows when you participate in public activities and meet new people. You may marry wealth or profit handsomely from a business partnership. Your close relationships are filled with optimism and generosity of spirit.

With Saturn: Your contacts with people seem to add to your responsibilities and obligations in coming months. You cherish the stability of your marriage or business partnership, as you have a strong sense of security. A political partnership is favored, as you have the public eye due to wise associations.

With Uranus: Ongoing changes create tension or indecision the next few months. You may break off a relationship now, but chances are you will change your mind again. Avoid major moves in a business partnership until conditions settle down.

With Neptune: Rely on intuition in dealing with people the next few months. You are sensitive to what others think of your close relationships—learn to put the feelings of those close to you first.

With Pluto: Contact with the public seems to resurrect past life acquaintances in coming months. This is an excellent time to participate in new group activities with your spouse or special friends. You all benefit from the togetherness.

Populus
In the 8th House
Alone, no planets: This is a fluctuating influence, sometimes mildly favorable, sometimes mildly adverse. You might enjoy a group past life regression session, or other occult classes. You profit from investments in common stocks and public companies.

With Sun: Your personality dominates public gatherings, where you have a definite effect on decisons. You are sexually attractive to a wide variety of members of the opposite sex. You radiate psychic as well as physical energy.

With Moon: You are completely attuned to the moods of the people and make an excellent representative. You would enjoy taking a tarot or other card-reading class now. You profit from public cooperative investments. You are strongly drawn to a popular member of the opposite sex now.

With Mercury: Public opinion is important to your interests the next few months. You excel as a public spokesperson. You succeed easily in mastering the occult subjects that interest you, and may be ready to teach or practice professionally. A good time to do tax work or have it done.

With Venus: You excel as a mediator of public disputes, and achieve cooperation among various groups. Your sexual charm wins you new admirers, so circulate more. Joint ventures can also be profitable. You enjoy your interests in the occult more.

With Mars: Increased interaction with people and involvement in public affairs absorbs your energy in coming months. You are sexually dynamic and can take the initiative with the opposite sex successfully. Joint financial ventures demand work, but are profitable; avoid excessive credit spending, however.

With Jupiter: Good fortune follows when you participate in public activities and meet new people. You may receive a legacy or profit from a cooperative investment; do not be too generous with your newly won good fortune. You may make friends with the opposite sex more easily now. Occult studies bring spiritual benefits.

With Saturn: Your contacts with people seem to add to your responsibilities and obligations in coming months. High magic is your best choice of occult interests now. Avoid public. or cooperative investments, as returns are too slow. You may be anxious about an intimate relationship, or feeling the lack thereof.

With Uranus: Ongoing changes create tension or indecision the next few months. Astrology interests you now, and is easy to comprehend. The opposite sex is unpredictable, so avoid the moody ones. You may have an unexpected financial opportunity.

With Neptune: Rely on intuition in dealing with people the next few months. Develop your mediumistic talents and practice astral travel now. You are highly attuned with a member of the opposite sex— knowledge is power. Play your hunches in a joint financial venture.

With Pluto: Contact with the public seems to resurrect past life acquaintances in coming months. Occult studies and practices are highly favored, as you can call on abundant spiritual energy. You may find your soul mate now.

Populus
In the 9th House
Alone, no planets: This is a fluctuating influence, sometimes mildly favorable, sometimes mildly adverse. A good time to study or travel with other groups—you learn more and expand your horizons when stimulated by the viewpoints of others.

With Sun: Your personality dominates public gatherings, where you have a definite effect on decisions. You, like the prophet, may be more popular and admired among those at a distance than you are in your own hometown. Travel enables you to publicly express your creative talents.

With Moon: You are completely attuned with the moods of the people and make an excellent representative. You especially get along with those from foreign cultures. Your writings or lectures may become more popular now. You are also interested in the new ideas affecting the public.

With Mercury: Public opinion is important to your interests the next few months. You excel as a public spokesperson. This is a good time to learn a foreign language, emphasizing actual practice with natives; or, you may have your own writings or lectures translated abroad. Foreign publishing and travel are favored.

With Venus: You excel as a mediator of public disputes, and achieve cooperation among various groups. You may find romance in a foreign setting; you are certainly attractive to people from other cultures, as you try to see and understand things from their point of view.

With Mars: Increased interaction with people and involvement in public affairs absorb your energy in coming months. Avoid getting involved in public disputes, but do participate in positive public activities. Travel is favored, and your ideas are sought by the crowds.

With Jupiter: Good fortune follows when you participate in public activities and meet new people. This is an excellent time for publishing, writing and travel to otherwise difficult areas, as you will have good luck and be welcomed. Religious activities are genuinely inspiring now.

With Saturn: Your contacts with people seem to add to your responsibilities and obligations in coming months. Be realistic in business dealings in foreign areas; avoid travel where governments are in trouble. You may assume added responsibilities in your religious affiliation.

With Uranus: Ongoing changes create tension or indecision the next few months. You are swept up by popular fads, particularly in religion and metaphysics. Keep an open mind, but examine all that this novel information really has to offer you.

With Neptune: Rely on intuition in dealing with people the next few months. An excellent time to practice psychometry, astral travel and card reading, as you are tuned into the higher astral plane.

With Pluto: Contacts with the public seem to resurrect past life acquaintances in coming months. An excellent time to examine the relevance of karma and reincarnation to your life; and to explore the hidden religions of the past.

Populus
In the 10th House
Alone, no planets: This is a fluctuating influence, sometimes mildly favorable, sometimes mildly adverse. Your professional standing or the success of your business depends on your ability to understand and cater to the needs of a wide variety of people.

With Sun: Your personality dominates public gatherings, where you have a definite effect on decisons. Your success is assured if you can maintain your appeal as a leader with the crowds. Put on a good display.

With Moon: You are completely attuned with the moods of the people and make an excellent representative. Watch for problems with the continuity of your career or business if you misjudge the whims of the people, or fail to keep pace with them.

With Mercury: Public opinion is important to your interests the next few months. You excel as a public spokesperson. You are capable of molding public opinion, and gaining fame for your writings or lectures. Make sure your goals are positive ones.

With Venus: You excel as a mediator of public disputes, and achieve cooperation among various groups. Promote the arts and cultural pursuits to the public to improve society and add to your own pleasure.

With Mars: Increased interaction with people and involvement in public affairs absorbs your energy in coming months. Your decisiveness and ability to make things happen greatly enhance your career success in dealing with people.

With Jupiter: Good fortune follows when you participate in public activities and meet new people. You are a pillar of trust and a fount of ethical behavior in an often cutthroat world; you gain popular affection as a result.

With Saturn: Your contacts with people seem to add to your responsibilities and obligations in coming months. You discharge your obligations to society with the needs of the common people first and foremost in your mind. You are respected as an elder statesperson.

With Uranus: Ongoing changes create tension or indecision the next few months. Follow your impulses and intuition in dealing with people in your work. Your original flair puts you in the forefront as a leader of the future.

With Neptune: Rely on intuition in dealing with people the next few months. Your mystical tendencies appeal to the crowds, who yearn for the kind of uplift your charitable instincts can give them. This is a highly favorable time for the artist and musical performer.

With Pluto: Contact with the public seems to resurrect past life acquaintances in coming months. Work to rebuild and renew those segments of society whose futures look dimmest. You may operate on the spiritual, physical or material planes successfully.

Populus
In the 11th House
Alone, no planets: This is a fluctuating influence, sometimes mildly favorable, sometimes mildly adverse. You are meeting and socializing with an ever-increasing number of people, and may be able to gain support for projects in the groups to which you belong. You may also represent a group to the public.

With Sun: Your personality dominates public gatherings, where you have a definite effect on decisions. You will be honored by friends or chosen leader of a public group. In the meantime, more casual friends still depend on your strength and stability.

With Moon: You are attuned to the moods of the people and make an excellent representative. Your ideas catch on quickly with the crowds, and your personality is considered an example of the ideal social person.

With Mercury: Public opinion is important to your interests the next few months. You excel as a public spokesperson. Your ideas are given full play in the groups to which you belong. This is a good time to join a foreign-language practice group.

With Venus: You excel as a mediator of public disputes, and achieve cooperation among various groups. Your charm and tact help smooth any divisions in groups, and you excel at planning pleasurable social events and cultural functions.

With Mars: Increased interaction with people and involvement in public affairs absorb your energy in coming months. You enjoy public conflicts, and excel at lobbying and protesting for the good of the people. You are also successful in social competitions and contests.

With Jupiter: Good fortune follows when you participate in public activities and meet new people. You are a fearless upholder of truth and justice, and people appreciate these qualities. You may be honored for your efforts to achieve social fair play.

With Saturn: Your contacts with people seem to add to your responsibilities and obligations in coming months. Your interest in proper government and the political process gain you a reputation for expertise in bridging the gap between the people and their government, through political action and reform groups.

With Uranus: Ongoing changes create tension or indecision the next few months. You are independent and self-contained in the midst of people, and make an excellent observer and recorder of the popular will and moods. You are in the forefront of groups seeking to improve the future.

With Neptune: Rely on intuition in dealing with people the next few months. You enjoy sharing artistic and musical interests, and are especially active in public charitable efforts.

With Pluto: Contact with the public seems to resurrect past life acquaintances in coming months. You may feel alone in the crowds at times, but your advice and support are eagerly sought.

Populus
In the 12th House

Alone, no planets: This is a fluctuating influence, sometimes mildly favorable, sometimes mildly adverse. Your health depends on your emotions, and you are also more subject to catching infectious ailments, such as colds, through public contacts.

With Sun: Your personality dominates public gatherings, where you have a definite effect on decisons. Your inner confidence increases through contact with the public. You also work in an occupation that improves the health of others.

With Moon: You are completely attuned to the moods of the people and make an excellent representative. Public health is particularly important to you, and you may work in a health field. You may also have premonitory dreams about events that affect large numbers of people.

With Mercury: Public opinion is important to your interests the next few months. You excel as a public spokesperson. You acquire good information about preventive medicine now, and how to build up your own health, possibly through a group lecture or the public media. You are active in charitable efforts.

With Venus: You excel as a mediator of public disputes, and achieve cooperation among various groups You are a persuasive collector for charities. You enjoy more privacy to get harmoniously balanced physically and spiritually.

With Mars: Increased interaction with people and involvement in public affairs absorb your energy in coming months. Release frustrations through group discussions or therapy. Avoid crowds, as you may come down with a feverish ailment.

With Jupiter: Good fortune follows when you participate in public activities and meet new people. Your generosity inclines you to action on the part of charitable causes. Your own health is excellent, and you may be able to help others improve their health as well. Dreams may involve premonitions and astral travel.

With Saturn: Your contacts with people seem to add to your responsibilities and obligations in coming months. You are anxious about the infectious ailments making the rounds. Get plenty of rest and keep your resistance built up now.

With Uranus: Ongoing changes create tension or indecision the next few months. Too much interaction with people may leave you overexcited and nervous, leading to insomnia. Limit your contacts to regain your equilibrium. Dreams may include a clairvoyant vision of the future.

With Neptune: Rely on intuition in dealing with people the next few months. Dreams may include a spiritual message. Meditation strengthens you for dealings with the public. You are sympathetic to others and work for charitable goals.

With Pluto: Contact with the public seems to resurrect past life acquaintances in coming months. Public lectures and discussions lead to self-understanding and greater inner strength. You stay healthy when others fall prey to colds and other infectious ailments.

CONJUNCTIO

This symbol is essentially favorable with all of the planets, regardless of their aspects.

Conjunctio is ruled by Mercury and associated with the sign Virgo, which is also ruled by Mercury. This is the Mercury of practical, material accomplishment. It represents the union between the generations created by the written word and the many human crafts. The combination of reason and observation is also related to Conjunctio.

Conjunctio always represents a point of concession, agreement or the joining of forces to accomplish a shared goal. The meaning of Conjunctio (Union) can symbolize marriage of two like-minded people, a business partnership, or a union in a skilled trade or other occupation. Conjunctio always indicates the action of two or more people, or the combination of two or more ingredients in a formula. It may also indicate two or more concepts in a hypothesis or scientific theory, or the addition or multiplication of the forces acting toward a specific goal. This may be a deliberate and conscious combination, or the result of natural forces, as when two rivers converge.

Conjunctio
In the 1st House
Alone, no planets: This is a favorable influence that remains in effect for the next few months. You are strongly under the influence of another in your personal life, and benefit from the objective insights others may bring into your future and interests.

With Sun: You are the dominant factor in a partnership or relationship which will be successful in coming months. Others rely on you for leadership and guidance toward goals that are of mutual interest and profit.

With Moon: You are the responsive person in a relationship or partnership which brings public attention in coming months. Your quick intuition establishes immediate rapport with individuals and the public, highly favorable for any sales, advertising or communications work in general.

With Mercury: You are the teacher or guide, or the recipient of teaching and worthwhile guidance in coming months. You are able to display the logic and reason of facts and theories in ways easily understood by others; you learn easily yourself as well.

With Venus: A friendship formed in coming months will prove happy and fruitful. A sympathetic shared appreciation of the arts and music, and cultural activities, brightens your life now.

With Mars: Combining your efforts with another greatly magnifies your rewards. Take the initiative to start new projects, and get others involved in new physical activities. Friendly competition is favored, and you may meet a challenging and stimulating opponent.

With Jupiter: Shared activities assume greater importance and bring correspondingly greater rewards in coming months. You are lucky and successful in new projects, feel more youthful and energetic, optimistic about the future. You may meet an astrological twin.

With Saturn: Activities shared with an older person or established group are more successful than solitary ones in coming months. Shared experiences can give you a new perspective on your plans and strategy for the future. You need this sense of security now.

With Uranus: Many beneficial changes are going on in your life in the next few months. Another person may influence you to assert your independence and freedom, and express yourself creatively in original ways. You become more oriented to New Age groups.

With Neptune: Enhanced intuitive understanding brings cooperation in coming months. Keep your ideals high and be prepared to share them with someone who may need a lift of spirits. Musical interests find an interesting sympathizer.

With Pluto: Contacts with the public seem to resurrect past life acquaintances in coming months. You may see your own good qualities and flaws reflected in the life of someone you meet for the first time. A good time to join a group devoted to self-improvement and good health.

Conjunctio
In the 2nd House

Alone, no planets: This is a favorable influence that remains in effect for the next few months. A good time to sign financial agreements, purchase items to be shared with others, and link your financial opportunities with a partner.

With Sun: You are the dominant factor in a partnership or relationship which will be successful in coming months. You will be shopping more for personal items and goods that you can use in creative projects that offer prospects of profit.

With Moon: You are the responsive person in a relationship or partnership which brings public attention in coming months. A cooperative venture now could be highly profitable, particularly in services and goods currently in great public demand.

With Mercury: You are the teacher or guide; or the recipient of teaching and worthwhile guidance in coming months. Lecturing, writing and communications in general are highly profitable. A good commission job may come your way.

With Venus: A friendship formed in coming months will prove happy and fruitful. You may receive a special gift, or advice that can improve your personal income.

With Mars: Combining your efforts with another greatly magnifies your rewards. Contests and competitions for couples or teams are particularly favored, and could bring nice profits. There is much action in money matters which are dependent on your ability to cooperate with others.

With Jupiter: Shared activities assume greater importance and correspondingly bring greater rewards in coming months. Cooperative ventures, publishing, and lecturing can bring excellent profits now. Your economic opportunities widen now.

With Saturn: Activities shared with an older person or established group are more successful than solitary ones in coming months. A conservative approach to investments is most profitable; antiques, old coins and other collectibles are favored.

With Uranus: Many beneficial changes are going on in your life in the next few months. Keep up with the news in your professional field, as opportunities abound for making a quick profit in combination with others.

With Neptune: Enhanced intuitive understanding brings coopera- tion in coming months. You may be lucky in a lottery, or have some inspired intuition about stocks and other investments. Follow your hunches.

With Pluto: You will join forces with a past life acquaintance in com- ing months. Material gain is your mutual objective, so cooperative ventures are highly favored. You may also be lucky in a lottery or sweepstakes.

Conjunctio
In the 3rd House
Alone, no planets: Your trips will bring the results you desire, and messages will bring good news. An excellent time to join in com- munity activities and promotions. Visit with relatives.

With Sun: You are the dominant factor in a partnership or relationship which will be successful in coming months. You may gain local recognition for your skills or personality, and take on a position of leadership in community affairs. Travel benefits your health. You communicate with authority now.

With Moon: You are the responsive person in a relationship or part- nership which brings public attention in coming months. Meetings enhance your position, so be open to contacts from neighbors and relatives. Excellent for sales and advertising, short communications.

With Mercury: You are the teacher or guide; or the recipient of teach- ing and worthwhile guidance in coming months. Excellent for sales, advertising, taking a short practical course, and above all, com- municating your ideas and goals to those around you. Make phone calls and write letters to keep in touch with friends, or for business purposes.

With Venus: A friendship formed in coming months will prove happy and fruitful. Your charm and sincerity bring you cooperation and attention from those around you. Enjoy and participate in local entertainment and cultural events.

With Mars: Combining your efforts with another greatly magnifies your rewards. If traveling, try a car pool or public transportation for regular trips, and save your car for personal travel. You will be participating in many community and neighborhood activities now. Enter contests of skill and wit now.

With Jupiter: Shared activities assume greater importance and correspondingly bring greater rewards in coming months. Excellent for any type of sales including self-promotion in your community. Your message of hope and cheer is greatly appreciated, and you will be asked to repeat it frequently. Travel for business and pleasure is also highly favored.

With Saturn: Activities shared with an older person or established group are more successful than solitary ones in coming months. By all means get in touch with old friends and professional acquaintances to promote both business and pleasure. A good time to shop for bargains, antiques and collectibles, and take an interest in community history.

With Uranus: Many beneficial changes are going on in your life in the next few months. You may have some clairvoyant messages now, and be surprised by the new activities and oprortunities opening up in your community. Catch up with New Age reading and travel to new places.

With Neptune: Enhanced intuitive understanding brings cooperation in coming months. You may hear spirit messages now, Consult with experts on these experiences, and try automatic writing also. Enjoy local artistic and musical entertainment to lift your spirits.

With Pluto: You will join forces with a past life acquaintance in coming months. You may travel to local places which hold past life memories or become more conscious of the effect of the past on the present. Group discussions and specialized studies are favored. Shop for reusable items.

Conjunctio
In the 4th House
Alone, no planets: This is a favorable influence that remains in effect for the next few months. You and your family unite now to solve problems and take better advantage of opportunities for each family member that contribute to the well-being of the entire family.

With Sun: You are the dominant factor in a partnership or relationship which will be successful in coming months. Your family looks to you for leadership, strength and continuity in times of stress, and for creative ideas to improve family life and relationships.

With Moon: You are the responsive person in a relationship or partnership which brings public attention in coming months. The mother—you if the mother, or your own mother—is the center of family interest and activities now. You may also achieve recognition for community activities.

With Mercury: You are the teacher or guide or the recipient of teaching and worthwhile guidance in coming months. Family discussions, travel, and studies are favored. Bring any problems into the open, and make agreed-upon plans to resolve them. Family games are more fun now also.

With Venus: A friendship formed in coming months will prove happy and fruitful. Invite your friends home to entertain your family, and vice versa, This is the time to get family cooperation in planning social events or home redecorating.

With Mars: Combining your efforts with another greatly magnifies your rewards. An excellent time to get the family together for home repair, a move, family outings and physical fitness efforts. There is much activity in the home, and cooperation can get more accomplished more quickly.

With Jupiter: Shared activities assume greater importance and correspondingly bring greater rewards in coming months. This is an excellent time to invest in real estate, purchase a new home, sell your present home, or start a business in your home. Family life is ideal, spiritually and materially.

With Saturn: Activities shared with an older person or established group are more successful than solitary ones in coming months. Another good time to purchase real estate at low prices to retain until values increase; mining and agriculture are also good investments. Research your family tree or hold a family reunion.

With Uranus: Many beneficial changes are going on in your life in the next few months. Family members depart in more independent and original directions, with mutual respect and appreciation. Purchase domestic conveniences now.

With Neptune: Enhanced intuitive understanding brings cooperation in coming months. Pay more attention to grandparents and their needs, and be sure to incorporate them into family plans and activities. You achieve greater peace and harmony in the home.

With Pluto: You will join forces with a past life acquaintance in coming months. You may be renovating your home and renewing family relationships now. If you are worrying about a family member, try talking the problems out.

Conjunctio
In the 5th House
Alone, no planets: This is a favorable influence that remains in effect for the next few months. You may meet your special love, or share a time of satisfying rapport with someone special. If expecting a child, you may have twins. Excellent for joint creative projects and luck in lotteries.

With Sun: You are the dominant factor in a partnership or relationship which will be successful in coming months. Your creative projects are successful now, particularly when shared. Speculative investments are also favored. Take the initiative in love. If expecting a child, you will have a son.

With Moon: You are the responsive person in a relationship or partnership which brings public attention in coming months. Creative projects achieve public acclaim, and you may win a supermarket sweepstakes. If expecting a child, you will have a daughter.

With Mercury: You are the teacher or guide; or the recipient of teaching and worthwhile guidance in coming months. Creative writing is successful, as are investments in communications in general. You achieve great mental rapport and agreement with a loved one.

With Venus: A friendship formed in coming months will prove happy and fruitful. Love is ideal now, so enjoy recreation with your loved one. If expecting a child, you will have a girl. You may also win a prize.

With Mars: Combining your efforts with another greatly magnifies your rewards. Take the initiative in love and be daring in competition and contests. If expecting a child you will have a son. Sports betting is favored.

With Jupiter: Shared activities assume greater importance and correspondingly bring greater rewards in coming months. Gambling can be profitable, as are investments. You are fortunate in love also. If expecting a child, you are likely to have a son. Creative ventures are favored now.

With Saturn: Activities shared with an older person or established group are more successful than solitary ones in coming months. You reminisce about the beginnings of love; enjoy anniversary festivities. Gambling is not favored, but a long-term creative project may be completed now. If expecting a child, you will have a son.

With Uranus: Many beneficial changes are going on in your life in the next few months. You may be lucky in games of chance, and a sudden investment opportunity should be pursued. If expecting a child, you will have a son. Apply your original creative ideas.

With Neptune: Enhanced intuitive understanding brings cooperation in coming months. You may be lucky in lotteries and sweepstakes
now. Love is ideal and romantic, and you may attune yourself psychi-
cally with someone special. If expecting a child, you are likely to have
a daughter. Musical and artistic creative efforts are favored.

With Pluto: You will join forces with a past life acquaintance in coming months. You may be lucky in lotteries and sweepstakes now. If
expecting a child, you will have a boy. A good time to work on a group
creative project. Love is rejuvenated.

Conjunctio
In the 6th House
Alone, no planets: This is a favorable influence that remains in effect
for the next few months. An excellent time to take job-related courses
of study or on-the-job training, and put your mind to developing better health routines. You make greatest progress with the company and
support of others.

With Sun: You are the dominant factor in a partnership or relationship
which will be successful in coming months. Take tests or submit
resumés to attain job advancement and a position of authority. Take
an active role in any union to which you may belong. Your health
is excellent.

With Moon: You are the responsive person in a relationship or
partnership which brings public attention in coming months. Sales,
advertising and other work dealing with the public are highly favored,
as you are attuned to public moods and desires. Take advantage of
opportunities to build health in a group setting.

With Mercury: You are the teacher or guide; or the recipient of teaching and worthwhile guidance in coming months. This is an excellent
time to take tests, such as civil service, for a better job; to take job courses, and participate in on-the-job training. A positive mental attitude
benefits your health.

With Venus: A friendship formed in coming months will prove happy and fruitful. Relations with coworkers and working conditions improve. You are more satisfied with your job due to greater cooperation and appreciation on the part of coworkers and supervisors. Your health benefits from your happier mood.

With Mars: Combining your efforts with another greatly magnifies your rewards. Your efficiency on the job is excellent, as you divide labors with others in a more productive way. An excellent time to compete for advancement and join a physical fitness group.

With Jupiter: Shared activities assume greater importance and correspondingly bring greater rewards in coming months. This is an excellent time to send out resumés and make job contacts to gain advancement, a better-paying job, or a change in job direction. Your health is excellent, but do not enter any eating contests, as you will gain weight.

With Saturn: Activities shared with an older person or established group are more successful than solitary ones in coming months. An excellent time to seek a civil service or other government job, or a long-term, stable job, or managerial position. Build up your endurance and take care of dental needs.

With Uranus: Many beneficial changes are going on in your life in the next few months. Make contacts in the job market, as a new opportunity for advancement or an entirely new career will arise soon. Watch for nervous tension and insomnia.

With Neptune: Enhanced intuitive understanding brings cooperation in coming months. Use your psychic ability to attune yourself better with coworkers, or seek out a better job. Heed your hunches. Your health depends on maintaining positive feelings.

With Pluto: You will join forces with a past life acquaintance in coming months. Your health improves and you feel physically rejuvenated. Join any union or work-related group now to gain a better perspective on future opportunities, and benefit from the experiences of others.

Conjunctio
In the 7th House

Alone, no planets: This is a favorable influence that remains in effect for the next few months. Marriage and business partnerships are stimulated positively by improved communications and greater similarity of goals and methods. Settle legal disputes and sign papers and agreements now.

With Sun: You are the dominant factor in a partnership or relationship which will be successful in coming months. An excellent time to marry or form a business partnership, as you and your partner share close mental and spiritual rapport, and strength of purpose in mutual goals.

With Moon: You are the responsive person in a relationship or partnership which brings public attention in coming months. An excellent time for a wedding or to announce a business partnership to the public. Settle any legal disputes while public opinion is in your favor.

With Mercury: You are the teacher or guide; or the recipient of teaching and worthwhile guidance in coming months. This is an excellent time for discussions, planning and better rapport with your spouse or business partner. You stimulate each other's thinking. Sign legal papers and make agreements.

With Venus: A friendship formed in coming months will prove happy and fruitful. Spend more time with spouse or special loved one, as your emotional rapport is ideal. This is an excellent time for a wedding. You profit from partnership business dealings.

With Mars: Combining your efforts with another greatly magnifies your rewards. You excel in initiatives and in competition and debates. Start legal actions now, as judgment will be in your favor, but avoid action on any pending issues.

With Jupiter: Shared activities assume greater importance and correspondingly bring greater rewards in coming months. Settle legal disputes, marry, form a business partnership—anything you touch that you share will turn into material or spiritual gold. Youthful people are especially stimulating.

With Saturn: Activities shared with an older person or established group are more successful than solitary ones in coming months. You and your spouse or partner share a realistic view of your relationship. Discuss needs before you accept new responsibilities to avoid resentment.

With Uranus: Many beneficial changes are going on in your life in the next few months. A new acquaintance may become a close friend swiftly because of mutual mental and creative stimulation. An elopement is favored if you are both in the same mood.

With Neptune: Enhanced intuitive understanding brings cooperation in coming months. Set the right mood and you will achieve ideal emotional rapport with your spouse. Use your intuition in legal matters and partnership affairs.

With Pluto: You will join forces with a past life acquaintance in coming months. You may meet your soul mate, or find a way to pay a karmic debt or gain karmic benefits in a close relationship. You profit from partnership ventures.

Conjunctio
In the 8th House:
Alone, no planets: This is a favorable influence that remains in effect for the next few months. You may meet your soul mate or share greater rapport with an intimate. This is an excellent time for occult studies and communications with the occult spirit world. Do joint financial paperwork now.

With Sun: You are the dominant factor in a partnership or relationship which will be successful in coming months. You can achieve success and gain protection and strength from occult activities and spiritual sources. Joint financial ventures prosper, and your sexual energy level is high.

With Moon: You are the responsive person in a relationship or partnership which brings public attention in coming months. Card reading and development of intuition are favored. Invest in cooperative and public service ventures. Relations with the opposite sex fluctuate because you are sensitive to your partner's moods.

With Mercury: You are the teacher or guide; or the recipient of teaching and worthwhile guidance in coming months. This is an excellent time for occult studies and spirit communications. Sign joint financial and tax papers. Discuss shared interests with an intimate, as your sexual drives are mentalized now.

With Venus: A friendship formed in coming months will prove happy and fruitful. Sexual rapport depends on ardent expressions of affection. Purchase occult jewelry and artistic items now. Joint ventures are profitable.

With Mars: Combining your efforts with another greatly magnifies your rewards. Your sexual drives are at a high point, and shared by your intimate partner. Excellent for occult studies in the use of spiritual energy. Avoid haste in joint financial dealings, but act on those that appear profitable.

With Jupiter: Shared activities assume greater importance and correspondingly bring greater rewards in coming months. Excellent for studies in prophetic dreams and inspirations. You profit handsomely from joint ventures, and may receive a legacy. You feel companionable rather than sexual toward an intimate now.

With Saturn: Activities shared with an older person or established group are more successful than solitary ones in coming months. Your sexual drive may diminish unless efforts are made to establish a happy mood, as you feel insecure. Settle taxes and debts now. High magic rituals are favored.

With Uranus: Many beneficial changes are going on in your life in the next few months. This is an excellent time for the study of astrology and development of clairvoyant abilities. A sudden sexual attraction may puzzle you—think it over. Avoid joint financial dealings as there are too many ups and downs now.

With Neptune: Enhanced intuitive understanding brings cooperation in coming months. This is an excellent time for development of mediumistic abilities, dowsing and psychometry, as well as divination in general. Your sexual drives are stimulated by romantic fantasies. Avoid financial dealings involving others, as deception or confusion may reign supreme.

With Pluto: You will join forces with a past life acquaintance in coming months. Excellent for any type of occult study or practice, as you can call on reserves of spiritual energy now. Your sexual drives are strong, but very specific. Joint and cooperative financial ventures are favored.

Conjunctio
In the 9th House
Alone, no planets: This is a favorable influence that remains in effect for the next few months. This is an excellent time to travel abroad or study a foreign language, as your mind is more receptive to new information and viewpoints. Long-range planning and philosophical studies are also favored.

With Sun: You are the dominant factor in a partnership or relationship which will be successful in coming months. Travel and contacts with other cultures give you a better perspective on your own thought processes. You may achieve prominence far from your place of birth.

With Moon: You are the responsive person in a relationship or partnership which brings public attention in coming months. You learn quickly and are easily swayed by new ideas. Check out new information carefully before applying it to your own life. Public transportation is favored for travel. Advertising and sales are also favorable.

With Mercury: You are the teacher or guide; or the recipient of teaching and worthwhile guidance in coming months. Excellent for any type of studies, writing, or lecturing. You absorb and transmit information easily. Read the foreign news for a new perspective on the world. Travel is favored.

With Venus: A friendship formed in coming months will prove happy and fruitful. Acquire a pen pal abroad and form personal relationships with those from different cultures. Travel for pleasure and artistic and musical studies are favored.

With Mars: Combining your efforts with another greatly magnifies your rewards. Explore new places and ideas through travel and study. Excellent for developing technical skills and acquiring practical knowledge. Avoid disputes over matters of opinion or belief.

With Jupiter: Shared activities assume greater importance and bring rewards in coming months. You are an immediate success in writing, publishing, teaching or lecturing. An excellent time to travel for both business and pleasure. You are open to spiritual enlightenment.

With Saturn: Activities shared with an older person or establishedd group are more successful than solitary ones in coming months. This is an excellent time to seek a master or guide in achieving both spiritual and material goals. Your mental persistence and demand for facts will bring you a body of reliable knowledge. Travel for business purposes.

With Uranus: Many beneficial changes are going on in your life in the next few months. You may have a revelation about your future, alone or shared with another, which inspires you with greater confidence and opens your mind to new ideas and opportunities. Avoid travel and extremist individuals.

With Neptune: Enhanced intuitive understanding brings cooperation in coming months. You are absorbed in mysticism and religious interests, and may have a vision or astral travel experience which changes your view of the world and your place in it. Sea travel is favored, as are studies in mathematics, chemistry, art and music.

With Pluto: You will join forces with a past life acquaintance in coming months. Occult studies will bring you in contact with sources of spiritual energy and inspiration. Your psychic abilities are more easily developed now. Group travel is favored.

Conjunctio
In the 10th House

Alone, no planets: This is a favorable influence that remains in effect for the next few months. Seek work with a team or a partner, join a job-related professional group, or pursue work in communications, writing, teaching and lecturing.

With Sun: You are the dominant factor in a partnership or relationship which will be successful in coming months. You may be a successful candidate for public office due to the support of an influential person and your own ability to communicate your ideas to the public.

With Moon: You are the responsive person in a relationship or partnership which brings public attention in coming months. You also gain prominence for your ability to understand and interpret the moods of the public, and communicate your knowledge on the job.

With Mercury: You are the teacher or guide; or the recipient of teaching and worthwhile guidance in coming months. You may be prominent in promoting a public cause or providing information to government agencies, or working in government in the communications area.

With Venus: A friendship formed in coming months will prove happy and fruitful. Attend and promote public social events. You may mediate the disputes of public groups. You receive praise and favors from those in authority.

With Mars: Combining your efforts with another greatly magnifies your rewards. Competing as part of a team on the job can bring advancement and solid accomplishments. Your natural leadership abilities are displayed well now. Good for a career in the military.

With Jupiter: Shared activities assume greater importance and correspondingly bring greater rewards in coming months. This is an excellent time for achieving prominence in the publishing world, travel industry, or in promoting religious values and justice. You may start a successful business with another now.

With Saturn: Activities shared with an older person or established group are more successful than solitary ones in coming months. Any type of work in government that involves sharing cooperation, and a practical approach to long-term goals is favorable. Stick to the status quo in your work, rather than seeking expansion in business.

With Uranus: Many beneficial changes are going on in your life in the next few months. This is an excellent time for work as an astrologer, scientist, computer specialist, or electrical engineer. Conjunctio brings greater independence in your career, and favors the start of a new businness with a unique product.

With Neptune: Enhanced intuitive understanding brings cooperation in coming months. Conjunctio favors work as a musician, artist, or professional psychic, but puts you alone on a peak except for one special partner. Work in community health and charities is also favored.

With Pluto: You will join forces with a past life acquaintance in coming months. This is an excellent time for efforts to transform society by taking a public stand on current issues. You prosper in any business devoted to public renovation and renewal, insurance and credit.

Conjunctio
In the 11th House
Alone, no planets: This is a favorable influence that remains in effect for the next few months. You excel at organizing group efforts, or starting a new group, as you are able to define and explain methods to achieve mutual goals. You may make a special new friend now.

With Sun: You are the dominant factor in a partnership or relationship which will be successful in coming months. You may assume leadership of a group you belong to, or gain recognition from friends for your special creative or personal qualities. This is an excellent time for the political activist.

With Moon: You are the responsive person in a relationship or partnership which brings public attention in coming months. Excellent for the promoter of charities and public causes—you understand the mood of the people well, and can appeal to large groups for support.

With Mercury: You are the teacher or guide; or the recipient of teaching and worthwhile guidance in coming months. You may be chosen spokesperson for a group because you identify personally with the goals of the group. Excellent for leading group discussions and studies.

With Venus: A friendship formed in coming months will prove happy and fruitful. You receive many favors and social invitations, and enjoy planning and putting on entertainment for groups to which you belong. You may make new friends now.

With Mars: Combining your efforts with another greatly magnifies your rewards. Your qualities of leadership show up best in casual group situations, where you can organize efforts toward real social accomplishments. Team competitions are favored.

With Jupiter: Shared activities assume greater importance and correspondingly bring greater rewards in coming months. A good time to join a fraternal organization where you can feel more like a part of a group that has closer ties than the average. Excellent for group travel and studies also.

With Saturn: Activities shared with an older person or established group are more successful than solitary ones in coming months. Political activism is especially favored. Look up friends and attend any reunions to renew old ties.

With Uranus: Many beneficial changes are going on in your life in the next few months. You will be breaking loose from old ties and social routines in search of new mental stimulation and social experiences.

With Neptune: Enhanced intuitive understanding brings cooperation in coming months. You will be seeking groups and friends who add peace and harmony to your life as an escape from the problems of workaday reality. A sympathetic friend will appear.

With Pluto: You will join forces with a past life acquaintance in coming months. Your acquaintance will become a closer friend as you seek to realize social goals and renew your sense of spiritual purpose.

Conjunctio
In the 12th House

Alone, no planets: This is a favorable influence that remains in effect for the next few months. You can achieve spiritual and physical harmony by integrating conscious understanding with your inner unconscious drives. A good time to explore past lives for valuable experience.

With Sun: You are the dominant factor in a partnership or relationship which will be successful in coming months. You can make progress in alleviating any ailments and building up your vitality and energy level now. You can also put in place new positive habits and thought patterns.

With Moon: You are the responsive person in a relationship or partnership which brings public attention in coming months. Your health responds to the lunar cycle, so take good advantage of energy highs, and relax more at low points. Your dreams may contain intuitively gathered information.

With Mercury: You are the teacher or guide; or the recipient of teaching and worthwhile guidance in coming months. An excellent time for introspection and resolution of inner problems that may have been hindering you from developing to your fullest potential: also good for studying dreams and dream analysis.

With Venus: A friendship formed in coming months will prove happy and fruitful. Greater inner contentment enables you to show a more positive attitude toward yourself and the world. You enjoy solitude to develop creative ideas.

With Mars: Combining your efforts with another greatly magnifies your rewards. You will either suffer from frustration at limitations in physical expression, or a feverish ailment. Seek mental distractions in solitude, and plan for more active days.

With Jupiter: Shared activities assume greater importance and correspondingly bring greater rewards in coming months. Take advantage of increased solitude to get projects off the back burner and organize your strategy for future accomplishment. You may have prophetic dreams, so keep track of them. Your health is excellent.

With Saturn: Activities shared with an older person or established group are more successful than solitary ones in coming months. You may suffer from anxiety or feelings of inadequacy now. A good time to eliminate bad health habits and take care of dental needs. Avoid dieting, but make sure you get plenty of rest and vitamins.

With Uranus: Many beneficial changes are going on in your life in the next few months. Nervous tension may keep you awake at night. Plan restful relaxation prior to bedtime, and jot down ideas or dreams, as you may have clairvoyant visions now.

With Neptune: Enhanced intuitive understanding brings cooperation in coming months. Solitude brings peace and harmony; examine dreams for psychic content and contacts, and organize your creative ideas for future action. Avoid alcohol and drugs.

With Pluto: You will join forces with a past life acquaintance in coming months. An excellent time to examine past-life experiences for useful hints for the future. All occult studies and practices are favored. Spiritual healing helps solve problems.

ALBUS

This symbol is essentially favorable with all of the planets, regardless of their aspects.

Albus is ruled by Mercury, and associated with the sign Cancer, ruled by the Moon. Albus or White Head not only represents the wisdom of tradition, reason and common sense, but also of the intuitive kind ruled by the Moon.

Albus in a chart always indicates a point where knowledge is required or revealed, knowledge that is both practical and spiritually valuable. Albus represents the traditions of the civilizations of the past, the scientific facts and speculations of modern times, the learning handed down by books and word of mouth. Albus always represents beneficial and constructive knowledge. In the querent's chart, it indicates an area of life in which further studies should be undertaken, or that the querent should be displaying and teaching knowledge to others.

Albus
In the 1st House
Alone, no planets: This is a favorable influence that remains in effect for the next few months. Love of knowledge stimulates you to explore your surroundings, start new study projects, and take a greater interest in the knowledge and experiences of the new people you meet.

With Sun: You have an insatiable desire to learn new things, particularly about yourself, in coming months. You can develop innate creative abilities by adding to your artistic, dramatic and musical knowledge—the basis for self-expression.

With Moon: Take advantage of your ability to persuade the public in advertising and sales in coming months. Your personal popularity is at a high point, so take advantage of your many contacts to expand your understanding and knowledge of human nature.

With Mercury: Excellent for the writer, public speaker, teacher—you communicate clearly and effectively in coming months. You may be published, or sought after for your special knowledge in a field of expertise, for lectures or for a career in the communications industry.

With Venus: Knowledge brings pleasure, and favorable messages come in the near future. You would benefit by polishing your charm and appearance with diet, beauty and other ornamental courses that focus on the ideal form. Express yourself in the arts, music and cultural interests.

With Mars: You have great mental energy to devote to a new learning objective. You are especially interested in self-learned improvement and development, both physical and mental. Reach out to meet new people and assert your qualities of leadership in new projects.

With Jupiter: Whatever you learn now will be both profitable and pleasurable in coming months. You are a beacon of enlightenment to the new people you meet. Your new projects succeed because you have your strategy well in mind, and all factors have been considered.

With Saturn: The wisdom of the past and your own experience are the keys to success in coming months. An excellent time to complete any pending projects, and renew contacts with helpful people you have not seen for awhile. Self-discipline benefits your physical health as well.

With Uranus: Many beneficial changes are going on in your life in the next few months. These changes may be preceded by clairvoyant visions of the future. Original creative ideas can lead to fulfilling self-expression and recognition from others. It is time to set a new course in life.

With Neptune: Exercise your psychic abilities to gain the information you need in coming months. Your knowledge of the spiritual plane is invaluable to the people who seek your guidance. Focus on spiritual healing for yourself and others.

With Pluto: A better understanding of occult sciences can help resolve conflicts in coming months. You gain great understanding of reincarnation and karma as you perceive and appply the experiences of past lives to present objectives.

Albus
In the 2nd House

Alone, no planets: This is a favorable influence that remains in effect for the next few months. Acquisition and dissemination of knowledge and information can be potent factors in financial success. Purchase books and other mind-developing materials now.

With Sun: You have an insatiable desire to learn new things, particularly about yourself, in coming months. Your inner resources and skills are valuable in increasing your income. Creative projects may be profitable. Assert authority over your expenses and income.

With Moon: Take advantage of your ability to persuade the public in advertising and sales in coming months. A seasonal job may also be profitable. Invest in agricultural commodities, shop for household items and family needs or gifts on sale. Restrain personal spending, as your tastes and desires fluctuate.

With Mercury: Excellent for the writer, public speaker, teacher—you communicate clearly and effectively in coming months. Excellent for profits from writing, teaching, and the communications and transportation industries. Keep up on the latest economic news.

With Venus: Knowledge brings pleasure, and favorable messages come in the near future. You may receive a gift or a bonus on the job. Invest in the arts, which will increase in value. Put your own artistic creations on the market. Shop for personal items and a new wardrobe.

With Mars: You have great mental energy to devote to a new learning objective. Improve your physical and technical skills to increase your income, take the initiative in pursuing new financial opportunities. Do-it-yourself efforts at home and on personal items can save you money and give pleasure in accomplishment as well.

With Jupiter: Whatever you learn now will be both profitable and pleasurable in coming months. Your financial ship may come in now. You profit handsomely from investments and gambling, and may receive a gift, legacy, or bonus on the job. Watch extravagant spending.

With Saturn: The wisdom of the past and your own experience are the keys to success in coming months. Invest in antiques and securities, bargain-hunt for necessities, and file taxes. Your income remains the same, but expenses can be cut more easily now.

With Uranus: Many beneficial changes are going on in your life in the next few months. These changes may be preceded by clairvoyant visions of the future. Financial independence is possible if you grasp new opportunities. You may also receive a windfall through games of chance or a contest.

With Neptune: Exercise your psychic abilities to gain the information you need in coming months. You may win a lottery or sweepstakes, or find a treasure, but you are more interested in purchasing a special or difficult-to-obtain personal item. Follow your hunches.

With Pluto: A better understanding of occult sciences can help resolve conflicts in coming months. Excellent for investments in cooperative ventures. Shop for reusable items, refurbish present possessions—you will be happy with the results and the low cost.

Albus
In the 3rd House
Alone, no planets: This is a favorable influence that remains in effect for the next few months. A course of study or application of knowledge already acquired is highly favored. The key to success is expansion of the mind and mental powers.

With Sun: You have an insatiable desire to learn new things, particularly about yourself, in coming months. Excellent for creative self-expression in speech and writing, for sales and advertising, for travel, studies and discussion groups. You may assume a position of leadership in a local group.

With Moon: Take advantage of your ability to persuade the public in advertising and sales in coming months. Excellent for sales, advertising, making public contacts, teaching or working with young children, and restaurant work. You are in touch with the public's tastes.

With Mercury: Excellent for the writer, public speaker, teacher—you communicate clearly and effectively in coming months. Travel, send letters and resumés, call friends and business contacts, and generally step up communications with those around you. A good time for a short study course, seminar or lecture.

With Venus: Knowledge brings pleasure, and favorable messages come in the near future. Attend lectures, seminars or a study course in the history and/or practice of your favorite arts and cultural interest. A good time to reconcile with friends and resolve disputes.

With Mars: You have great mental energy to devote to a new learning objective. Your mind is quick and sharp, and your feet are restless. Find new places and new ideas to explore through short trips, books, lectures, seminars and classes. Good for success in debates and contests.

With Jupiter: Whatever you learn now will be both profitable and pleasurable in coming months. A good time to expand your influence into local activities, for both business and pleasure. Settle disputes. Advertising, sales, studies and publishing are favored.

With Saturn: The wisdom of the past and your own experiences are the keys to success in coming months. A good time to organize your daily routines and set up a schedule to make the most efficient use of your time and energy. A course in business communications is favored.

With Uranus: Many beneficial changes are going on in your life in the next few months. These changes may be preceded by clairvoyant visions of the future. Develop your clairvoyant abilities and astrological understanding through regular studies. You are open to new ideas and enjoy a little variety in your daily activities.

With Neptune: Exercise your psychic abilities to gain the information You need in coming months. You are very receptive to psychic influences operating around you, and can tune in easily to helpful spiritual forces with the help of a study course and regular practice.

With Pluto: A better understanding of occult sciences can help resolve conflicts in coming months. You may become part of a community educational program to reform problems in your locale. Any practical course in self-improvement areas is favored.

Albus
In the 4th House

Alone, no planets: This is a favorable influence that remains in effect for the next few months. Excellent for valuing property and work in real estate, agriculture, or architecture. You are a source of inspiration and advice to family members.

With Sun: You have an insatiable desire to learn new things, particularly about yourself, in coming months. Assume a role of leadership in resolving family or domestic problems, as you have the common sense and intuitive understanding to handle whatever comes.

With Moon: Take advantage of your ability to persuade the public in advertising and sales in coming months. Your home or a family member may be the focus of public attention. Pay special attention to young children in the family circle—interesting things are happening in their lives.

With Mercury: Excellent for the writer, public speaker, teacher—you communicate clearly and effectively in coming months. Excellent for home studies and domestic subjects, real estate, architecture, family relations. Discuss issues openly with family members, as viewpoints are more positive and flexible now.

With Venus: Knowledge brings pleasure, and favorable messages come in the near future. Excellent for a family reunion, family outing, or home entertaining and redecorating. Family unity and affection reach a firm footing.

With Mars: You have great mental energy to devote to a new learning objective. Study do-it-yourself courses in home repairs and gardening, or physical routines you can share with family members to improve health and increase vitality.

With Jupiter: Whatever you learn now will be both profitable and pleasurable in coming months. You will profit from real estate sales and dealings in agriculture and mining. Home studies and family travel are also favored. You may inherit property.

With Saturn: The wisdom of the past and your own experiences are the keys to success in coming months. Mining, business property, and antiques are sources of profit and pleasure. Pay more attention to older members of the family—their memories and experiences can be invaluable.

With Uranus: Many beneficial changes are going on in your life in the next few months. These changes may be preceded by clairvoyant visions of the future. Family relationships and domestic arrangements are subject to radical changes. Be flexible, but avoid impulsive decisions in home and family affairs.

With Neptune: Exercise your psychic abilities to gain the information you need in coming months. Grandparents are the focus of family attention. Bridge the generation gap and discuss varying interests and viewpoints to increase family harmony.

With Pluto: A better understanding of occult sciences can help resolve conflicts in coming months. Excellent for rejuvenating family relationships and resolving misunderstandings and doubts. Home renovations and investment in cooperative properties are favored.

Albus
In the 5th House
Alone, no planets: This is a favorable influence that remains in effect for the next few months. Love of wisdom dominates your relations with children and loved ones, to whom you are a constant source of inspiration and understanding. You may be successful in a lottery or literary creative project.

With Sun: You have an insatiable desire to learn new things, particularly about yourself, in coming months. If expecting a child, it is likely to be a son. Success in mental contests and creative self-expression comes easily to you. Your strength of will and character reassure loved ones.

With Moon: Take advantage of your ability to persuade the public in advertising and sales in coming months. If expecting a child, it is likely to be a girl. You are dominated by concern for loved ones and children, and moody when your efforts are unappreciated. You may win a supermarket sweepstakes.

With Mercury: Excellent for the writer, public speaker, teacher—you communicate clearly and effectively in coming months. If expecting a child, it is likely to be a boy or twins. You share easy mental rapport with loved ones and children, and enjoy success in literary creative efforts and verbal contests.

With Venus: Knowledge brings pleasure, and favorable messages come in the near future. If expecting a child, it is likely to be a girl. Artistic calligraphy and studies in harmony, both musical and social, appeal to you. Romance is based on mutual understanding.

With Mars: You have great mental energy to devote to a new learning objective. Apply strategy and initiative to establish a romantic relationship. Share sports and activities that contribute to coordination and learning with children. If expecting a child, it is likely to be a boy.

With Jupiter: Whatever you learn now will be both profitable and pleasurable in coming months. If expecting a child, it is likely to be a boy. You are fortunate in all forms of gambling and speculation. Romance offers spiritual as well as emotional satisfaction. Creative efforts are successful.

With Saturn: The wisdom of the past and your own experiences are the keys to success in coming months. Avoid gambling and concentrate on contests of skill and persistence. You may complete a creative project now. You feel a little insecure in romance, or inclined to reminisce.

With Uranus: Many beneficial changes are going on in your life in the next few months. These changes may be preceded by clairvoyant visions of the future. Sudden attractions and repulsions dominate your romantic life. Children are unpredictable. You may be lucky in games of chance.

With Neptune: Exercise your psychic abilities to gain the information you need in coming months. Music stimulates a romantic or creative mood. The arts are highly favored. You may be lucky in a lottery or sweepstakes. If expecting a child, it is likely to be a girl.

With Pluto: A better understanding of occult sciences can help resolve conflicts in coming months. If expecting a child, it is likely to be a son. An old romance may rise from the ashes. Group creative efforts are favored.

Albus
In the 6th House
Alone, no planets: This is a favorable influence that remains in effect for the next few months. Excellent for on-the-job training, a work study course, or work in the communications industry. You will be giving a lot of thought to your job plans for the future. Now is the time to look over the job market.

With Sun: You have an insatiable desire to learn new things, particularly about yourself, in coming months. You may assume a position of leadership and management on the job. Your health is excellent, and you make a point of maintaining a good diet and exercise routine.

With Moon: Take advantage of your ability to persuade the public in advertising and sales in coming months. You may take a seasonal or temporary job now, to gain experience which will develop new career opportunities for you. Your energy level fluctuates somewhat.

With Mercury: Excellent for the writer, public speaker, teacher—you communicate clearly and effectively in coming months. Submit resumés, discuss job plans and interests with helpful people, and seek work that offers mental challenges. You may suffer from some nervous tension now.

With Venus: Knowledge brings pleasure, and favorable messages come in the near future. Work in the arts, beauty, social relations, counseling, and luxury items is favored. You gain the cooperation and support of coworkers easily.

With Mars: You have great mental energy to devote to a new learning objective. Excellent for physical labor, and work in the skilled trades and technical fields. Your energy level is high and you are productive on the job. Compete for advancement.

With Jupiter: Whatever you learn now will be both profitable and pleasurable in coming months. An excellent time to seek a better-paying job or a promotion. Your health is excellent, although you may gain a little weight.

With Saturn: The wisdom of the past and your own experiences are the keys to success in coming months. A good time to make long-range career plans, but avoid changing jobs at this time. You may rise to a managerial position. Improve your endurance with diet, exercise and rest.

With Uranus: Many beneficial changes are going on in your life in the next few months. These changes may be preceded by clairvoyant visions of the future. You may succeed in more technical careers, or in computer work. Keep your eyes open for new job fields of potential interest.

With Neptune: Exercise your psychic abilities to gain the information you need in coming months. Seek a job where you attain emotional as well as material satisfaction. A good time to determine and cure any allergies.

With Pluto: A better understanding of occult sciences can help resolve conflicts in coming months. Membership in a union or work-related group will advance your ultimate career opportunities. Your health is good and recuperative abilities excellent.

Albus
In the 7th House

Alone, no planets: This is a favorable influence that remains in effect for the next few months. Sign legal papers, resolve legal disputes, and seek greater mental rapport with your spouse and partners. A good time to make plans for joint social and business activities.

With Sun: You have an insatiable desire to learn new things, particularly about yourself, in coming months. You define your own ideas more clearly when you discuss plans and issues with your spouse and partners. Let your inner self show through to those who will appreciate you. You are successful in competition and legal disputes.

With Moon: Take advantage of your ability to persuade the public in advertising and sales in coming months. An excellent time to hold a wedding, sign partnership legal papers, and give or get advice on important issues. Professional counseling work is favored.

With Mercury: Excellent for the writer, public speaker, teacher—you communicate clearly and effectively in coming months. You are successful in debates and contests of wit and skill. An excellent time to sign papers, settle disputes through arbitration, and to discuss plans with spouse. Travel with a loved one is favored.

With Venus: Knowledge brings pleasure, and favorable messages come in the near future. A romantic wedding is favored. You bask in the affection of special people now. Settle legal disputes.

With Mars: You have great mental energy to devote to a new learning objective. Initiatives may confirm a profitable business partnership. Dynamic interaction marks your relations with partners and spouse.

With Jupiter: Whatever you learn now will be both profitable and pleasurable in coming months. You may marry someone with material wealth or great qualities of character and spirit. Be grateful for your good fortune in close relationships. You will succeed in any legal disputes.

With Saturn: The wisdom of the past and your own experiences are the keys to success in coming months. Avoid legal disputes, which will be prolonged. Spend time with old friends in comfortable social activities. Weigh the benefits before you accept new partnership obligations and responsibilities.

With Uranus: Many beneficial changes are going on in your life in the next few months. These changes may be preceded by clairvoyant visions of the future. An elopement or the breakup of a bondage-type relationship opens new opportunities for shared stimulation and accomplishment.

With Neptune: Exercise your psychic abilities to gain the information you need in coming months. A romantic ideal may become a reality now. Be sensitive to the needs and desires of a partner, but do not become a willing slave.

With Pluto: A better understanding of occult sciences can help resolve conflicts in coming months. You may meet your soul mate now, or revitalize a failing relationship. Try to resolve disputes before resorting to law.

Albus
In the 8th House
Alone, no planets: This is a favorable influence that remains in effect for the next few months. You can attain a state of mastery in an occult art if you study hard and pay attention to messages and information from the spiritual plane as well as your books and other tools. Sign legal papers.

With Sun: You have an insatiable desire to learn new things, particularly about yourself, in coming months. You gain spiritual insights, strength and self-confidence from your occult studies and practices. You dominate an intimate relationship and assure your partner. Good for cooperative financial ventures.

With Moon: Take advantage of your ability to persuade the public in advertising and sales in coming months. You excel especially in card reading, psychometry and mediumship if you study and exercise your psychic abilities. Cooperative ventures are favored. Your mood with the opposite sex fluctuates.

With Mercury: Excellent for the writer, public speaker, teacher—you communicate clearly and effectively in coming months. Excellent for the study of handwriting analysis and the practice of automatic writing. Your philosophical studies in the occult also prosper. Complete joint financial paperwork and sign agreements. Mental rapport with the opposite sex is more easily achieved.

With Venus: Knowledge brings pleasure, and favorable messages come in the near future. Harmony, effection and romantic encounters dominate your relations with the opposite sex. Spiritual peace is your goal in occult studies. You may receive a small legacy.

With Mars: You have great mental energy to devote to a new learning objective. Psychic energies are generated through your contacts with the opposite sex. Take the initiative in relationships and joint financial ventures.

With Jupiter: Whatever you learn now will be both profitable and pleasurable in coming months. You may receive a legacy or other benefits through joint financial ventures. Occult philosophy and prophecy interest you, along with divination, and you receive great spiritual and material benefits from your studies. Friendship is your goal in relations with the opposite sex.

With Saturn: The wisdom of the past and your own experience are the keys to success in coming months. High magic is a source of spiritual and material benefit, as long as your goals involve the many, rather than purely selfish ends. Avoid joint dealings financially. You are realistic in your relations with the opposite sex.

With Uranus: Many beneficial changes are going on in your life in the next few months. These changes may be preceded by clairvoyant visions of the future. Astrology, geomancy, and revelations are of interest to you in the occult world. Avoid joint financial dealings and be cautious with the opposite sex.

With Neptune: Exercise your psychic abilities to gain the information you need in coming months. You can achieve excellence in divination if you try. Avoid get-rich-quick schemes and deceptions practiced on or by the opposite sex.

With Pluto: A better understanding of occult sciences can help resolve conflicts in coming months. Reincarnation, karma and spiritual healing hold your attention. Cooperative financial ventures are favored. Don't expect to be easily appreciated by the opposite sex.

Albus
In the 9th House
Alone, no planets: This is a favorable influence that remains in effect for the next few months. Enroll in a study course or take an educational trip, as you learn quickly and easily. Languages, communications in general, and speech are favored.

With Sun: You have an insatiable desire to learn new things, particularly about yourself, in coming months. Travel to benefit your health and vitality, and to achieve recognition for your talents. Creative studies, those which develop your ability to express yourself, are most favored.

With Moon: Take advantage of your ability to persuade the public in advertising and sales in coming months. Excellent for group travel, contacts with the foreign public, and foreign sales and advertising. A short term study course in a subject of interest is favored.

With Mercury: Excellent for the writer, public speaker, teacher—you communicate clearly and effectively in coming months. Broaden the scope of your audience through travel and efforts to achieve rapport with those from different cultures.

With Venus: Knowledge brings pleasure, and favorable messages come in the near future. A pleasure trip with a friend or loved one is favored. Studies in the arts, culture and music may appeal to you.

With Mars: You have great mental energy to devote to a new learning objective. An excellent time to explore new places and ideas, to travel, develop your communicative abilities, and make decisions on long range plans.

With Jupiter: Whatever you learn now will be both profitable and pleasurable in coming months. You succeed in the publishing, education and travel industries, and may pursue a career abroad successfully. Philosophy appeals to you now.

With Saturn: The wisdom of the past and your own experience are the keys to success in coming months. Antiquity in history and archeology interests you, and you may enjoy traveling to the sites of monuments, or simply to places that hold fond memories.

With Uranus: Many beneficial changes are going on in your life in the next few months. These changes may be preceded by clairvoyant visions of the future. Your religious viewpoint and philosophy of life may change dramatically. Studies and travel open your mind to new ideas.

With Neptune: Exercise your psychic abilities to gain the information you need in coming months. You enjoy travel by sea, books about the ancient mariners, and mystical religious materials. You may astral travel also.

With Pluto: A better understanding of occult sciences can help resolve conflicts in coming months. A distant land of a past life may appeal to you now. Travel is both physically and spiritually rejuvenating.

Albus
In the 10th House
Alone, no planets: This is a favorable influence that remains in effect for the next few months, bringing success in careers in communications, travel, teaching. You may become spokesperson for a group demanding public action. Seek support or advice for a business of your own.

With Sun: You have an insatiable desire to learn new things, particularly about yourself, in coming months. Excellent for winning public office, or assuming leadership in the business world. You may be honored for public service activities.

With Moon: Take advantage of your ability to persuade the public in advertising and sales in coming months. You are popular with the public, and both your personality and any business you engage in will bring material benefits. Communications work is particularly favored.

With Mercury: Excellent for the writer, public speaker, teacher—you communicate clearly and effectively in coming months. Advertising and sales are favored, as is work with educational materials, in publishing, and in creative writing.

With Venus: Knowledge brings pleasure, and favorable messages come in the near future. Attend and promote public social events for pleasure and to advertise your business. Success comes in the arts, home decorating and luxury items.

With Mars: You have great mental energy to devote to a new learning objective. Excellent for the military and skilled trades. Compete for advancement or start a business of your own.

With Jupiter: Whatever you learn now will be both profitable and pleasurable in coming months. Excellent for work in publishing, higher education, foreign relations and law. Your rise to prominence will be easy and swift.

With Saturn: The wisdom of the past and your own experience are the keys to success in coming months. Your advancement is slow, but assured. You excel as an organizer and manager, particularly in government or a business of your own.

With Uranus: Many beneficial changes are going on in your life in the next few months. These changes may be preceded by clairvoyant visions of the future. You may introduce advanced computers and technology to the workplace easily now. A radical job change may occur.

With Neptune: Exercise your psychic abilities to gain the information you need in coming months. Your talents are sought by social service agencies. You may also work as a professional in a psychic field, or for a charity.

With Pluto: A better understanding of occult sciences can help resolve conflicts in coming months. You may succeed as a psychologist or group analyst, working for government or a large social agency. Career aspirations are subtly changing.

Aldus
In the 11th House
Alone, no planets: This is a favorable influence that remains in effect for the next few months. An expanded social life will provide you with many new learning experiences, and also enable you to share your own expertise.

With Sun: You have an insatiable desire to learn new things, particularly about yourself, in coming months. You assume a role of leadership and authority because of your wide knowledge in an area of group interest.

With Moon: Take advantage of your ability to persuade the public in advertising and sales in coming months. Your ability to popularize group interests and attract support from the public brings you responsibilities and recognition.

With Mercury: Excellent for the writer, public speaker, teacher—you communicate clearly and effectively in coming months. Your ability to express group interests clearly, define group plans and organize efforts accordingly bring you many invitations to join with others.

With Venus: Knowledge brings pleasure, and favorable messages come in the near future. Your charm and persuasiveness enable you to organize group efforts harmoniously and bring them to a successful conclusion.

With Mars: You have great mental energy to devote to a new learning objective. You are adept at initiating new activities and stimulating the groups to which you belong in pursuit of worthwhile goals. Good for team competitions.

With Jupiter: Whatever you learn now will be both profitable and pleasurable in coming months. You make many new friends and are welcomed to various groups for your optimism and generosity of spirit.

With Saturn: The wisdom of the past and your own experience are the keys to success in coming months. Political action and other social groups with serious purposes welcome your sense of responsibility, persistence and reliability.

With Uranus: Many beneficial changes are going on in your life in the next few months. These changes may be preceded by clairvoyant visions of the future. Your originality and ingenuity spur group effort, even though you yourself remain independent.

With Neptune: Exercise your psychic abilities to gain the information you need in coming months. Charitable and social reform groups benefit from your sympathy and genuine concern. You have the ability to inspire others to action.

With Pluto: A better understanding of occult sciences can help resolve conflicts in coming months. You are a staunch supporter of groups which seek economic improvement for all.

Albus
In the 12th House
Alone, no planets: This is a favorable influence that remains in effect for the next few months. Spiritual and mental healing are highly beneficial. You may build up physical health and develop psychic self-defenses successfully now.

With Sun: You have an insatiable desire to learn new things, particularly about yourself, in coming months. Due to forethought and self-discipline in applying knowledge to protect your health, you are in excellent condition. Meditation increases inner spiritual confidence and power.

With Moon: Take advantage of your ability to persuade the public in advertising and sales in coming months. Aware that you are subject to infectious ailment, you use vitamins and get plenty of rest to avoid colds and flu. You may have psychic dreams, so read up on dream analysis.

With Mercury: Excellent for the writer, public speaker, teacher—you communicate clearly and effectively in coming months. You have great mental self-discipline, and apply good preventive medicine routines to protect yourself. Sleep-learning and meditation are beneficial.

With Venus: Knowledge brings pleasure, and favorable messages come in the near future. Beneficial self-love keeps you positive and effective in maintaining good health routines. Your love of peace and solitude strengthens your inner self.

With Mars: You have great mental energy to devote to a new learning objective. Physical exercise and self-development are a major part of your plan to maintain good health, and a good way to eliminate emotional frustrations.

With Jupiter: Whatever you learn now will be both profitable and pleasurable in coming months. You were born with naturally excellent health and are generally drawn to a healthful life style, as long as you do not overindulge your appetites. You may have prophetic dreams, and practice astral travel successfully.

With Saturn: The wisdom of the past and your own experience are the keys to success in coming months. You were born with some physical limitations, particularly in your energy level, but have wisely built up your endurance and learned to use your energy efficiently, and get enough rest. Dreams may reveal anxieties.

With Uranus: Many beneficial changes are going on in your life in the next few months. These changes may be preceded by clairvoyant visions of the future. Your health depnds on your nervous system, so healthful foods, meditation, relaxation build up your resistance to tension and strain. You may have clairvoyant visions or dreams of the future.

With Neptune: Exercise your psychic abilities to gain the information you need in coming months. You are closely attuned to your physical well-being and use the right remedies for any ailment. You apply drug therapy, spiritual healing and mental healing well. You may have psychic dreams and astral travel experience.

With Pluto: A better understanding of occult sciences can help resolve conflicts in coming months. You have great recuperative powers and make the effort to support your inner energies with rest and a good diet. Past life experiences may appear in your dreams.

PUELLA

This mildly adverse symbol is mitigated by Sun, Venus and Jupiter; made somewhat more adverse by Saturn, Uranus, Mars, Neptune and Pluto; and dissipated to some extent by Mercury and the Moon.

Puella is ruled by Venus, the feminine planet of love and beauty, and is associated with the sign Libra, representing marriage and cooperation, the better side of Venus; but also representing indecisive and fickle Venus, in which case Puella can be mildly adverse.

Puella in a chart always indicates a point where the affections of the individual are involved, be it love of an individual, love of one's work, pleasure in creative efforts, or a universal love that results in strivings for peace and harmony in all of society. Puella can also represent affection or desire for not-so-beneficial objectives: gluttony, lust, envy. Puella represents adjustments to conditions of the house involved, the need for catering to others and cooperation for success.

Puella
In the 1st House
Alone, no planets: A pleasant but not always beneficial influence prevails the next few months. You indulge your appetites, are lazy in pursuing personal projects, and expect others to help you without reward and sometimes without any appreciation on your part. Favorable for artistic self-expression.

With Sun: Your personal charm and attractiveness are at a peak and bring cooperation where you desire it. Learn to express your appreciation for cooperation. Your artistic ideas deserve persistent efforts to achieve real accomplishment. You may receive a gift.

With Moon: Your popularity is fleeting, but enjoy it while you can, and try to build stronger ties. A good time to arrange a showing or sale of your artistic and creative works. You may also successfully improve your appearance.

With Mercury: You are persuasive in speech and charming in manner, qualities which gain support in the right places. Excellent for the salesperson dealing in art and beauty items, cultural studies and luxury items. Literary creative efforts are favored.

With Venus: Bask in the approval and affection you gain now, but reciprocate if you want deeper relationships. Your personal life is geared to a romantic relationship or an artistic creative goal. Excellent for those working to help people improve their physical appearances.

With Mars: You are gripped by a romantic infatuation or an artistic ambition in coming months. Your appeal to the opposite sex is at a high point—use your powers wisely. Exercise to improve appearance and health is favored.

With Jupiter: You can form new friendly relationships and express your artistic talents successfully now. Avoid over-indulging your appetites or letting others take advantage of your generosity and good humor. Excellent for pleasure trips.

With Saturn: Your normal charm will not help you evade the restrictions put on you in coming months. Work in architecture and design is favored. You can successfully complete any creative projects now.

With Uranus: Pleasant changes create excitement in the next few months. You are fickle and flirtatious, in love with excitement. This combination favors artistic originality and sudden inspirations.

With Neptune: Infatuation and illusion undermine the realities in this area of your life for the next few months. Create a glamorous image and fulfill personal fantasies now in harmless but pleasurable ways. Musical self-expression is favored.

With Pluto: Fate frequently tempts you to give in to negative desires in coming months. A good time to renew your appearance and take the weariness from your face and attitudes. Group social creative activities help.

Puella
In the 2nd House
Alone, no planets: A pleasant but not always beneficial influence prevails the next few months. Emotional spending for purely pleasurable items is fun, but limit yourself, as your tastes may change. An extra source of income is temporary, and gifts may have strings attached.

With Sun: Your personal charm and attractiveness are at a peak and bring cooperation where you desire it. A good time to get a wardrobe and jewelry that do the most to express your unique inner self. Work in luxury sales is profitable.

With Moon: Your popularity is fleeting, but enjoy it while you can, and try to build stronger ties. Excellent for beauty, luxury and clothing sales work. Modeling and other beauty-oriented occupations are also favored.

With Mercury: You are persuasive in speech and charming in manner, qualities which gain support in the right places. Work in the arts, counseling, and communications is highly favored. Your taste is excellent, so shop for gifts now.

With Venus: Bask in the approval and affection you gain now, but reciprocate if you want deeper relationships. Excellent for success in the arts and beauty-oriented occupations. You may receive a special gift now.

With Mars: You are gripped by a romantic infatuation or an artistic ambition in coming months. Excellent for sales of perfumes, exotic clothing and magazines which emphasize sexual allure. Take the initiative to improve your income.

With Jupiter: You can form new friendly relationships and express your artistic talents successfully now. You are generous with your funds and possessions; fortunately, you also have a good income now.

With Saturn: Your normal charm will not help you evade the restrictions put on you in coming months. Expenses tend to rise. Put the brakes on the whims and self-indulgence of those who depend on you financially. Good for investments in art and antiques.

With Uranus: Pleasant changes create excitement in the next few months. You spend more for the latest innovations and fad items; shop comparatively if your heart is set on these items. Your income may increase briefly.

With Neptune: Infatuation and illusion undermine the realities in this area of your life for the next few months. Avoid get-rich-quick schemes; but you may be mildy lucky in lottery or sweepstakes. You spend more emotionally.

With Pluto: Fate frequently tempts you to give in to negative desires in coming months. Shop for reusable items, and sell items you no longer need. You profit from investments in cooperatives.

Puella
In the 3rd House
Alone, no planets: A pleasant but not always beneficial influence prevails the next few months. Travel for pleasure and enjoy local entertainment. Purchase new games, books and other items just for fun.

With Sun: Your personal charm and attractiveness are at a peak and bring cooperation where you desire it. You assume a role of leadership in community activities. A good time for an art or fashion show, or to present entertainment to the public.

With Moon: Your popularity is fleeting, but enjoy it while you can, and try to build stronger ties. Advertising and sales are highly favored, particularly entertainment items, luxuries, and beauty preparations and programs.

With Mercury: You are persuasive in speech and charming in manner, qualities which gain support in the right places. Excellent for the sale of self-improvement programs and items. You enjoy local travel and socializing.

With Venus: Bask in the approval and affection you gain now, but reciprocate if you want deeper relationships. Excellent for fashion sales, home decor, catering and all the products that beautify life and provide comfort and pleasure.

With Mars: You are gripped by a romantic infatuation or an artistic ambition in coming months. You may feel or reciprocate a strong sexual attraction to someone around you whom you have taken for granted in the past. Romantic entertainment is favored.

With Jupiter: You can form new friendly relationships and express your artistic talents successfully now. You may receive a gift through the mail, or receive some good news. A good time to visit with relatives, particularly brothers and sisters.

With Saturn: Your normal charm will not help you evade the restrictions put on you in coming months. You feel discontented with your daily routines. Get together with old friends for local entertainment that will cheer you up.

With Uranus: Pleasant changes create excitement in the next few months. A good time to purchase a car or electronic equipment for pleasure. You enjoy visiting new entertainment places in your locale.

With Neptune: Infatuation and illusion undermine the realities in this area of your life for the next few months. Excellent for a pleasure trip or retreat, where you can escape and indulge artistic and musical interests.

With Pluto: Fate frequently tempts you to give in to negative desires in coming months. You may meet a friend from a past lifetime and give each other an emotional lift. Join community improvement groups, particularly beautification projects.

Puella
In the 4th House
Alone, no planets: A pleasant but not always beneficial influence prevails the next few months. Excellent for home decorating

and entertaining if you choose the right items, and scan your guest list carefully. Good for a family reunion or wedding in the home.

With Sun: Your personal charm and attractiveness are at a peak and bring cooperation where you desire it. You are the mediator of family disputes, the arbiter of good decorating and social taste, and the planner of entertainment.

With Moon: Your popularity is fleeting, but enjoy it while you can, and try to build stronger ties. A family reunion is favored, as is greater rapport with your mother and other female relatives.

With Mercury: You are persuasive in speech and charming in manner, qualities which gain support in the right places. Good for family discussions and planning, a family outing, and purchasing a new home or household items.

With Venus: Bask in the approval and affection you gain now, but reciprocate if you want deeper relationships. Excellent for home entertaining and redecorating, improving family relationships.

With Mars: You are gripped by a romantic infatuation or an artistic ambition in coming months. Excellent for home repairs, family activities, gardening and agriculture, making the move to a new home.

With Jupiter: You can form new friendly relationships and express your artistic talents successfully now. Excellent time to purchase a new home, work in real estate, landscaping or decorating, and entertain at home.

With Saturn: Your normal charm will not help you evade the restrictions put on you in coming months. A good time to invest in business real estate, start a business in your home catering to luxury items or works of art; good for purchasing antiques.

With Uranus: Pleasant changes create excitement in the next few months. A good time to purchase appliances and decorate your home in a modern style. You may make a move successfully now.

With Neptune: Infatuation and illusion undermine the realities in this area of your life for the next few months. You share rapport with grandparents, or may reveal the talents of your ancestors in the arts or music. Excellent for peace and seclusion at home.

With Pluto: Fate frequently tempts you to give in to negative desires in coming months. Excellent for home renovating and renewing ties with family members. Do not risk security.

Puella
In the 5th House
Alone, no planets: A pleasant but not always beneficial influence prevails the next few months. If expecting a child, you are likely to have a girl. You make small winnings in gambling—know when to quit. Artistic creative efforts are favored; love is pleasant, but fickle.

With Sun: Your personal charm and attractiveness are at a peak and bring cooperation where you desire it. Love can be lasting if you make an effort. If expecting a child, you will have your heart's desire. You are successful in gambling and creative projects.

With Moon: Your popularity is fleeting, but enjoy it while you can, and try to build stronger ties. If expecting a child, it will resemble the mother. You may be lucky in supermarket sweepstakes. You achieve excellent rapport with children.

With Mercury: You are persuasive in speech and charming in manner, qualities which gain support in the right places. If expecting a child, you may have twin girls. You enjoy romantic exchanges and ideas, but are not ready to settle down. Good for luck in contests and literary creative efforts.

With Venus: Bask in the approval and affection you gain now, but reciprocate if you want deeper relationships. Love is charming and enchanting while times are good. Favorable for artistic creative projects.

With Mars: You are gripped by a romantic infatuation or an artistic ambition in coming months. If expecting a child, it is likely to be an attractive or artistic boy. You are successful in sports and creative projects. Love is stormy, but making up is fun.

With Jupiter: You can form new friendly relationships and express your artistic talents successfully now. If expecting a child, it will fulfill your every hope, boy or girl. You are lucky in all forms of gambling. Excellent for investments.

With Saturn: Your normal charm will not help you evade the restrictions put on you in coming months. If expecting a child, you will have a responsible, serious one who needs shows of affection frequently. Excellent for mastering ancient artistic or creative techniques. Avoid gambling.

With Uranus: Pleasant changes create excitement in the next few months. If expecting a child, it will be independent and need much freedom. Good for luck in games of chance, such as casino gambling. A romance may be broken off.

With Neptune: Infatuation and illusion undermine the realities in this area of your life for the next few months. Lucky in sweepstakes and lotteries, not so fortunate in life, as you are living in a dream. If expecting a child, it will have musical or artistic talents.

With Pluto: Fate frequently tempts you to give in to negative desires in coming months. If expecting a child, you will relive your own youth with him or her. Excellent for luck in sweepstakes and lotteries.

Puella
In the 6th House
Alone, no planets: A pleasant but not always beneficial influence prevails the next few months. Pleasure in your work may be more important than the salary you receive. Try to take a practical as well as personal approach to your job. Avoid overindulging your appetites.

With Sun: Your personal charm and attractiveness are at a peak and bring cooperation where you desire it. An excellent time to seek advancement, a better job, or better working conditions, as authorities and supervisors look on you favorably.

With Moon: Your popularity is fleeting, but enjoy it while you can, and try to build stronger ties. Excellent for seeking work in sales, particularly beauty and luxury items, and promoting your own products on the job or to the public.

With Mercury: You are persuasive in speech and charming in manner, qualities which gain support in the right places. Excellent for work in sales, advertising, communications and travel industries.

With Venus: Bask in the approval and affection you gain now, but reciprocate if you want deeper relationships. Excellent for attaining recognition and advancement in any artistic occupation; also favors counseling and beauty work.

With Mars: You are gripped by a romantic infatuation or an artistic ambition in coming months. You may find a coworker particularly attractive now. Excellent for accomplishing the goals you set for yourself, as desire plays an important part in your productivity.

With Jupiter: You can form new friendly relationships and express your artistic talents successfully now. Excellent for starting a new job, taking up a new line of work, or seeking a raise and advancement.

With Saturn: Your normal charm will not help you evade the restrictions put on you in coming months. You will, however, receive what you desire in terms of pay and appreciation for the added responsibilities you take on now.

With Uranus: Pleasant changes create excitement in the next few months. Artistic originality is favored. You may start on an entirely new type of job with ease now.

With Neptune: Infatuation and illusion undermine the realities in this area of your life for the next few months. Excellent for work with counseling, charities, the occult professions. You prefer to work alone now, and have excellent working conditions.

With Pluto: Fate frequently tempts you to give in to negative desires in coming months. Excellent for cooperative efforts on the job, and in dealing with supervisors.

Puella
In the 7th House
Alone, no planets: A pleasant but not always beneficial influence prevails the next few months. You receive much attention from spouse and close friends, but some may have devious motives. Share more recreational time with loved ones, but form no business partnerships.

With Sun: Your personal charm and attractiveness are at a peak and bring cooperation where you desire it. You may marry or form a successful business partnership, as long as you realize you will have to remain the strong person in the relationship.

With Moon: Your popularity is fleeting but enjoy it while you can, and try to build stronger ties. Good for a public wedding, a special outing with a loved one, and a romantic interlude. Resolve legal disputes.

With Mercury: You are persuasive in speech and charming in manner, qualities which gain support in the right places. Your charm wins you new friends and favors reconciliation with enemies and settlement of legal disputes. Discussions with loved ones are amiable.

With Venus: Bask in the approval and affection you gain now, but reciprocate if you want deeper relationships. Excellent for marriage based on genuine affection. Settle legal disputes, and enjoy social events with a loved one.

With Mars: You are gripped by a romantic infatuation or an artistic ambition in coming months. Share your ideas with a loved one. Excellent for a profitable business partnership. You are ardent in expressing affection, and successful in competition.

With Jupiter: You can form new friendly relationships and express your artistic talents successfully now. You may marry someone with material wealth or an uplifting spiritual influence on your life. Competition and legal disputes will go your way.

With Saturn: Your normal charm will not help you evade the restrictions put on you in coming months. You feel more secure and contented with old friends. You are shrewd in dealing with partnership affairs and competition.

With Uranus: Pleasant changes create excitement in the next few months. A sudden romantic attraction could bring new meaning and a close relationship that broadens your perspectives and offers new stimulation in shared activities.

With Neptune: Infatuation and illusion undermine the realities in this area of your life for the next few months. You may come face to face with a romantic ideal in the flesh. Shared activities bring new emotional rapport.

With Pluto: Fate frequently tempts you to give in to negative desires in coming months. You are especially doubtful or jealous in a close relationship. Avoid competition and legal disputes.

Puella
In the 8th House
Alone, no planets: A pleasant but not always beneficial influence prevails the next few months. Romantic flirtation is favored, along with benefits from joint financial ventures with members of the opposite sex. Avoid being too self-indulgent or generous to others on credit.

With Sun: Your personal charm and attractiveness are at a peak and bring cooperation where you desire it. Your sexual energies depend on the romantic setting you need to create. You are successful in all joint ventures and in occult activities devoted to love and peace.

With Moon: Your popularity is fleeting, but enjoy it while you can, and try to build stronger ties. Excellent for psychometry and occult arts which depend on material objects, such as gemstone healing and design of occult jewelry.

With Mercury: You are persuasive in speech and charming in manner, qualities which gain support in the right places. Good or fruitful discussions with an intimate, and signing any joint venture financial papers. You receive fortunate messages from the spiritual plane.

With Venus: Bask in the approval and affection you gain now, but reciprocate if you want deeper relationships. Romance is highly favored; you can attract the person of your dreams now. You may receive a small legacy.

With Mars: You are gripped by a romantic infatuation or an artistic ambition in coming months. You achieve great rapport and satisfaction in a sexual relationship, and sex magic is favored. Excellent for profits from aggressive joint ventures.

With Jupiter: You can form new friendly relationships and express your artistic talents successfully now. You may receive a legacy now. Relations with the opposite sex are easy and beneficial now. Happy prophetic dreams or spiritual messages come to you now.

With Saturn: Your normal charm will not help you evade the restrictions put on you in coming months. Excellent for work with talismans and gemstones for occult purposes. High magic is helpful. Relations with the opposite sex are friendly, but at a low energy level.

With Uranus: Pleasant changes create excitement in the next few months. Excellent for occult entertainment, such as psychic fairs, and the practice of astrological counseling, particularly dealing with close relationships. Avoid joint ventures and credit spending.

With Neptune: Infatuation and illusion undermine the realities in this area of your life for the next few months. Avoid joint financial ventures, as you may be deceived; and restrain credit spending. Excellent for working with occult arts such as divination.

With Pluto: Fate frequently tempts you to give in to negative desires in coming months. You may receive a legacy; credit is easy and joint financial ventures highly favored. Your sex drive depends on a sense of well-being and affectionate interest.

Puella
In the 9th House

Alone, no planets: A pleasant but not always beneficial influence prevails the next few months. You enjoy the prospect of travel and undertaking new studies, but will need persistence to complete what you start once the initial pleasure wears off and effort is required. Excellent for studies in the arts and diplomacy.

With Sun: Your personal charm and attractiveness are at a peak and bring cooperation where you desire it. You are honored abroad and may meet your dream romance in a foreign land. The creative arts are a source of inspiration and a good focus for study and skill development.

With Moon: Your popularity is fleeting, but enjoy it while you can and try to build stronger ties. Excellent for the study of any type of beauty work and the popular arts. You enjoy travel and may take a pleasure cruise soon.

With Mercury: You are persuasive in speech and charming in manner, qualities which gain support in the right places. Excellent for the development of sales and other persuasive techniques, and for art criticism. You may develop skills in a foreign language, preparatory to a pleasure trip.

With Venus: Bask in the approval and affection you gain now, but reciprocate if you want deeper relationships. Studies in the arts, culture and beauty are favored, for both personal pleasure and professional ambitions. Excellent for a pleasure trip to a foreign land.

With Mars: You are gripped by a romantic infatuation or an artistic ambition in coming months. Excellent for a romantic trip with a loved one, an elopement, or a shipboard romance. You are attracted to exotic new places.

With Jupiter: You can form new friendly relationships and express your artistic talents successfully now. A good time to relocate to a new area in search of study and writing opportunities and material. You radiate optimism and cheer.

With Saturn: Your normal charm will not help you evade the restrictions put on you in coming months. Excellent for business travel and the study of art history, architecture, and landscaping. You enjoy monuments and would like to leave a personal one to posterity.

With Uranus: Pleasant changes create excitement in the next few months. You may suddenly fall in love with a foreign land, while traveling, and decide to remain permanently. Excellent for the study of modern art and art techniques.

With Neptune: Infatuation and illusion undermine the realities in this area of your life for the next few months. Religious mysticism and secretive, mysterious oriental lands appeal to you now. Take a voyage of escape from the mundane if possible.

With Pluto: Fate frequently tempts you to give in to negative desires in coming months. You become consciously aware of the impact of past lives on your present, and may explore the distant lands you once knew so well.

Puella
In the 10th House
Alone, no planets: A pleasant but not always beneficial influence prevails the next few months. Favors work in counseling, the social sciences, arts, beauty, music, culture, and luxury items. Your personal charm is an important part of your success.

With Sun: Your personal charm and attractiveness are at a peak and bring cooperation where you desire it. You may become an authority on some area of the arts and social psychology or philosophy. A good time to run for elective office.

With Moon: Your popularity is fleeting, but enjoy it while you can, and try to build stronger ties. Excellent for publicizing your creative efforts, particularly in the arts, and attending public social events.

With Mercury: You are persuasive in speech and charming in manner, qualities which gain support in the right places. Excellent for speaking in public, mediating public disputes, and promoting cultural events.

With Venus: Bask in the approval and affection you gain now, but reciprocate if you want deeper relationships. Excellent for the performing and creative artist; now is the time to display your talents and productions. Public social events can promote your business interests as well.

With Mars: You are gripped by a romantic infatuation or an artistic ambition in coming months. Business success is guaranteed if you take the initiative in providing a product or service that has a strong emotional appeal to the public.

With Jupiter: You can form new friendly relationships and express your artistic talents successfully now. Excellent for publishing or producing books and artistic or luxury items for mass consumption.

With Saturn: Your normal charm will not help you evade the restrictions put on you in coming months. You can, however, rely on established customers for business expansion if you make the effort to promote your wares in an emotionally appealing way.

With Uranus: Pleasant changes create excitement in the next few months. You have the flexibility and clear sight to take advantage of public fads in your business. Emotionally appealing new ideas and products are favored.

With Neptune: Infatuation and illusion undermine the realities in this area of your life for the next few months. Cater to the escapist and illusionary moods of the public with products and services that have a strong emotional appeal. Social work, the arts and music are favored.

With Pluto: Fate frequently tempts you to give in to negative desires in coming months. Products that offer emotional, spiritual or physical rejuvenation or at least improvements are a business success now.

Puella
In the 11th House

Alone, no planets: A pleasant but not always beneficial influence prevails the next few months. Expand your social life, focusing on groups and activities purely for fun and relaxation. You get along especially well with women now. Cultural and artistic events are favored.

With Sun: Your personal charm and attractiveness are at a peak and bring cooperation where you desire it. You assume a role of leadership in social and cultural activities, and may be active in a peace group.

With Moon: Your popularity is fleeting, but enjoy it while you can, and try to build stronger ties. You are attracted to and join several groups, but only one will hold your interest. You benefit from attending public social events.

With Mercury: You are persuasive in speech and charming in manner, qualities which gain support in the right places. You may be invited to speak on cultural and social issues, or simply get together with friends for a gabfest or card games and other friendly contests.

With Venus: Bask in the approval and affection you gain now, but reciprocate if you want deeper relationships. Seek romance at the social events you attend. Display your artistic talents and products, and promote cultural values.

With Mars: You are gripped by a romantic infatuation or an artistic ambition in coming months. Your favors are spread among many new acquaintances, who respond in a satisfying manner. Excellent for team and sporting recreation.

With Jupiter: You can form new friendly relationships and express your artistic talents successfully now. You are interested in educational as well as purely pleasurable groups, and may take a group tour.

With Saturn: Your normal charm will not help you evade the restrictions put on you in coming months. You are in a reminiscent mood, and may look up old friends to talk over old times. Excellent for socializing for business purposes.

With Uranus: Pleasant changes create excitement in the next few months. A new friend introduces you to exciting groups and stimulating social activities. Spread yourself around.

With Neptune: Infatuation and illusion undermine the realities in this area of your life for the next few months. You are especially successful in promoting charitable and social improvement objectives; avoid being a soft touch for con artists, however.

With Pluto: Fate frequently tempts you to give in to negative desires in coming months. You may join a health and beauty-oriented group for exercise and improvement of your vitality and energy level.

Puella
In the 12th House
Alone, no planets: A pleasant but not always beneficial influence prevails the next few months. You are contented with solitude, enjoy meditation, and try to keep your health up because it affects your appearance. Your dreams are mainly wish-fulfillments.

With Sun: Your personal charm and attractiveness are at a peak and bring cooperation where you desire it. Your physical health is excellent, and you are more interested in building up your spiritual energies. A good time to set special inner goals for yourself.

With Moon: Your popularity is fleeting, but enjoy it while you can, and try to build strong ties. You may suffer from a minor skin rash or brief ailment. Your dreams are intuitive and may reveal the future, but only in areas of personal interest to you.

With Mercury: You are persuasive in speech and charming in manner, qualities which gain support in the right places. Keep track of your dreams for creative ideas in the arts and writing. You are aware of your own weaknesses and can apply methods to strengthen yourself.

With Venus: Bask in the approval and affection you gain now, but reciprocate if you want deeper relationships. You are serene and contented alone or in company. A secret romance is indicated.

With Mars: You are gripped by a romantic infatuation or an artistic ambition in coming months. Emotional or romantic frustrations can be directed into private creative efforts and improving your physical health.

With Jupiter: You can form new friendly relationships and express your artistic talents successfully now. You may be happier dreaming than waking, spending time meditating and communing with your inner self rather than other people.

With Saturn: Your normal charm will not help you evade the restrictions put on you in coming months. Your nostalgic mood inclines you to look over old mementos, letters, and photographs in private. Make a resolution to seek out people you have not seen for a while.

With Uranus: Pleasant changes create excitment in the next few months. You may have clairvoyant dreams of the future. You are in a state of suppressed romantic excitement. Original creative ideas come easily.

With Neptune: Infatuation and illusion undermine the realities in this area of your life for the next few months. Your charitable feelings may lead you to volunteer to help the less fortunate. You may have astral travels, other psychic experiences and dreams now.

With Pluto: Fate frequently tempts you to give in to negative desires in coming months. However, you can recuperate from romantic disappointments and other emotional frustrations more easily now.

AMISSIO

This adverse symbol is intensified by Saturn, Uranus, Neptune, Pluto and Mars; mitigated by Sun, Venus and Jupiter; and simply emphasized by the Moon and Mercury, which are neutral planets.

Amissio (Loss) is ruled by Venus and associated with the sign Scorpio, where Venus is in detriment, and represents the lust and self-indulgence of perverted Venus. Scorpio represents the intimacy with others which can lead to loss through association.

Amissio always indicates a point of loss or lack in the querent's chart. Loss of love, of money, of children, of self-esteem, of material goods; or theft of the above, can be suggested by Amissio. The need for a skill, an object, even a purpose in life can be indicated by Amissio. This leads to efforts to satisfy whatever need is felt, and these efforts, too, can be fruitless, if the goal is unrealistic; and so more losses are incurred.

Amissio
In the 1st House

Alone, no planets: This is an adverse influence that remains relatively unchanged in the next few months. You may suffer from weight loss, loss of sleep, loss of enthusiasm for life. Be careful with new contacts and avoid starting new financial projects now.

With Sun: Egotism, touchy sensitivity, dictatorial attitudes and self-centered behavior can be sources of loss. You lack the self-confidence to take control of your own life and persist in your projects until you achieve success.

With Moon: Moodiness, changeability, slavish adherence to fads or popular beliefs can be sources of loss. You are inconsistent and changeable, unable to take advantage of opportunities to deal with the public profitably, and inclined to drift instead of standing firm in your goals.

With Mercury: Indecision, saying anything to please another, and carelessness with facts can be sources of loss. You have too many new projects started and too many new ideas to be able to handle them all successfully. Sort the wheat from the chaff and plan in advance.

With Venus: Fickleness, self-indulgence, neglect of duties in pursuit of pleasure, can be sources of loss. You may also be too friendly and pleasant to people who waste your time and take advantage of your desire to please others.

With Mars: Excessive drains on your energy may cause tiredness or weight loss in coming months. You may also be attracted to too many new people and activities, and need to be more persistent to achieve success in a few new projects.

With Jupiter: Extravagance, carelessness and self-indulgence are the problems to watch for in the near future. Your willingness to trust new people and generously spend time on optimistic projects can lead to lack of personal accomplishment.

With Saturn: Whatever is lost now will be permanently lost—a good time to break old habits. You may hesitate too long to take advantage of new opportunities. Past experience may not always help in starting new projects.

With Uranus: Disturbing and disruptive changes occur during the next few months. Too many distractions and changes of mind prevent success in completing new projects. You tend to leap without looking into new situations.

With Neptune: Mysterious losses, some minor, some more significant, afflict you the next few months. You are too sensitive to the opinions of new people, and too vague in starting new projects. Dreams rather than reality dominate your personal life.

With Pluto: You are suffering from a drain of spiritual energies which is difficult to pin down in the near future. Excessive suspicion or desire for privacy can prevent you from taking advantage of new opportunities for personal success.

Amissio
In the 2nd House

Alone, no planets: This is an adverse influence that remains relatively unchanged in the next few months. Watch for loss of income or possessions. Make sure you get a good price for anything you sell; and limit your purchasing to reliable sources.

With Sun: Egotism, touchy sensitivity, dictatorial attitudes and self-centered behavior can be sources of loss. You are too proud to accept advice in financial matters, and too eager to make a public showing of your possessions. Loss by poor investment or theft may result.

With Moon: Moodiness, changeability, slavish adherence to fads or popular beliefs can be sources of loss. You may have to rely on temporary jobs or self-employment to satisfy income needs while you try to decide how best to apply your moneymaking talents.

With Mercury: Indecision, saying anything to please another, and carelessness with facts can be sources of loss. Avoid starting any moneymaking projects now, and focus on your regular sources of income. Do not order anything by mail or telephone—see what you are getting.

With Venus: Fickleness, self-indulgence, neglect of duties in pursuit of pleasure, can be sources of loss. Resist emotional spending, particularly on wardrobe and other personal items, and do not buy any expensive gifts—they will not be appreciated.

With Mars: Excessive drains on your energy may cause tiredness or weight loss in coming months. Do not waste time or energy on repairing items that are better replaced. Avoid frantic physical efforts in pursuit of money where planning ahead would halve the labor.

With Jupiter: Extravagance, carelessness and self-indulgence are the problems to watch for in the near future. Avoid being too trusting, getting involved in expansive investments, or making financial commitments you cannot fulfill. Restrain spending for luxuries.

With Saturn: Whatever is lost now will be permanently lost—a good time to break old habits. Ultra-conservatism can lead to lost financial opportunities. Avoid buying cheap bargains that are not really bargains.

With Uranus: Disturbing and disruptive changes occur during the next few months. Sudden personal expenses or impulsive buying can put you easily in the red. Do not make snap financial decisions or commitments now.

With Neptune: Mysterious losses, some minor, some more significant, afflict you the next few months. Forgetfulness and confusion lead to lost financial opportunities, but avoid get-rich-quick schemes and shoddy purchases.

With Pluto: You are suffering from a drain of spiritual energies which is difficult to pin down in the near future. Avoid sinking money into items that are not repairable, but appraise items you are ready to get rid of for their true value. Avoid pig-in-a-poke purchases.

Amissio
In the 3rd House
Alone, no planets: This is an adverse influence that remains relatively unchanged in the next few months. Indiscreet speech can lose a friend, susceptibility to flattery can bring unwanted obligations, and carelessness in travel can be costly.

With Sun: Egotism, touchy sensitivity, dictatorial attitudes and self-centered behavior can be sources of loss. Be less opinionated and more receptive to the ideas of others, but do not go to the other extreme and decide everyone else knows your business better than you do.

With Moon: Moodiness, changeability, slavish adherence to fads or popular beliefs can be sources of loss.

With Mercury: Indecision, saying anything to please another, and carelessness with facts can be sources of loss. Indiscreet speech, hasty or thoughtless business communications, failure to maintain your car and telephone, can lead to losses.

With Venus: Fickleness, self-indulgence, neglect of duties in pursuit of pleasure, can be sources of loss. Too much running around and gossiping with neighbors and relatives leaves you little reserve to achieve the major desires in your life.

With Mars: Excessive drains on your energy may cause tiredness or weight loss in coming months. Haste and impatience in travel can lead to accident potential, while argumentativeness can lose the good will of supportive neighbors and relatives.

With Jupiter: Extravagance, carelessness and self-indulgence are the problems to watch for in the near future. Confine your sense of human kinship to those who merit your generosity. Avoid indulging the bad habits of others.

With Saturn: Whatever is lost now will be permanently lost—a good time to break old habits. Over-rigidity of daily habits and mental inflexibility can lead to losses through lack of information or under-standing of new ideas and opportunities.

With Uranus: Disturbing and disruptive changes occur during the next few months. Do not indulge impulses to travel or try out fads or extremist ideas. Be prepared for disruptions in communications and travel.

With Neptune: Mysterious losses, some minor, some more signifi-cant, afflict you the next few months. Misinformation, confused com-munications and misdirection in travel can waste your time and delay important projects.

With Pluto: You are suffering from a drain of spiritual energies which is difficult to pin down in the near future. Subversive local influences, from bad plumbing, to dubious gossip, to adverse weather, can cause doubts as to the success of your intentions.

Amissio
In the 4th House
Alone, no planets: This is an adverse influence that remains relatively unchanged in the next few months. You may feel the loss of a family member, or the lack of family companionship. You may also worry about losing your home or your security for the future.

With Sun: Egotism, touchy sensitivity, dictatorial attitudes and self-centered behavior can be sources of loss. Excessive self-confidence may cost you security; do not take chances with your home, or invest in real estate now. You feel the absence of a parent strongly.

With Moon: Moodiness, changeabililty, slavish adherence to fads or popular beliefs can be sources of loss. You miss the company of your mother, but you may not be able to spend as much time as you would like with your family, due to the demands of public life.

With Mercury: Indecision, saying anything to please another, and carelessness with facts can be sources of loss. You are in a state of mental turmoil about the affairs of a family member, or out of touch family members. Sign no real estate papers.

With Venus: Fickleness, self-indulgence, neglect of duties in pursuit of pleasure, can be sources of loss. Avoid excessive costly home entertaining or luxury purchases, and do not take family cooperation for granted.

With Mars: Excessive drains on your energy may cause tiredness or weight loss in coming months. Avoid hasty or laborious work around the house, as you may make costly mistakes. Avoid quarrels that lose you family cooperation.

With Jupiter: Extravagance, carelesssness and self-indulgence are the problems to watch for in the near future. Avoid real estate dealings or the purchase of a new home, as you may pay a greatly inflated price for your desires. Better for selling a home at a high price, though you will miss the home if you leave it.

With Saturn: Whatever is lost now will be permanently lost—a good time to break old habits. Avoid being cheap in buying household appliances, as you will not find many genuine bargains. Do not sell property now, as prices are deflated.

With Uranus: Disturbing and disruptive changes occur during the next few months. Expect electrical and other problems connected with household conveniences, and erratic demands from guests and family members.

With Neptune: Mysterious losses, some minor, some more significant, afflict you the next few months. Do not invest in property or dubious conveniences or luxuries for your home. Family members are difficult to get in touch with and include in family planning.

With Pluto: You are suffering from a drain of spiritual energies which is difficult to pin down in the near future. The plumbing and foundations of your home may present problems. Family members are secretive and seek privacy, making you feel like odd man out.

Amissio
In the 5th House
Alone, no planets: This is an adverse influence that remains relatively unchanged in the next few months. Avoid gambling or speculation, as you are likely to lose money. Children's needs or desires can be costly. A romantic relationship may fizzle out. Creative projects may require more effort than the ultimate result is worth.

With Sun: Egotism, touchy sensitivity, dictatorial attitudes and self-centered behavior can be sources of loss. Avoid being domineering with loved ones, or too authoritarian and demanding with children. Your creative impulses are good, but your techniques may need improvement.

With Moon: Moodiness, changeability, slavish adherence to fads or popular beliefs can be sources of loss. You are too distracted to work on creative projects. You overindulge children and loved ones with little appreciation in return. Avoid gambling.

With Mercury: Indecision, saying anything to please another, and carelessness with facts can be sources of loss. Lack of communication with loved ones can lead to misunderstandings; lack of supervision of children can also lead to problems. Avoid gambling, no matter how good your system seems to be.

With Venus: Fickleness, self-indulgence, neglect of duties in pursuit of pleasure, can be sources of loss. You may be juggling several romantic interests, but sooner or later you will lose control. Avoid favoritism with children, or gambling.

With Mars: Excessive drains on your energy may cause tiredness or weight loss in coming months. Quarrels with loved ones, disobedience from children, frustrations in recreation and creative projects, and losses in gambling are typical.

With Jupiter: Extravagance, carelessness and self-indulgence are the problems to watch for in the near future. You spend too much on children and loved ones, indulge in excessive recreation, and waste money on gambling. Do not neglect creative impulses.

With Saturn: Whatever is lost now will be permanently lost—a good time to break old habits. He who hesitates in love is lost. Avoid worrying about children, gambling when you do not really feel like it, or dismissing creative ideas which may actually prove viable.

With Uranus: Disturbing and disruptive changes occur during the next few months. A romantic relationship may be broken off suddenly through no fault of your own. Avoid gambling or hazardous recreation, and be prepared for surprises from children who are becoming very independent.

With Neptune: Mysterious losses, some minor, some more significant, afflict you the next few months. Resolutely ignore get-rich-quick investments, as it is the other person who will get rich, not you. A romantic illusion fades, and your creative energies are ebbing. Do not make promises to children in an absent-minded moment.

With Pluto: You are suffering from a drain of spiritual energies which is difficult to pin down in the near future. Avoid getting carried away with gambling or the pursuit of romance or recreation. You find it difficult to maintain your perspectives now.

Amissio
In the 6th House
Alone, no planets: This is an adverse influence that remains relatively unchanged in the next few months. You may lose your job, or an opportunity for career advancement. You should avoid excessive dieting or physical activity, as your system needs balanced building up.

With Sun: Egotism, touchy sensitivity, dictatorial attitudes and self-centered behavior can be sources of loss. Avoid conflicts with your boss on the job, as this could cost you; your advice, whether good or bad, is not welcomed. You may be burning the candle at both ends— get more rest and build up your vitality.

With Moon: Moodiness, changeability, slavish adherence to fads or popular beliefs can be sources of loss. You are not successful in public contact jobs as you do not make a firm impression on people in the workplace. Watch for infectious ailments when out in the crowds.

With Mercury: Indecision, saying anything to please another, and carelessness with facts can be sources of loss. Do not believe gossip, but do pay attention to the commands of supervisors, to the letter, on the job. Focus on mental clarity in building up your health; sleep is important.

With Venus: Fickleness, self-indulgence, neglect of duties in pursuit of pleasure, can be sources of loss. Avoid counting on the cooperation of coworkers, who may be envious. Avoid overindulging your appetites.

With Mars: Excessive drains on your energy may cause tiredness or weight loss in coming months. You may be saddled with overtime work or added job responsibilities; use your energy efficiently, and get plenty of rest to maintain your level of vitality.

With Jupiter: Extravagance, carelessness and self-indulgence are the problems to watch for in the near future. Inattention or irresponsibility could put your job in jeopardy. Exaggerating your skills can lead to problems when you can not achieve your claims. Avoid junk foods.

With Saturn: Whatever is lost now will be permanently lost—a good time to break old habits. Depression or anxiety may affect your appetite and energy level. Get plenty of rest, vitamins and a good diet. Do not get stuck in a job with no future.

With Uranus: Disturbing and disruptive changes occur during the next few months. You may have problems adjusting to a new job or learning new skills, particularly if the financial incentive is minimal. Watch for nervous tension.

With Neptune: Mysterious losses, some minor, some more significant, afflict you the next few months. Daydreaming could lower job efficiency, and create problems for you. Avoid alcohol and drugs.

With Pluto: You are suffering from a drain of spiritual energies which is difficult to pin down in the near future. Doubts and a hostile work environment can limit your job productivity. Avoid indulging appetites in strange places, or with exotic foods.

Amissio
In the 7th House
Alone, no planets: This is an adverse influence that remains relatively unchanged in the next few months. You lack companionship and may need the advice of an expert in some field. Avoid legal disputes, which are losing propositions; and business partnerships which cost more than they bring in.

With Sun: Egotism, touchy sensitivity, dictatorial attitudes and self-centered behavior can be sources of loss. Domineering attitudes can lose you close friends and create barriers with loved ones. Do not let wounded pride keep you from strengthening a good relationship. Avoid competition no matter how tempting.

With Moon: Moodiness, changeability, slavish adherence to fads or popular beliefs can be sources of loss. Do not give way to the unreasonable demands of partners, as they will not appreciate it and will simply lose respect for you.

With Mercury: Indecision, saying anything to please another, and carelessness with facts can be sources of loss. Confusion in communications or unwillingness to discuss matters can lose you a close friend or a lawsuit.

With Venus: Fickleness, self-indulgence, neglect of duties in pursuit of pleasure, can be sources of loss. You may be wasting your affections on one who is unworthy, or trying to cooperate with a selfish partner.

With Mars: Excessive drains on your energy may cause tiredness or weight loss in coming months. Avoid competition and lawsuits, and let loved ones come to you rather than taking the initiative. Be quick but tactful in your responses.

With Jupiter: Extravagance, carelessness and self-indulgence are the problems to watch for in the near future. You are entirely too trusting or generous in legal matters and love, and too honest yourself to recognize unfair competition.

With Saturn: Whatever is lost now will be permanently lost—a good time to break old habits. Excessive caution, hesitation, and delays can put stress on relationships, or lose you new opportunities in business. Old friends may take all your time, limiting expansion of new relationships.

With Uranus: Disturbing and disruptive changes occur during the next few months. A romantic encounter or business deal adversely changes your attitudes or relations with partners. Avoid new commitments now.

With Neptune: Mysterious losses, some minor, some more significant, afflict you the next few months. Illusions and excessive sympathy make you a soft touch for self-seekers and devious business people.

With Pluto: You are suffering from a drain of spiritual energies which is difficult to pin down in the near future. Any expressions of doubt or jealousy could jeopardize a close personal relationship. Avoid partnership dealings now, as dubious elements are on the prowl.

Amissio
In the 8th House

Alone, no planets: This is an adverse influence that remains relatively unchanged in the next few months. Expect losses in credit and joint financial dealings. You may feel the loss of someone close, through death or relocation. Your sexual energy and interest are at a low point now, or frustrated.

With Sun: Egotism, touchy sensitivity, dictatorial attitudes and self-centered behavior can be sources of loss. Do not cosign loans or get involved as the supporter of any joint financial ventures. Avoid being over-assertive with the opposite sex, and refrain from expansive occult purchases.

With Moon: Moodiness, changeability, slavish adherence to fads or popular beliefs can be sources of loss. Your psychic sensitivity leaves you open to too many distracting influences. You are also hypersensitive and inclined to exaggerate your feelings in an intimate relationship. Do not forget to pay bills on time.

With Mercury: Indecision, saying anything to please another, and carelessness with facts can be sources of loss. Ignore gossip and fast sales pitches, particularly when shopping on credit. You are too easily talked into spending. Sign no legal papers.

With Venus: Fickleness, self-indulgence, neglect of duties in pursuit of pleasure, can be sources of loss. A romantic disappointment or a cooling off process may occur in an intimate relationship. Avoid spending on credit, no matter how appealing the item. Avoid wishful thinking in interpreting occult arts.

With Mars: Excessive drains on your energy may cause tiredness or weight loss in coming months. Sexual frustration can lead to loss of interest in an intimate relationship. Watch for negative energy in occult activities. Avoid hasty spending on credit.

With Jupiter: Extravagance, carelessness and self-indulgence are the problems to watch for in the near future. You are too generous with funds to partners, and should avoid signing legal papers now. Do not let an intimate take advantage of your trustfulness. Occult arts are favored, but you may not like the answers you get.

With Saturn: Whatever is lost now will be permanently lost—a good time to break old habits. Avoid occult practices, as you will attract too many adverse influences. Organize your debts, and expect payments due you to be late. Avoid credit spending. Do not be too anxious or possessive in an intimate relationship.

With Uranus: Disturbing and disruptive changes occur during the next few months. You may have some startling psychic premonitions. Watch for sudden expenses, as credit is not easily obtained. An intimate relationship may also be broken off suddenly.

With Neptune: Mysterious losses, some minor, some more significant, afflict you the next few months. Get rid of romantic illusions about an intimate relationship. Avoid get-rich-quick partnership financial schemes, or easy credit payment plans.

With Pluto: You are suffering from a drain of spiritual energies which is difficult to pin down in the near future. Doubts arise in occult and metaphysical studies, and in your intimate relationship. Avoid joint financial dealings now.

Amissio
In the 9th House
Alone, no planets: This is an adverse influence that remains relatively unchanged in the next few months. Be careful in travel, as you may lose a prized possession. You may lose contact with friends who are relocating. Studies may be costly, and unprofitable in the end.

With Sun: Egotism, touchy sensitivity, dictatorial attitudes and self-centered behavior can be sources of loss. Avoid expressing your opinions too loudly, or giving unsought advice, as you may put your foot in your mouth. Travel is costly, so estimate the value of a trip before starting.

With Moon: Moodiness, changeability, slavish adherence to fads or popular beliefs can be sources of loss. Travel plans may fall through or have to be changed at the last minute. Be sure you know what is being presented in any study course you sign up for.

With Mercury: Indecison, saying anything to please another, and carelessness with facts can be sources of loss. Plan your travel in advance, and prepare with language studies, but be discreet once abroad. Avoid taking repetitive study courses by examining a prospectus.

With Venus: Fickleness, self-indulgence, neglect of duties in pursuit of pleasure, can be sources of loss. A foreign or shipboard romance will be ephemeral, but pleasant. Be sure to get background before pursuing art purchases.

With Mars: Excessive drains on your energy may cause tiredness or weight loss in coming months. Avoid haste or impatience in travel or studies, and avoid quarrels with those of differing opinions.

With Jupiter: Extravagance, carelessness and self-indulgence are the problems to watch for in the near future. Do not spend lavishly on travels, as you will not get your money's worth now. The same holds true for study courses, particularly by mail.

With Saturn: Whatever is lost now will be permanently lost—a good time to break old habits. A poor time to review studies or revisit places that hold fond memories. Delays in travel could be costly.

With Uranus: Disturbing and disruptive changes occur during the next few months. Avoid air travel, as minor accident potential exists. Studies may be disrupted by demands of work or family.

With Neptune: Mysterious losses, some minor, some more significant, afflict you the next few months. Watch for loss of property when traveling, and be cautious with people you meet while traveling. Studies may be too confusing and the teacher inadequate.

With Pluto: You are suffering from a drain of spiritual energies which is difficult to pin down in the near future. Avoid travel to out-of-the-way places, as natural phenomena such as the weather may blight your trip. Be sure of the qualifications of the teacher in any study course, as well as the adequacy of your own background.

Amissio
In the 10th House

Alone, no planets: This is an adverse influence that remains relatively unchanged in the next few months. You may lose status or the approval of supervisors, or face cutbacks on the job. Avoid competing for advancement or public office, and keep your eyes open for other opportunities.

With Sun: Egotism, touchy sensitivity, dictatorial attitudes and self-centered behavior can be sources of loss. You may be thrust into a position of authority for which you are unprepared. Do not be afraid to get help and advice.

With Moon: Moodiness, changeability, slavish adherence to fads or popular beliefs can be sources of loss. Popularity can be a detriment if it keeps you from accomplishment. You will have your share of cranks and time-wasters to contend with on the job now.

With Mercury: Indecision, saying anything to please another, and carelessness with facts can be sources of loss. Be extremely discreet on the job and ignore office gossip. Keep up carefully with paperwork and seek instructions if in doubt.

With Venus: Fickleness, self-indulgence, neglect of duties in pursuit of pleasure, can be sources of loss. Do not be talked into taking on the responsibilities of others "just to be nice," or you will not get your own work finished.

With Mars: Excessive drains on your energy may cause tiredness or weight loss in coming months. A poor time to take the initiative on the job. Avoid open conflicts with irritating supervisors and put off competition for advancement temporarily.

With Jupiter: Extravagance, carelesssness and self-indulgence are the problems to watch for in the near future. Avoid over-expanding your business or promising more on the job than you can deliver; underestimate, so that you can take up any slack if business drops off.

With Saturn: Whatever is lost now will be permanently lost—a good time to break old habits. Dealings with government may find you in the wrong or in debt, so delay confrontations until conditions are more favorable. Avoid taking on too many responsibilities at work.

With Uranus: Disturbing and disruptive changes occur during the next few months. Innovation is costly and inefficient for your business at this time. Avoid making job changes, as you will come out the loser.

With Neptune: Mysterious losses, some minor, some more significant, afflict you the next few months. Request clarification of any obscure demands by supervisors, and be prepared to put up with the emotionalism of others on the job.

With Pluto: You are suffering from a drain of spiritual energies which is difficult to pin down in the near future. Economic trends may phase out your job or business; be alert to such signs, and have alternatives in mind.

Amissio
In the 11th House
Alone, no planets: This is an adverse influence that remains relatively unchanged in the next few months. Social life may be financially or emotionally costly now. You may lose a friend through misunderstanding or simply a move to a distant locale.

With Sun: Egotism, touchy sensitivity, dictatorial attitudes and self-centered behavior can be sources of loss. Avoid taking leadership in a group with internal difficulties, or you will end up with blame instead of praise. Do not dictate to friends.

With Moon: Moodiness, changeability, slavish adherence to fads or popular beliefs can be sources of loss. Disassociate yourself from public action groups that are going no place or being taken over by extremists. Be discreet about the problems of friends.

With Mercury: Indecision, saying anything to please another, and carelessness with facts can be sources of loss. Choose the groups you speak to or for, to screen out those who are using you as a front or dupe. Be discreet about your personal life now.

With Venus: Fickleness, self-indulgence, neglect of duties in pursuit of pleasure, can be sources of loss. Your peacemaking efforts may be wasted on quarreling friends—avoid being drawn in, or spending too much on social life.

With Mars: Excessive drains on your energy may cause tiredness or weight loss in coming months. Quarrels can lose you friends, but initiatives can waste your time, as groups are sluggish and unwilling to act.

With Jupiter: Extravagance, carelessness and self-indulgence are the problems to watch for in the near future. Scrutinize carefully the charities to which you devote time and funds. Do not let friends turn you into a simple soft touch, whether financial or emotional.

With Saturn: Whatever is lost now will be permanently lost—a good time to break old habits. Avoid getting embroiled in political disputes or activism, as your efforts will be fruitless. Better to be lonely than spend time with people who are uncongenial.

With Uranus: Disturbing and disruptive changes occur during the next few months. Friends seem to change in front of your eyes, entertainment places close, and you must seek new groups to join to promote personal and social goals, all taking more time and energy.

With Neptune: Mysterious losses, some minor, some more significant, afflict you the next few months. Avoid being a soft touch for casual friends, and avoid people who indulge too much in drugs or alcohol—they are nothing but trouble. Save your sympathy for recognized charities.

With Pluto: You are suffering from a drain of spiritual energies which is difficult to pin down in the near future. A search for renewed youth or popular action may lead you into strange and dangerous places. Avoid extremist groups, and curb your natural curiosity, as you will hear little of the truth.

Amissio
In the 12th House
Alone, no planets: This is an adverse influence that remains relatively unchanged in the next few months. Loss of weight, sleep, self-confidence or inner purpose may afflict you now. You tend to lie back and let life roll past or over you. Sort out priorities and seek only major goals.

With Sun: Egotism, touchy sensitivity, dictatorial attitudes and self—centered behavior can be sources of loss. You feel helpless and lacking in self-confidence, as you are limited in opportunities for self-expression and inner development. Strive to maintain control and build up your health.

With Moon: Moodiness, changeability, slavish adherence to fads or popular beliefs can be sources of loss. You sleep lightly and have vivid dreams that seem more real than life itself. You feel the loss of contacts with the public, due to lack of energy, time or opportunity.

With Mercury: Indecision, saying anything to please another, and carelessness with facts can be sources of loss. You are self-absorbed and hearing and seeing things only through the framework of your own inner needs and biases. Be especially discreet about any secrets or private projects in your life.

With Venus: Fickleness, self-indulgence, neglect of duties in pursuit of pleasure, can be sources of loss. Love of good food puts you in need of a diet, while a secret romance creates more problems than your affection can surmount. Do not worry so much about your external appearance, but build up inner qualities of attractiveness.

With Mars: Excessive drains on your energy may cause tiredness or weight loss in coming months. You may suffer from inner frustration, but practice a course of masterly inactivity to improve your health.

Check out eyes, kidneys, and allergies if you have headaches.

With Jupiter: Extravagance, carelessness and self-indulgence are the problems to watch for in the near future. Pure laziness is due to absorption in the conception of new ideas and goals; do not explain to critics, who waste your time, but do organize your projects for an ultimate push to success. Excess weight is a problem now.

With Saturn: Whatever is lost now will be permanently lost—a good time to break old habits. A good time to diet, as long as you maintain your protein, vitamin and mineral intakes, and exercise *mildly* to keep body contours correct. Avoid depressants such as alcohol and drugs.

With Uranus: Disturbing and disruptive changes occur during the next few months. Insomnia and nervous tension may result from keeping problems bottled up. Unload on a friend or professional, and avoid stimulants such as caffeine. Put an unpleasant psychic vision out of your mind.

With Neptune: Mysterious losses, some minor, some more significant, afflict you the next few months. Your psychic sensitivity responds to negative events going on around you. Music and other relaxing components of environment can help dispel this cloud.

With Pluto: You are suffering from a drain of spirituual energies which is difficult to pin down in the near future. Watch for an apparently minor infectious ailment that could create problems if not attended to promptly. Do not become the confidant of people with problems now—tell them to consult professionals.

PUER

This favorable symbol is supported by Sun, Venus, Jupiter, Mars and Mercury; weakened or dispersed by Moon, Neptune, and Pluto; emphasized by Uranus; and controlled by Saturn.

Puer (Male) is ruled by Mars and is associated with Aries, also ruled by Mars, and symbolizes the pioneering spirit, with courage, daring, intellectual sharpness, initiative and physical energy. Aries is the sign of new beginnings, and Puer represents the spirit that ever strives after new experiences.

Puer in a chart always indicates a point in life where initiative, daring, courage and energy can win the desired goal. Puer also recommends physical exercise and healthy competition, as in sports. Puer may also represent a young man who can be helpful, or in a woman's chart, an important man in a personal relationship, who dominates the area of life indicated by the house Puer is in. In a man's chart, Puer may indicate a competitor who helps the querent by compelling him to exert himself; or is a comrade in an arduous task.

Puer
In the 1st House
Alone, no planets: This is a favorable influence that remains in effect for the next few months. You take the initiative in personal affairs. You make new beginnings, and start new projects with ambition.

With Sun: You feel a surge of energy, decisiveness and competitiveness in coming months. You have a high level of energy, and strike out in new directions with confidence. Favorable for projects of long term interest, and for dealing with authorities and leaders.

With Moon: You take an active lead in public affairs and in dealings with the public. Favorable for presenting your ideas to the public. You bring emotional and psychic energy to bear on personal interests.

With Mercury: Exploration, travel and information-seeking absorb you in coming months. Thinking, communications and travel are swifter. You respond quickly to new ideas, and are successful in debate.

With Venus: A powerful romantic urge comes over you—it may be love in the near future. A dynamic or daring person may enter your life. Favorable for expressing emotions and sensuality. You are popular, making this an excellent time to meet others and date.

With Mars: A competitive spirit and daring initiatives achieve all your objectives. You can start an exercise program, or projects that require great physical effort.

With Jupiter: You have an abundance of energy and enthusiasm to succeed beyond all expectations in coming months. You will have enthusiasm and physical energy for large projects and initiatives. A good time to begin expansion projects for personal goals.

With Saturn: Your efficiency and productivity are at a peak in coming months. You are resolute, and have indomitable will power. You are constructive and industrious in regards to self, and personal concerns.

With Uranus: Many beneficial changes are going on in your life in the next few months. You undertake revolutionary and inventive changes in your personal appearance, presentation and actions.

With Neptune: You strive with zeal and enthusiasm to achieve a lofty goal the next few months. You will begin a crusade in a matter you feel deeply about. You can be heroic in your actions.

With Pluto: Positive spiritual forces are impelling you into a rewarding new situation in coming months. You are driven to actions that will affect the masses.

Puer
In the 2nd House
Alone, no planets: This is a favorable influence that remains in effect for the next few months. You take action in regards to personal property, personal possessions, investments and income.

With Sun: You feel a surge of energy, decisiveness and competitiveness in coming months. Fortunate for investments in gold and diamonds. You win the gold in a contest or gamble.

With Moon: You take an active lead in public affairs and in dealings with the public. You will find ways to make money from activities you perform in your home. These appeal to public tastes, or have broad public interest.

With Mercury: Exploration, travel and information-seeking absorb you in coming months. Daring actions in commerce, trade or exchange are favored now.

With Venus: A powerful romantic urge comes over you—it may be love in the near future. The manufacture of jewelry is profitable. Architectural and decorative projects begun now will increase the value of your property.

With Mars: A competitive spirit and daring initiatives achieve all your objectives. Manufacturing with metals, working with metal tools and engineering projects increase your income, or the value of your property.

With Jupiter: You have an abundance of energy and enthusiasm to succeed beyond all expectations in coming months. An excellent time to launch a promotion and sales campaign. Bold investment in a large undertaking, or expansion project lead to large returns.

With Saturn: Your efficiency and productivity are at a peak in coming months. Real estate construction, the mining or refining of precious metals and gemstones, and persistent energy applied to real property are favored now.

With Uranus: Many beneficial changes are going on in your life in the next few months. Advanced technologies, scientific breakthroughs and pioneering efforts lead to financial gain.

With Neptune: You strive with zeal and enthusiasm to achieve a lofty goal the next few months. The performing arts, especially dance or theatre, can increase income. Efforts spent at alluring and attracting others increase the value of your possessions, or your income.

With Pluto: Positive spiritual forces are impelling you into a reward-ing new situation in coming months. A matter of inheritance, insurance, credit or taxes is favorably aspected for your direct action.

Puer
In the 3rd House
Alone, no planets: This is a favorable influence that remains in effect for the next few months. Your ambitions turn towards studies, or local affairs in regard to relatives, neighbors, short trips and communi-cations.

With Sun: You feel a surge of energy, decisiveness and competitive-ness in coming months. You assume a leadership role in communicat-ing. Pursuit of your ideas leads to positive results.

With Moon: You take an active lead in public affairs and in dealings with the puublic. You take the initiative in contacting people from your past, or you return to familiar places in your locale.

With Mercury: Exploration, travel and information-seeking absorb you in coming months. Your mind is quick, and your actions swift, as you implement your ideas.

With Venus: A powerful romantic urge comes over you—it may be love in the near future. Favorable for initiating friendly contact—send a gift, card or flowers.

With Mars: A competitive spirit and daring initiatives achieve all your objectives. Firm words and decisive action in your immediate locale lead to favorable results.

With Jupiter: You have an abundance of energy and enthusiasm to succeed beyond all expectations in coming months. You speak with confidence, and those near to you are won over by your optimistic ideas for the future.

With Saturn: Your efficiency and productivity are at a peak in coming months. You take authority in beginning local projects of a utilitarian nature. Your ideas are well thought out, and you obtain practical results.

With Uranus: Many beneficial changes are going on in your life in the next few months. You obtain sudden and surprising good fortune on a short trip, or from making contact with a relative or neighbor.

With Neptune: You strive with zeal and enthusiasm to achieve a lofty goal the next few months. You study inspirational subjects with enthusiasm. Favorable for visiting beautiful places in your immediate locality.

With Pluto: Positive spiritual forces are impelling you into a rewarding new situation in coming months. You initiate contact with a religious or spiritual guide nearby. You learn quickly and will have a positive spiritual awakening.

Puer
In the 4th House
Alone, no planets: This is a favorable influence that remains in effect for the next few months. Your energies are directed towards affairs of the home, family or people and events from the past.

With Sun: You feel a surge of energy, decisiveness and competitiveness in coming months. You take command of your children, or those that are dependent on you. Favorable for a party in your home.

With Moon: You take an active lead in public affairs and in dealings with the public. You undertake changes that affect your family, or the larger public, in regards to basic security.

With Mercury: Exploration, travel and information-seeking absorb you in coming months. Send a message, or take a trip, and make contact with someone from your past; perhaps a parent. Applying what you learn brings many changes.

With Venus: A powerful romantic urge comes over you—it may be love in the near future. A romance is in your neighborhood, or with a person from your past.

With Mars: A competitive spirit and daring initiatives achieve all your objectives. You will undertake tough or physically taxing jobs in your home or neighborhood. You could be moving from your home.

With Jupiter: You have an abundance of energy and enthusiasm to succeed beyond all expectations in coming months. Pioneering a large undertaking brings you benefits from your community, family or parents.

With Saturn: Your efficiency and productivity are at a peak in coming months. Practical and patient application of your energies helps you establish your roots, and secure your future for home and family.

With Uranus: Many beneficial changes are going on in your life in the next few months. A surprise visit from someone in your past, or the return of a long forgotten matter, stirs you to initiate new projects.

With Neptune: You strive with zeal and enthusiasm to achieve a lofty goal the next few months. You begin a project to beautify your home, neighborhood or community. Initiate activities with grandparents.

With Pluto: Positive spiritual forces are impelling you into a rewarding new situation in coming months. You initiate personal renewal and regeneration in regards to a matter from the past, or a situation close to home.

Puer
In the 5th House
Alone, no planets: This is a favorable influence that remains in effect for the next few months. You take action or risk in regard to romance, children, creative expression or pleasurable pursuits.

With Sun: You feel a surge of energy, decisiveness and competitiveness in coming months. You pursue who or what you love with ardent passion.

With Moon: You take an active lead in public affairs and in dealings with the public. Gamble on sports events or supermarket sweep-stakes.

With Mercury: Exploration, travel and information-seeking absorb you in coming months. Contact the one you love, and take a trip for pleasure and entertainment.

With Venus: A powerful romantic urge comes over you—it may be love in the near future. You pursue a person of refinement and nobility. If pregnant, the baby will be a girl.

With Mars: A competitive spirit and daring initiatives achieve all your objectives. Your boldness and courage win over in a creative or romantic competition. If pregnant, the baby will be a boy.

With Jupiter: You have an abundance of energy and enthusiasm to succeed beyond all expectations in coming months. Your heartfelt love expands, and you pursue your love to your great benefit.

With Saturn: Your efficiency and productivity are at a peak in coming months. Your efforts bring concrete results in a gamble, or creative pursuit.

With Uranus: Many beneficial changes are going on in your life in the next few months. Creative inventiveness brings surprising results. Gamble on a lottery.

With Neptune: You strive with zeal and enthusiasm to achieve a lofty goal the next few months. You take charge of creative or romantic energies, and are willing to sacrifice to obtain the object of your affection.

With Pluto: Positive spiritual forces are impelling you into a rewarding new situation in coming months. You have a sudden sexual attraction towards another.

Puer
In the 6th House
Alone, no planets: This is a favorable influence that remains in effect for the next few months. You are stronger, and bring great energy to bear on matters of work and health.

With Sun: You feel a surge of energy, decisiveness and competitiveness in coming months. You can apply great energy to a tough chore with immense success.

With Moon: You take an active lead in public affairs and in dealings with the public. A service you perform in public, or for the public, brings useful results.

With Mercury: Exploration, travel and information-seeking absorb you in coming months. You are precise and exacting as you analyze and take action in a matter of work or health.

With Venus: Exploration, travel and information-seeking absorb you in coming months. Make the first approach toward a romantic interest in your workplace—you benefit.

With Mars: A competitive spirit and daring initiatives achieve all your objectives. Compete with coworkers, or in the open market, for a better job.

With Jupiter: You have an abundance of energy and enthusiasm to succeed beyond all expectations in coming months. Your health improves, your energy increases, and you are able to do more work.

With Saturn: Your efficiency and productivity are at a peak in coming months. You apply the hammer to the anvil, and achieve lasting results from your work.

With Uranus: Many beneficial changes are going on in your life in the next few months. You take the initiative, and make inventive changes in your work, or your health habits.

With Neptune: You strive with zeal and enthusiasm to achieve a lofty goal the next few months. You can sacrifice your energy in the service of another, benefiting all concerned.

With Pluto: Positive spiritual forces are impelling you into a rewarding new situation in coming months. Organize or be active in your union. Good for physical rejuvenation through exercise and health foods.

Puer
In the 7th House
Alone, no planets: This is a favorable influence that remains in effect for the next few months. You take the initiative, and are ambitious in matters of marriage, partnerships and contracts.

With Sun: You feel a surge of energy, decisiveness and competitiveness in coming months. You successfully pursue social activities, a partnership, or marriage.

With Moon: You take an active lead in public affairs and in dealings with the public. You can be attracted to someone younger, or someone in public life. You express your feelings to your partner with vigor.

With Mercury: Exploration, travel and information-seeking absorb you in coming months. You communicate and travel to secure commitment from another.

With Venus: A powerful romantic urge comes over you—it may be love in the near future. You obtain the contract or commitment you have fought for. A marriage or partnership is active and harmonious.

With Mars: A competitive spirit and daring initiatives achieve all your objectives. You compete for the commitment of another, and win. You overcome in combat and competition.

With Jupiter: You have an abundance of energy and enthusiasm to succeed beyond all expectations in coming months. Pursue a partnership or contract that has the promise of large benefits, or is undertaken in regard to a large and expansive project.

With Saturn: Your efficiency and productivity are at a peak in coming months. An older individual, or one from your past, will become a stable and dependable partner.

With Uranus: Many beneficial changes are going on in your life in the next few months. You are attracted to someone unique, unusual or highly creative.

With Neptune: You strive with zeal and enthusiasm to achieve a lofty goal the next few months. You are attracted to and pursue someone mysterious or strange. They may be psychic or artistic.

With Pluto: Positive spiritual forces are impelling you into a rewarding new situation in coming months. You can team up with a large organization, or the masses. You are victorious in competitive team undertakings.

Puer
In the 8th House
Alone, no planets: This is a favorable influence that remains in effect for the next few months. Your procreative powers are stirred and strengthened. Your activities are directed toward finances, sex and occult mysteries.

With Sun: You feel a surge of energy, decisiveness and competitiveness in coming months. Your desire to procreate is intense. You pursue your deepest and most secret desires.

With Moon: You take an active lead in public affairs and in dealings with the public. Your psychic and occult powers are strong. You direct them with intensity, authority and effectiveness.

With Mercury: Exploration, travel and information-seeking absorb you in coming months. Occult studies or collaborative efforts will bring renewal of your resources.

With Venus: A powerful romantic urge comes over you—it may be love in the near future. You initiate union with another, and produce offspring.

With Mars: A competitive spirit and daring initiatives achieve all your objectives. You are intense and unconquerable in every desire you pursue. You are victorious in a lawsuit.

With Jupiter: You have an abundance of energy and enthusiasm to succeed beyond all expectations in coming months. Your courage and daring will bring large benefits. You make large financial gains from associations or marriage.

With Saturn: Your efficiency and productivity are at a peak in coming months. Your staying power is tremendous. You will retain whatever you achieve or acquire.

With Uranus: Many beneficial changes are going on in your life in the next few months. You pioneer and explore into other planes of existence. An unexpected inheritance comes to you.

With Neptune: You strive with zeal and enthusiasm to achieve a lofty goal the next few months. Your unconscious powers are great. Exploring the psychic mysteries leads to renewal and regeneration of libidinal energies.

With Pluto: Positive spiritual forces are impelling you into a rewarding new situation in coming months. Your actions lead to renewal of your health or resources. You seek a new mode of life.

Puer
In the 9th House
Alone, no planets: This is a favorable influence that remains in effect for the next few months. You explore and expand in the larger world around you, by travel or by exploratory studies.

With Sun: You feel a surge of energy, decisiveness and competitiveness in coming months. You explore and expand into foreign lands, or into foreign fields of self expression.

With Moon: You take an active lead in public affairs and in dealings with the public. Publish popular works that appeal to current fads and tastes. You may move far from present location.

With Mercury: Exploration, travel and information-seeking absorb you in coming months. Study textbooks to learn more details about subjects of interest. Your thoughts are fast and deep.

With Venus: A powerful romantic urge comes over you—it may be love in the near future. Favorable relationships in foreign lands, or with foreigners in regard to love or finances.

With Mars: A competitive spirit and daring initiatives achieve all your objectives. You compete with foreigners and overcome those at a distance by your strength and courage.

With Jupiter: You have an abundance of energy and enthusiasm to succeed beyond all expectations in coming months. Learn law, religion or philosophy. Publish textbooks on subjects ruled by Mars: manufacturing, competition, war, law enforcement.

With Saturn: Your efficiency and productivity are at a peak in coming months. Study serious or conservative subjects such as history, agriculture, economics.

With Uranus: Many beneficial changes are going on in your life in the next few months. You may take a trip by plane. Sudden surprises from unusual people from foreign lands.

With Neptune: You strive with zeal and enthusiasm to achieve a lofty goal the next few months. Contact with foreigners of a mysterious, psychic or spiritual nature.

With Pluto: Positive spiritual forces are impelling you into a rewarding new situation in coming months. You may move to a foreign land, or far from home. You pursue great changes in your education or philosophical outlook.

Puer
In the 10th House
Alone, no planets: This is a favorable influence that remains in effect for the next few months. You apply great physical strength and stamina to achieving solid results in business and career.

With Sun: You feel a surge of energy, decisiveness and competitiveness in coming months. Entertainment and speculation surround business affairs. You become a leader in your field—with honors.

With Moon: You take an active lead in public affairs and in dealings with the public. You are popular with the public, especially women.

With Mercury: Exploration, travel and information-seeking absorb you in coming months. Commercial trade and exchange are favored for action. Scientific and literary business is successful.

With Venus: A powerful romantic urge comes over you—it may be love in the near future. The arts, clothing, decorations, pleasures and romance are areas in which business success is signified—the beautiful.

With Mars: A competitive spirit and daring initiatives achieve all your objectives. Take daring and dangerous actions for career success. Physical work, work with metals, and work in dangerous environments favored.

With Jupiter: You have an abundance of energy and enthusiasm to succeed beyond all expectations in coming months. Favors attorneys, professors, the higher professions, and business that deals with these.

With Saturn: Your efficiency and productivity are at a peak in coming months. Your authority in business is unassailable, and you can overcome competitors, or those that oppose you.

With Uranus: Many beneficial changes are going on in your life in the next few months. You initiate creative business changes, and introduce new technologies—mechanical and electrical.

With Neptune: You strive with zeal and enthusiasm to achieve a lofty goal the next few months. Favors business actions in the arts, cinema and theater. Also favorable for dealings in liquids and oils.

With Pluto: Positive spiritual forces are impelling you into a rewarding new situation in coming months. Excellent for profit in all undertakings involving large numbers of people. Insurance or finance businesses are activated.

Puer
In the 11th House

Alone, no planets: This is a favorable influence that remains in effect for the next few months. You take the initiative, and have sudden and fortunate encounters with friends, social groups and informal cliques.

With Sun: You feel a surge of energy, decisiveness and competitiveness in coming months. You meet influential people, and associate with leaders and the famous.

With Moon: You take an active lead in public affairs and in dealings with the public. Women's groups and clubs will bring many exciting events. If a man, you win the support of women.

With Mercury: Exploration, travel and information-seeking absorb you in coming months. Excellent for association with intellectual and literary groups.

With Venus: A powerful romantic urge comes over you—it may be love in the near future. Refined and harmonious friendships and associations are favored. Excellent for meeting the opposite sex.

With Mars: A competitive spirit and daring initiatives achieve all your objectives. Association with sports and athletic groups brings favorable results.

With Jupiter: You have an abundance of energy and enthusiasm to succeed beyond all expectations in coming months. An influential friend may become a patron. Favors association with professionals.

With Saturn: Your efficiency and productivity are at a peak in coming months. Stable and dependable friends help you direct your energy and ambition in constructive ways. Meet with authorities, and the influential.

With Uranus: Many beneficial changes are going on in your life in the next few months. Scientists, intellectuals, inventors and the creative are the types that bring changes into your life now.

With Neptune: You strive with zeal and enthusiasm to achieve a lofty goal the next few months. Artists, actors, dancers, or those with refined tastes are favored friends now.

With Pluto: Positive spiritual forces are impelling you into a rewarding new situation in coming months. You eliminate dying friendships, while renewing old friendships that show promise for the future.

Puer
In the 12th House
Alone, no planets: This is a favorite influence that remains relatively unchanged in the next few months. You are stimulated to take action in the psychic realms, and to explore your unconcious mind and dreams.

With Sun: You feel a surge of energy, decisiveness and competitiveness in coming months. You feel more certain of your inner strength, and are intuitive in creative, romantic and speculative affairs.

With Moon: You take an active lead in public affairs and in dealings with the public. Your behind-the-scenes activities will lead to public recognition.

With Mercury: Exploration, travel and information-seeking absorb you in coming months. You investigate and analyze the secrets behind things, both in yourself, and in the outer realms of psychic activity.

With Venus: A powerful romantic urge comes over you—it may be love in the near future. Favorable for meditation and psychic balance, as you take steps to achieve inner peace.

With Mars: A competitive spirit and daring initiatives achieve all your objectives. You take action against psychic enemies, unconscious phobias, and overcome them.

With Jupiter: You have an abundance of energy and enthusiasm to succeed beyond all expectations in coming months. Prophetic dreams and messages stir you to action.

With Saturn: Your efficiency and productivity are at a peak in coming months. Solitary meditation, and digging into the past brings greater psychic stability.

With Uranus: Many beneficial changes are going on in your life in the next few months. The occult sciences provide the stimulus to creatively alter your unconcious and psychic mind.

With Neptune: You strive with zeal and enthusiasm to achieve a lofty goal the next few months. You obtain psychic or clairvoyant messages, and your powers of visualization help you achieve your ends.

With Pluto: Positive spiritual forces are impelling you into a rewarding new situation in coming months. Your higher guide will lead you to renew your psychic energies, and achieve greater power.

RUBEUS

This adverse symbol is intensified by Saturn, Uranus, Neptune, Pluto and Mars; mitigated by Sun, Venus and Jupiter; and simply emphasized by the Moon and Mercury, which are neutral planets.

Rubeus (Anger) is ruled by Mars, but is related to the sign Gemini, the Twins. The assignment is based on the Roman twins, Castor and Pollux, who appeared in battle with the Romans as divine helpers, riding great white horses. Castor and Pollux were honored as gods of battle in ancient Rome; herein lies the association with Rubeus, representing the anger and destruction of war; and lesser expressions of violence, passion, and anger.

Rubeus in a chart always denotes a point of *danger*, either from the querent's own acts, through his or her associates, enemies, or adverse circumstances, such as war, riots, volcanoes, fires. Whether it is the anger of nature, as in dangerous animals or upheavals of the earth, or of other people, this anger can be life-threatening. A personal example is high blood pressure or dangerous cuts and wounds, as Mars rules the blood. The best antidote for Rubeus is calm consideration and consultation with experts on either physical or emotional problems. Stimulants should be avoided as should stressful situations on the job or in personal relationships.

Rubeus
In the 1st House
Alone, no planets: This is an adverse influence that remains relatively unchanged in the next few months. Angry emotions lead to rash and impetuous actions.

With Sun: You are challenged by frustrating obstacles, your efforts are not always successful. Conflicts and struggles will arise if you charge ahead in a stubborn manner.

With Moon: You respond emotionally to frustrations and may waste energy in fruitless protests. Mental and emotional irritation can lead to disputes, especially with women or children.

With Mercury: You respond loudly and vocally to frustrations when careful thought is more productive of results. You may say things you later regret. Your words can arouse anger in others.

With Venus: Be wary of feelings of jealousy or envy, when seeking your own rewards is the more positive course of action. You can create a scandal if your actions are motivated by ignoble self-interest. Cautions against a split with a partner.

With Mars: Try to avoid being rushed into hasty or careless action, however strong the provocation. You are in no mood to compromise, and your fiery emotions can cause you to break with another.

With Jupiter: Overconfidence can lead to rash, impulsive and costly action in coming months. Extravagant and extremist behavior must be guarded against now.

With Saturn: Frequent delays and disappointments leave you frustrated in coming months. Restrictions and disciplines imposed on you can lead to simmering anger, and self-destructive actions.

With Uranus: Disturbing and disruptive changes occur during the next few months. Your emotions can lead to sudden and destructive actions that are out of character.

With Neptune: The source of your irritability is difficult to pin down in coming months. Delusions of grandeur, or illusions of persecution can be the hidden cause behind your passionate actions.

With Pluto: Fate seems to delight in frustrating you in strange ways in coming months. Your intense and extreme reaction to events or to others lies behind your present frustrations.

Rubeus
In the 2nd House
Alone, no planets: This is an adverse influence that remains relatively unchanged in the next few months. Possessions and finances are afflicted by accidents, rash actions or conflict.

With Sun: You are challenged by frustrating obstacles, and your efforts are not always successful. An urge to gamble your way out of financial strains can bring financial ruin.

With Moon: You respond emotionally to frustrations and may waste energy in fruitless protests. Waste or extravagance in spending on home and family can bring conflicts.

With Mercury: You respond loudly and vocally to frustrations when careful thought is more productive of results. Fault-finding and criticism in regard to finances leads to explosive verbal wars.

With Venus: Be wary of feelings of jealousy or envy, when seeking your own rewards is the more positive course of action. An intense desire for material gain can lead to conflicts with partners.

With Mars: Try to avoid being rushed into hasty or careless action, however strong the provocation. Protect your possessions from theft. Restrain the impulse to spend.

With Jupiter: Overconfidence can lead to rash, impulsive and costly action in coming months. The tendency is to overspending and extravagance. Wait on any big investments now.

With Saturn: Frequent delays and disappointments leave you frustrated in coming months. Do not let frustration cause you to suddenly change directions in regard to long-term security interests.

With Uranus: Disturbing and disruptive changes occur during the next few months. Protect your property and finances from sudden and unexpected damage.

With Neptune: The source of your irritable moods is difficult to pin down in coming months. Do not make rash moves in finances—you could be deceived.

With Pluto: Fate seems to delight in frustrating you in strange ways in coming months. Protect property and possessions from destruction by acts of nature, or from theft by criminal and underworld elements.

Rubeus
In the 3rd House
Alone, no planets: This is an adverse influence that remains relatively unchanged in the next few months. Aggravating communications with relatives or neighbors, and the potential for accidents or breakdowns in travel are prevalent.

With Sun: You are challenged by frustrating obstacles, and your efforts are not always successful. Communication with children and romantic partners is frustrating.

With Moon: You respond emotionally to frustrations and may waste energy in fruitless protests. Disputes with family members in the home can lead to deep psychic wounds.

With Mercury: You respond loudly and vocally to frustrations when careful thought is more productive of results. Extreme mental irritability. Watch for accidents to hands and arms.

With Venus: Be wary of feelings of jealousy or envy, when seeking your own rewards is the more positive course of action. You could stick your foot in your mouth when communicating with loved ones or partners. Avoid verbal conflicts, if at all possible.

With Mars: Try to avoid being rushed into hasty or careless action, however strong the provocation. Do not speed when traveling. Bite your tongue and hold back angry words.

With Jupiter: Overconfidence can lead to rash, impulsive and costly action in coming months. Pride comes before a fall, and egotistical boasting can cause you to take one.

With Saturn: Frequent delays and disappointments leave you frustrated in coming months. Watch your words with authorities, the police and your elders. You could damage your own long term interests.

With Uranus: Disturbing and disruptive changes occur during the next few months. Sudden events can throw your mental balance off. Caution in air travel, and with electrical appliances.

With Neptune: The source of your irritability is difficult to pin down in coming months. Caution with depressant drugs. You could over use. Avoid arguments with those under the influence.

With Pluto: Fate seems to delight in frustrating you in strange ways in coming months. Danger of explosion during travel. Communications with unsavory types can be dangerous.

Rubeus
In the 4th House
Alone, no planets: This is an adverse influence that remains relatively unchanged in the next few months. Tension surrounds you in the affairs of family and home, and can lead to an accident or arguments.

With Sun: You are challenged by frustrating obstacles, and your efforts are not always successful. A domineering or bossy approach with family members will lead to their resisting and frustrating your plans.

With Moon: You respond emotionally to frustrations and may waste energy in fruitless protests. Your emotions boil in regards to family matters. Try to stabilize your feelings.

With Mercury: You respond loudly and vocally to frustrations when careful thought is more productive of results. Rushing and hurrying can bring mental distractions, and lead to physical injury around the home.

With Venus: Be wary of feelings of jealousy or envy, when seeking your own rewards is the more positive course of action. Domestic disputes over finances or personal property can heat up. Be diplomatic.

With Mars: Try to avoid being rushed into hasty or careless action, however strong the provocation. Use care with sharp tools and fire around the home. Guard against theft and burglary.

With Jupiter: Overconfidence can lead to rash, impulsive and costly action in coming months. Be on guard against accidents to your parents in the home. Restrain your impulsiveness.

With Saturn: Frequent delays and disappointments leave you frustrated in coming months. Cautions to guard against a possible fire in the home.

With Uranus: Disturbing and disruptive changes occur during the next few months. Caution with electrical appliances, and explosion potential in the home.

With Neptune: The source of your irritability is difficult to pin down in coming months. Caution with gas or drugs in the home. A danger of explosion, asphyxiation or poisoning.

With Pluto: Fate seems to delight in frustrating you in strange ways in coming months. Guard against explosion or eruption of subterranean or hidden structures in your home—wells, water, gas and sewage pipes, foundations.

Rubeus
In the 5th House
Alone, no planets: This is an adverse influence that remains relatively unchanged in the next few months. Affairs of children, romantic partners or pleasurable pursuits can bring anger or aggravation.

With Sun: You are challenged by frustrating obstacles, and your efforts are not always successful. Gambling sports and competition can lead to loss or accident.

With Moon: You respond emotionally to frustrations and may waste energy in fruitless protests. Troubles and difficulties with children or women.

With Mercury: You respond loudly and vocally to frustrations when careful thought is more productive of results. Unlucky for gambling. Brings inconsistency in love.

With Venus: Be wary of feelings of jealousy or envy, when seeking your own rewards is the more positive course of action. Your passions can lead to dangerous or violent liaisons.

With Mars: Try to avoid being rushed into hasty or careless action, however strong the provocation. Jealous anger can lead to quarrels. Caution in the affairs of children.

With Jupiter: Overconfidence can lead to rash, impulsive and costly action in coming months. Excess and carelessness can lead to losses in love or speculation.

With Saturn: Frequent delays and disappointments leave you frustrated in coming months. Tension surrounds your love life, and pleasurable pursuits bring upsets and losses.

With Uranus: Disturbing and disruptive changes occur during the next few months. Chances and risks taken now will lead to sudden and upsetting losses.

With Neptune: The source of your irritable moods is difficult to pin down in coming months. Your passions can lead you to seduce the wrong person—scandal can result.

With Pluto: Fate seems to delight in frustrating you in strange ways in coming months. Intense desire can backfire, and lead to conflicts in love or speculative affairs.

Rubeus
In the 6th House
Alone, no planets: This is an adverse influence that remains relatively unchanged in the next few months. Work and health produce tension, stress and potential for extremes, arguments and accidents.

With Sun: You are challenged by frustrating obstacles, and your efforts are not always successful. Tough jobs and overwork can lead to conflict with others, and dangers to your health.

With Moon: You respond emotionally to frustrations and may waste energy in fruitless protests. Emotional over-reaction is due to extremes in health and work habits.

With Mercury: You respond loudly and vocally to frustrations when careful thought is more productive of results. Cautions against arguments with coworkers.

With Venus: Be wary of feelings of jealousy or envy, when seeking your own rewards is the more positive course of action. Conflicts with coworkers or partners in the workplace can produce fiery and emotional splits.

With Mars: Try to avoid being rushed into hasty or careless action, however strong the provocation. Overwork dissipates your energy, and creates accident potential in the workplace.

With Jupiter: Overconfidence can lead to rash, impulsive and costly action in coming months. Weight and blood pressure can cause illness if you let extremism carry you away.

With Saturn: Frequent delays and disappointments leave you frustrated in coming months. You put too much stress on yourself. Relax, before a health affliction forces you to.

With Uranus: Disturbing and disruptive changes occur during the next few months. Accidents and hazards surround electrical and explosive items in the workplace.

With Neptune: The source of your irritable moods is difficult to pin down in coming months. Do not sacrifice your health to your work. Danger from gases and chemicals in the workplace.

With Pluto: Fate seems to delight in frustrating you in strange ways in coming months. Unions in the workplace can cause conflict. Guard against explosions or eruptions in the workplace.

Rubeus
In the 7th House
Alone, no planets: This is an adverse influence that remains relatively unchanged in the next few months. Angry arguments with partners

can lead to break-ups.

With Sun: You are challenged by frustrating obstacles, but your efforts are not always successful. Control your anger, or you could clash with those that have great power and authority.

With Moon: You respond emotionally to frustrations and may waste energy in fruitless protests. Difficulties and changes bring aggravation in mutual affairs.

With Mercury: You respond loudly and vocally to frustrations when careful thought is more productive of results. Quarrels and arguments can lead to breaking important partnerships.

With Venus: Be wary of feelings of jealousy or envy, when seeing your own rewards is the more positive course of action. You may feel as though you are competing with your partners.

Mars: Try to avoid being rushed into hasty or careless action, however strong the provocation. Passion and extremism can cause open conflict with partners, and bring accidents and hazards in competition.

With Jupiter: Overconfidence can lead to rash, impulsive and costly action in coming months. Enlarging your aggressive behavior with partners can be your self-undoing now.

With Saturn: Frequent delays and disappointments leave you frustrated in coming months. Restrictions others place on you could cause you to overreact with anger. Control your temper.

With Uranus: Disturbing and disruptive changes occur during the next few months. Stress and anger surround your partnerships, due to sudden or erratic changes.

With Neptune: The source of your irritable moods is difficult to pin down in coming months. Control your anger if you discover fraud, debt or theft among your partners. They could turn and attack you.

With Pluto: Fate seems to delight in frustrating you in strange ways in coming months. Buried anger can erupt and cause the end of relationships.

Rubeus
In the 8th House

Alone, no planets: This is an adverse influence that remains relatively unchanged in the next few months. Aggravation and impulsive reactions bring difficulties in sex or joint financial affairs. Protect yourself against crime.

With Sun: You are challenged by frustrating obstacles but your efforts are not always successful. You can burn up your resources in pursuit of what you want—remain conservative.

With Moon: You respond emotionally to frustrations and may waste energy in fruitless protests. Emotions in regards to your sex partner can be angry, changeable and dangerous.

With Mercury: You respond loudly and vocally to frustrations when careful thought is more productive of results. Watch your words, or you could be sued for slander.

With Venus: Be wary of feelings of jealousy or envy, when seeking your own rewards is the more positive course of action. Materialistic passions can cause you to take imprudent actions.

With Mars: Try to avoid being rushed into hasty or careless action, however strong the provocation. Danger from criminals and assault. Cautions against intense and passionate anger.

With Jupiter: Overconfidence can lead to rash, impulsive and costly action in coming months. Over-expansion of your borrowing can be careless at this time.

With Saturn: Frequent delays and disappointments leave you frustrated in coming months. Your attempts to borrow money can meet with frustrations due to others resistance.

With Uranus: Disturbing and disruptive changes occur during the next few months. Erratic and impatient actions will frustrate your attempts to bring about change in your sex life or financial affairs.

With Neptune: The source of your irritable moods is difficult to pin down in coming months. Sex or passion can be alluring, but dangerous. Do not rush in where angels fear to tread.

With Pluto: Fate seems to delight in frustrating you in strange ways in coming months. Sexual passions can be intense, and cause you scandal or disease. Have no dealings with criminal types.

Rubeus
In the 9th House
Alone, no planets: This is an adverse influence that remains relatively unchanged in the next few months. Higher education, distant travel or affairs to do with foreigners can lead to conflict or accident.

With Sun: You are challenged by fruustrating obstacles, but your efforts are not always successful. You can burn up energy pursuing your aspirations, with little to show for it in the end. Take things slower.

With Moon: You respond emotionally to frustrations and may waste energy in fruitless protests. Changes in plans and changes in opinions surround this influence. Keep frustrations from boiling over into anger.

With Mercury: You respond loudly and vocally to frustrations when careful thought is more productive of results. A rushed or careless attitude can lead to collisions in communications or travel.

With Venus: Be wary of feelings of jealousy or envy, when seeking your own rewards is the more positive course of action. Investments or relationships at a distance can leave you frazzled and frustrated. Maintain your balance.

With Mars: Try to avoid being rushed into hasty or careless action, however strong the provocation. Intolerance and conflict surround affairs at a distance. Cautions against theft while you travel.

With Jupiter: Overconfidence can lead to rash, impulsive and costly action in coming months. Teachers and benefactors will frustrate your desires if you act childish.

With Saturn: Frequent delays and disappointments leave you frustrated in coming months. Authorities can place you under restriction if you do not control impulsive or aggressive behavior.

With Uranus: Disturbing and disruptive changes occur during the next few months. Fanaticism can take hold of you. Caution if traveling by plane.

With Neptune: The source of your irritable moods is difficult to pin down in coming months. Be cautious of strangers if traveling abroad, and of strange offers made by people at a distance.

With Pluto: Fate seems to delight in frustrating you in strange ways in coming months. Big changes considered now may have destructive results. Grand promises can tempt you, and lead to terrible consequences.

Rubeus
In the 10th House
Alone, no planets: This is an adverse influence that remains relatively unchanged in the next few months. Watch for conflicts with supervisors on the job and government officials. Danger of accidents and conflicts in career and profession.

With Sun: You are challenged by frustrating obstacles and your efforts are not always successful. Your rush for success can lead to errors, accidents or physical exhaustion.

With Moon: You respond emotionally to frustrations and may waste energy in fruitless protests. Conflict and controversy surround your public relations and business. Do not push others now.

With Mercury: You respond loudly and vocally to frustrations when careful thought is more productive of results. Misunderstandings and missed messages can lead to costly errors in business and career.

With Venus: Be wary of feelings of jealousy or envy, when seeking your own rewards is the more positive course of action. Rushing on contracts and partnership affairs can lead to conflict. Others may question your motives.

With Mars: Try to avoid being rushed into hasty or careless action, however strong the provocation. Threatens the physical breakdown of machinery, or your body, if you push too hard in business.

With Jupiter: Overconfidence can lead to rash, impulsive and costly action in coming months. You may feel you cannot lose in a big business deal. Think twice, before taking chances.

With Saturn: Frequent delays and disappointments leave you frustrated in coming months. Pushing your weight around in career or business can bring delays, frustration and loss. Soften your approach.

With Uranus: Disturbing and disruptive changes occur during the next few months. Murphy's Law applies here. If something can go wrong, this is when it will happen. Cover all the bases.

With Neptune: The source of your irritable moods is difficult to pin down in coming months. You may be tempted by get-rich-quick schemers. Pass up offers that seem too good to be true—they are.

With Pluto: Fate seems to delight in frustrating you in strange ways in coming months. Insurance, debt or stock and bond matters can present frustrating problems. Use patience now.

Rubeus
In the 11th House
Alone, no planets: This is an adverse influence that remains relatively unchanged in the next few months. Conflicts and arguments with friends or social groups are potential now.

With Sun: You are challenged by frustrating obstacles, and your efforts are not always successful. Your attempts to win friends and influence people are too aggressive. Take a lighter approach.

With Moon: You respond emotionally to frustrations and may waste energy in fruitless protests. Public social life can produce hazards and angry emotions.

With Mercury: You respond loudly and vocally to frustrations when careful thought is more productive of results. You can alienate friends and acquaintances through rash speech.

With Venus: Be wary of feelings of jealousy or envy, when seeking your own rewards is the more positive course of action. Conflicts with close friiends can arise over shared costs and expenses, or sensitive feelings that are hurt.

With Mars: Try to avoid being rushed into hasty or careless action, however strong the provocation. You can injure your social standing if you press for open conflict with others.

With Jupiter: Overconfidence can lead to rash, impulsive and costly action in coming months. Do not think you are so big that you cannot be brought down. Friends can take offense if you ignore their needs or desires.

With Saturn: Frequent delays and disappointments leave you frustrated in coming months. Those in authority will force you to slow down if you try to move too fast in the social or club circuit.

With Uranus: Disturbing and disruptive changes occur during the next few months. You could have a sudden split with a friend. Is it necessary, or are you just overreacting?

With Neptune: The source of your irritable moods is difficult to pin down in coming months. Cautions against drinking too much with friends, or at social gatherings. Keep your senses sharp in social groups.

With Pluto: Fate seems to delight in frustrating you in strange ways in coming months. Secret enemies among social groups can be waiting to pounce if you step out of line. Restrain yourself if you are angry.

Rubeus
In the 12th House

Alone, no planets: This is an adverse influence that remains relatively unchanged in the next few months. Hidden aggravations, or buried anger can lead to nightmares, illness or inner turmoil.

With Sun: You are challenged by frustrating obstacles but your efforts are not always successful. Failure to make headway can leave you physically drained and bring on illness. Get enough rest.

With Moon: You respond emotionally to frustrations and may waste energy in fruitless protests. Thoughts and feelings are in a flux right now. Do not make any drastic decisions under this influence.

With Mercury: You respond loudly and vocally to frustrations when careful thought is more productive of results. Your nerves can become frayed, and your mind overactive. Try to relax and meditate.

With Venus: Be wary of feelings of jealousy or envy, when seeking your own rewards is the more positive course of action. Secret liaisons with the opposite sex can produce scandal—or worse. Control sensual drives.

With Mars: Try to avoid being rushed into hasty or careless action, however strong the provocation. Your enemies are active, and the danger of accidents is high. Try to keep a low profile.

With Jupiter: Overconfidence can lead to rash, impulsive and costly action in coming months. Your lack of foresight, and self-indulgent impulses can be your downfall. Maintain a conservative approach.

With Saturn: Frequent delays and disappointments leave you frustrated in coming months. If you break the law, you are certain to pay the full penalty. Maintain your patience with authorities that may be frustrating your goals.

With Uranus: Disturbing and disruptive changes occur during the next few months. If you go out on a limb, you could take a big fall. Cautions against sudden attack by secret enemies. Protect yourself.

With Neptune: The source of your irritable moods is difficult to pin down in coming months. You may feel picked on, or persecuted, and react in a destructive manner. Restrain your impulse to strike back.

With Pluto: Fate seems to delight in frustrating you in strange ways in coming months. Impulsive or aggressive behavior can bring your self-undoing. Enemies are active, so avoid betrayal or arrest.

ACQUISITIO

This symbol is essentially favorable with all of the planets, regardless of their aspects.

Acquisitio (Success, Attainment) is ruled by Jupiter and associated with the sign Aries, where the Sun, or soul, is exalted, and in this respect indicates success that is not only material but also spiritual. However, Acquisitio does stress material gain, financial success, and social status.

Acquisitio always represents a point of gain in life: higher social status, many more material possessions, plenty of money, the esteem and respect of others, a position of leadership and command. In health houses, it can indicate gain in weight. Acquisitio generally is concerned with human gain, but it can represent political acquisitions of land and power, or the accretion of land at the mouths of rivers. Acquisitio is always a symbol of *more* of anything.

Aquisitio
In the 1st House
Alone, no planets: This is a favorable influence that remains in effect for the next few months. You receive honors, favors or gifts. Your personal goals and desires easily materialize.

With Sun: Success and self-fulfillment are assured in coming months. You receive a promotion, or obtain more authority in your life. You receive favors from those in power.

With Moon: Success, popularity and public attention are yours in coming months. Remaining sensitive to your emotional and intuitive urges can lead to large benefits in your personal affairs.

With Mercury: Communications and information are your keys to success in coming months. Enlarging your experience through study or travel leads to greater success in life.

With Venus: Gifts and windfalls come your way in coming months. Your resources improve; perhaps from a loved one, a partnership or a fortunate contract.

With Mars: A competitive spirit and daring initiatives achieve all your objectives. You can draw on a large store of energy to overcome the obstacle, win the race and obtain the prize.

With Jupiter: You are extremely lucky and opportunities for success and happiness abound in coming months. Go after the thing that has been just out of reach. You are more likely to obtain it now.

With Saturn: Any success or attainment of material goods will be permanent. Excellent for starting a business of your own. Pursue your most solid and stable ideas. They lead to long term success and fulfillment.

With Uranus: Many beneficial changes are going on in your life in the next few months. You may receive an unusual or unique proposition. Consider it carefully, as it could lead to great rewards.

With Neptune: Your intuition and imagination are your keys to success in coming months. Your ability to visualize and conceptualize a better future is the key to your success.

With Pluto: You have the promise of physical and spiritual rejuvenation and expansion in coming months. Making large changes, or taking a big step, will lead to success and achievement.

Acquisitio
In the 2nd House
Alone, no planets: This is a favorable influence that remains in effect for the next few months. Your property and finances increase, and income-producing activities are blessed with good luck.

With Sun: Success and self-fulfillment are assured in coming months. You may recieve a luxury gift. Favorable for business dealing with public entertainment, jewels, luxuries and speculation.

With Moon: Success, popularity and public attention are yours in coming months. You may acquire a boat, home or place of residence. Favorable for business in real estate, restaurant, home or family items or services.

With Mercury: Communications and information are your keys to success in coming months. You may obtain a profitable message or information. Favors business in communication and travel.

With Venus: Gifts and windfalls come your way in coming months. You may receive a gift of jewelry or clothing. Favors business in the arts, decorations, adornments, clothing and negotiation.

With Mars: A competitive spirit and daring initiatives achieve all your objectives. You may obtain new tools or machinery. Favorable for metalworking trades, engineering, manufacturing and competition.

With Jupiter: You are extremely lucky and opportunities for success and happiness abound in coming months. You may receive an opportunity to invest, and reap large profits. Favors business with professionals, bankers and educators.

With Saturn: Any success or attainment of material goods will be permanent. Excellent for starting a business of your own. You may obtain land or property. Favors business in real estate, mining, farming and conservative investments.

With Uranus: Many beneficial changes are going on in your life in the next few months. You may recieve a unique or unusual financial proposition. Favors business in autos, electronics, computers and aviation.

With Neptune: Your intuition and imagination are your keys to success in coming months. You may receive financial help from a charity or benefactor. Favors business in liquids, oil, chemicals and other peoples' secrets.

With Pluto: You have the promise of physical and spiritual rejuvenation and expansion in coming months. You may obtain a legacy, or money from a large organization. Favors business in demolition, renovation, waste management, insurance, taxes and investigation.

Acquistio
In the 3rd House

Alone, no planets: This is a favorable influence that remains in effect for the next few months. Your studies, communications and travels are fortunate, and bring great success for the effort.

With Sun: Success and self-fulfillment are assured in coming months. Communication and travel in regard to your most personal goals and desires bring good luck and success.

With Moon: Success, popularity and public attention are yours in coming months. Favors writing and communicating for public appeal. You can receive favorable publicity. You may have a rewarding encounter with someone from your past.

With Mercury: Communications and information are your keys to success in coming months. Learning from what you hear now can lead to greater success. Apply yourself to thought and study to gain the largest benefits.

With Venus: Gifts and windfalls come your way in coming months. You gain from social contacts you make. Communicate, travel, and negotiate to obtain your desires.

With Mars: A competitive spirit and daring initiatives achieve all your objectives. You are powerful in thought, debate and argument. Quickly apply your energies to what you learn for greatest success.

With Jupiter: You are extremely lucky and opportunities for success and happiness abound in coming months. Favors affairs to do with professionals, higher education, publishing and the courts. Speak up and be heard, for greater success and gain.

With Saturn: Any success or attainment of material goods will be permanent. Excellent for starting a business of your own. Favors long term business interests, and long term planning. Authorities and government officials can be the source of abundant gain.

With Uranus: Many beneficial changes are going on in your life in the next few months. Favors high tech communications and travel, mental creativity and invention for improvement and reward.

With Neptune: Your intuition and imagination are your keys to success in coming months. Intuition or spiritual guidance directs your thoughts to the most rewarding and fortunate course you should follow.

With Pluto: You have the promise of physical and spiritual rejuvenation and expansion in coming months. Rejuvenate the old, restore the damaged, and rebuild what was destroyed for greatest gain and attainment.

Acquisitio
In the 4th House
Alone, no planets: This is a favorable influence that remains in effect for the next few months. Home and family are favored with material gain, and an abundance of material blessings.

With Sun: Success and self-fulfillment are assured in coming months. Affairs to do with the family, parents, children and entertainment in the home are favored for gain and pleasurable reward.

With Moon: Success, popularity and public attention are yours in coming months. You may enlarge your present quarters, or move to a larger place. You can obtain the support and aid of women.

With Mercury: Communications and information are your keys to success in coming months. You can achieve improvements in communications and travel as they relate to property, home and family.

With Venus: Gifts and windfalls come your way in coming months. You may receive a gift for your home. Favors home redecorating, refinancing and sociable gatherings in the home.

With Mars: A competitive spirit and daring initiatives achieve all your objectives. Apply your energy to home and family concerns. The strongest members of the family will aid you now.

With Jupiter: You are extremely lucky and opportunities for success and happiness abound in coming months. Your home will become more comfortable, or perhaps larger. Prosperity pours over, and improves conditions for the whole family.

With Saturn: Any success or attainment of material goods will be permanent. Excellent for starting a business of your own. You may buy a permanent home, or invest in property for the long term. You receive the favors of the elderly, and if older, the young benefit you.

With Uranus: Many beneficial changes are going on in your life in the next few months. You may acquire the latest technology for your home. For greatest success and gain, stay creative and inventive in affairs of family and home.

With Neptune: Your intuition and imagination are your keys to success in coming months. Matters and affairs from the past come back to bring you good luck and gain. Benefits may come from grandparents.

With Pluto: You have the promise of physical and spiritual rejuvenation and expansion in coming months. You may receive benefits for home or family from government, insurance, banking or large community development projects.

Acquisitio
In the 5th House
Alone, no planets: This is a favorable influence that remains in effect for the next few months. Creativity, romance and speculation are favored for easy success and big gains.

With Sun: Success and self-fulfillment are assured in coming months. The things you most enjoy bring a great deal of pleasure. Your creative or romantic urges are satisfied.

With Moon: Success, popularity and public attention are yours in coming months. Following your intuitions can lead to rewarding creative activities. Your intuitive feel makes you a winner in speculative matters.

With Mercury: Communications and information are your keys to success in coming months. You may receive a love letter, or a request for a rendezvous. Expand your contacts for greatest benefit.

With Venus: Gifts and windfalls come your way in coming months. New clothes, jewelry, perfume or . . . ? You are favored to receive material benefits from a romantic partner, or a creative endeavor.

With Mars: A competitive spirit and daring initiatives achieve all your objectives. You can win what you want in love or in competition. Energy and dominance are your means to success.

With Jupiter: You are extremely lucky and opportunities for success and happiness abound in coming months. You have the Midas touch, and your actions transmute small investments into large rewards.

With Saturn: Any success or attainment of material goods will be permanent. Excellent for starting a business of your own. The affairs of authorities, executives or the elderly combine with new and enthusiastic initiatives for big rewards. Favors business in gold or diamonds.

With Uranus: Many beneficial changes are going on in your life in the next few months. Stay creative, inventive and open to change, and new or unusual ideas. Catching a sudden opportunity promises great success.

With Neptune: Your intuition and imagination are your keys to success in coming months. Stay in touch with your higher powers, and your inner feelings. You gain in love or pleasure by following your heart.

With Pluto: You have the promise of physical and spiritual rejuvenation and expansion in coming months. New loves, new infatuations and new enthusiasm are yours. Let the past rest, and expand into the future for greatest fulfillment.

Acquisitio
In the 6th House
Alone, no planets: This is a favorable influence that remains in effect for the next few months. Work and health improve. You obtain financial, material or physical aid.

With Sun: Success and self-fulfillment are assured in coming months. Responding to your duties brings personal success and rewards.

With Moon: Success, popularity and public attention are yours in coming months. You are favored in the company of fellow workers. Emotional sympathy brings benefits in working relationships.

With Mercury: Communications and information are your keys to success in coming months. Put on your thinking cap, and limber up your muscles, for achievement and gain from work. Seeing the large picture, and acting quickly, brings rewards.

With Venus: Gifts and windfalls come your way in coming months. Working relationships improve, and monetary gain from work increases. Socialize with working companions.

With Mars: A competitive spirit and daring initiatives achieve all your objectives. Applying yourself to your work, and increasing your work activities, brings large gains and benefits.

With Jupiter: You are extremely lucky and opportunities for success and happiness abound in coming months. Benefits you receive from your employers or superiors bring personal happiness, and financial security.

With Saturn: Any success or attainment of material goods will be permanent. Excellent for starting a business of your own. Expanding your work responsibilities will lead to larger and more lasting rewards.

With Uranus: Many beneficial changes are going on in your life in the next few months. Debate, create and innovate in job, duty and health for good results.

With Neptune: Your intuition and imagination are your keys to success in coming months. Follow the guidance of your higher powers, or those that have your best interests at heart, in regards to work and health. Your inner feelings guide you to success.

With Pluto: You have the promise of physical and spiritual rejuvenation and expansion in coming months. Clean house, remove waste and renew outworn approaches to health and work.

Acquisitio
In the 7th House
Alone, no planets: This is a favorable influence that remains in effect for the next few months. Partnerships, contracts, marriage and public affairs are favored for reward and gain.

With Sun: Success and self-fulfillment are assured in coming months. You attract the right partners, and make the right agreements. Favorable for marriage.

With Moon: Success, popularity and public attention are yours in coming months. If a man, you may make a profitable agreement. If a woman, you express your inner feelings to others better, leading to greater rewards.

With Mercury: Communications and information are your keys to success in coming months. Contact by message, conversation or travel brings fortunate partners into your life.

With Venus: Gifts and windfalls come your way in coming months. The bonding you achieve with another can bring deep emotional fulfillment, as well as great material blessings.

With Mars: A competitive spirit and daring initiatives achieve all your objectives. If someone has you up against a wall, you can win if you want to fight back. Combine foresight with action to get the best out of all your relationships.

With Jupiter: You are extremely lucky and opportunities for success and happiness abound in coming months. Your prince charming or lady fair may be found. Expand your contacts, and seek favorable agreements.

With Saturn: Any success or attainment of material goods will be permanent. Excellent for starting a business of your own. If a long term commitment has been up in the air, now is the time to finalize it for your greatest benefit.

With Uranus: Many beneficial changes are going on in your life in the next few months. Socialize with friends or groups to which you belong. An encounter with a unique individual can brighten up your life.

With Neptune: Your intuition and imagination are your keys to success in coming months. The charity you now show another can rebound to your advantage later. Sensitive, artistic and spiritual types are favored for your personal gain.

With Pluto: You have the promise of physical and spiritual rejuvenation and expansion in coming months. Old relationships or neglected agreements can now be renewed, and lead to great rewards and returns.

Acquisitio
In the 8th House
Alone, no planets: This is a favorable influence that remains in effect for the next few months. Finances can improve through loans or legacies. Investments, the occult arts and sex are favored for gain and fulfillment.

With Sun: Success and self-fulfillment are assured in coming months. Material benefits, and personal pleasures increase when you unite with others.

With Moon: Success, popularity and public attention are yours in coming months. The powerful, the transforming and the occult are intuitively understood by you now. Plumb the depths of your subconcious for expanded pleasure and attainment.

With Mercury: Communications and information are your keys to success in coming months. You can gain financially through collaboration. Agents and representatives benefit you.

With Venus: Gifts and windfalls come your way in coming months.

You make financial gains from partnerships, and benefit from deeper involvement with partners.

With Mars: A competitive spirit and daring initiatives achieve all your objectives. You are unbeatable in financial matters. Your emotional depth and sexual prowess lead to fulfillment.

With Jupiter: You are extremely lucky and opportunities for success and happiness abound in coming months. Expand your knowledge of mysterious matters, and dig into the depths of research and investigation, to achieve your greatest desires and pleasures.

With Saturn: Any success or attainment of material goods will be permanent. Excellent for starting a business of your own. You can breeze through the most difficult matters, and achieve your long term goals.

With Uranus: Many beneficial changes are going on in your life in the next few months. Creative ideas in the occult, the sciences, or the nature of things, brings sudden and large gain.

With Neptune: Your intuition and imagination are your keys to success in coming months. You obtain guidance from the higher realms. An inheritance, refund, or funds from a partner may mysteriously appear.

With Pluto: You have the promise of physical and spiritual rejuvenation and expansion in coming months. You can obtain profound insight. All occult studies and regenerative practices will lead to favorable results.

Acquisitio
In the 9th House
Alone, no planets: This is a favorable influence that remains in effect for the next few months. Higher education, long trips, and foreign places and people bring large benefits and rewards.

With Sun: Success and self-fulfillment are assured in coming months. Your expansive ambitions meet with great success. Promote and publicize for greatest benefit.

With Moon: Success, popularity and public attention are yours in coming months. Publishing, public affairs, foreign affairs and long distance contacts bring fortunate changes.

With Mercury: Communications and information are your keys to success in coming months. Study, teaching and writing in your profession brings greater financial returns.

With Venus: Gifts and windfalls come your way in coming months. You may receive financial grants for education, business or a charity. Signifies financial gain from professional activities.

With Mars: A competitive spirit and daring initiatives achieve all your objectives. Your inspirations motivate your actions, and you achieve constructive results from expansion projects.

With Jupiter: You are extremely lucky and opportunities for success and happiness abound in coming months. Educators, professionals, diplomats or the courts are all favored to bring you promotion and gain.

With Saturn: Any success or attainment of material goods will be permanent. Excellent for starting a business of your own. Your careful, conservative and well considered plans for expansion meet with approval, and bring good results.

With Uranus: Many beneficial changes are going on in your life in the next few months. Signifies scientific breakthroughs, spiritual revelations and professional genius. Explore the distant and unusual for greatest benefit.

With Neptune: Your intuition and imagination are your keys to success in coming months. Favors long journeys, in body, spirit or mind. You receive aid from distant places, or from a foreign source.

With Pluto: You have the promise of physical and spiritual rejuvenation and expansion in coming months. You may change your perspective, your philosophy or your approach to matters of great importance. You benefit from the change.

Acquisitio
In the 10th House
Alone, no planets: This is a favorable influence that remains in effect for the next few months. You achieve great gains, honors or recognition in career, business and worldly achievement.

With Sun: Success and self-fulfillment are assured in coming months. You obtain exceptional rewards from business or profession. Signifies promotion and financial gain.

With Moon: Success, popularity and public attention are yours in coming months. Favors self-employment, or business operated from the home. Favors managerial activities and businesses.

With Mercury: Communications and information are your keys to success in coming months. Favors all business communications fields, as well as journalism and printing. Also benefits agents and transportation businesses.

With Venus: Gifts and windfalls come your way in coming months. Favorable for business in the arts, banking, real estate, fashionable adornments and entertainment.

With Mars: A competitive spirit and daring initiatives achieve all your objectives. Business gains and benefits derive from manufacturing, engineering, construction and competitive action.

With Jupiter: You are extremely lucky and opportunities for success and happiness abound in coming months. Excellent for all businesses. Most fortunate for publishing, shipping, foreign trade, the legal profession and politicians.

With Saturn: Any success or attainment of material goods will be permanent. Excellent for starting a business of your own. Favors business with government and elected officials, and all activities to do with products from the earth.

With Uranus: Many beneficial changes are going on in your life in the next few months. Favors high tech industries, electronics, computers, aviation, scientific research and social reform.

With Neptune: Your intuition and imagination are your keys to success in coming months. Brings benefits from advertising and promotion campaigns. Favors the film industry, and businesses in chemicals, drugs, oil and all liquids and gasses.

With Pluto: You have the promise of physical and spiritual rejuvenation and expansion in coming months. If business is floundering, it will revive. Favors business in demolition, renovation and insurance, taxes and the goods of the dead.

Acquisitio
In the 11th House
Alone, no planets: This is a favorable influence that remains in effect for the next few months. Friends, groups and socializing lead to fortunate events, and aid you in attaining your dreams and hopes.

With Sun: Success and self-fulfillment are assured in coming months. Success in all public affairs, and favors from friends in high places.

With Moon: Success, popularity and public attention are yours in coming months. Friendships and socializing centering around the home and family lead to rewarding results.

With Mercury: Communications and information are your keys to success in coming months. Making friends in literary, educational or intellectual groups brings benefits.

With Venus: Gifts and windfalls come your way in coming months. Favors all your social and public interests, and dealings with friends. Matters to do with the arts or with women benefit you.

With Mars: A competitive spirit and daring initiatives achieve all your objectives. Brings benefits from activities with groups, and physically demanding group projects lead to greater gains.

With Jupiter: You are extremely lucky and opportunities for success and happiness abound in coming months. Your friendships bring great luck. You are favored by the influential and powerful friends you have.

With Saturn: Any success or attainment of material goods will be permanent. Excellent for starting a business of your own. Friendships with those older than you, or those in politics or administration, bring enduring benefits.

With Uranus: Many beneficial changes are going on in your life in the next few months. Friends among occult, metaphysical, astrological or scientific groups are fortunate.

With Neptune: Your intuition and imagination are your keys to success in coming months. Favorable for association with psychic, spiritual or magical groups and friends.

With Pluto: You have the promise of physical and spiritual rejuvenation and expansion in coming months. Adverse conditions will come to an end, and rebound in your favor. Genuine friends are looking out for your best interests.

Acquisitio
In the 12th House
Alone, no planets: This is a favorable influence that remains in effect for the next few months. Your spiritual and inner life expands to your great advantage. You receive great benefits from inner development, or from hidden benefactors.

With Sun: Success and self-fulfillment are assured in coming months. You can obtain the favors of those in authority, and influential friends aid your cause.

With Moon: Success, popularity and public attention are yours in coming months. Favors meditation and psychic development. You may receive secret aid from artists, women or family members.

With Mercury: Communications and information are your keys to success in coming months. Investigation and occult studies are favored. Transmute small thoughts into expanded visions for success.

With Venus: Gifts and windfalls come your way in coming months.

Sharing secret pleasures brings fulfillment. You obtain formerly unrealized benefits from relationships.

With Mars: A competitive spirit and daring initiatives achieve all your objectives. Favors self healing, and the application of inner energies to successfully renew your psychic and occult powers.

With Jupiter: You are extremely lucky and opportunities for success and happiness abound in coming months. You obtain great aid from hidden benefactors. Favors philosophical, spiritual and religious benefits coming your way.

With Saturn: Any success or attainment of material goods will be permanent. Excellent for starting a business of your own. Meditating on where you have been, and long term planning on where you want to go, will bring long term benefits.

With Uranus: Many beneficial changes are going on in your life in the next few months. Favors the occult sciences, esoteric astrology, and things very modern, or very ancient for your benefit and gain.

With Neptune: Your intuition and imagination are your keys to success in coming months. Favors intimacy and union with higher powers, and your inner occult power. You benefit from mystical liasons.

With Pluto: You have the promise of physical and spiritual rejuvenation and expansion in coming months. You regenerate your inner resources and energy, and obtain beneficial results in the outer world.

LAETITIA

This symbol is essentially favorable with *all* of the planets, regardless of their aspects.

Laetitia or Joy is ruled by Jupiter, and is related to the sign Taurus, a material Earth sign, denoting the pleasures of the flesh as well as the spirit. It represents Joy that is spread among the many, and incorporates plenty which suffices not only for the individual, but can be shared through charity and personal generosity. Laetitia represents the material comfort of Taurus, and the generosity of Jupiter.

Laetitia always symbolizes a point of abundance in life, whether material, social or spiritual. Laetitia represents abundant good health, high vitality, positive attitudes, strong self-confidence, favorable circumstances to achieve success, and bliss in romantic relationships. Laetitia in a house means that any opposition or obstacles will soon evaporate, and all the wishes connected with the affairs of that house will be fulfilled.

Laetitia
In the 1st House
Alone, no planets: This is a favorable influence that remains in effect for the next few months. Your efforts bring praise, favors or gifts from others, while you are protected against loss.

With Sun: You are radiant with good health and happiness, and filled with creative impulses. You achieve personal success, due to ambition and determination.

With Moon: You are happy in the limelight of public attention and cooperation. Your show of affection and feelings brings the blessings of others to you, especially the public, women or children.

With Mercury: You take pleasure in communicating your ideas to others and gaining new information as well. Your mental and communicative abilities help bring quick achievement of your personal goals.

With Venus: Social life, romance, cooperative dealings with others bring you great pleasure. Your personal charm and cheerful attitude help attract benefits and good fortune in your personal affairs.

With Mars: Pleasure in developing physical skills and in action for its own sake absorbs you in the next few months. You can apply a great deal of physical energy to your pursuits, and will reap equally great rewards.

With Jupiter: Life is filled with pleasure and good fortune in the coming months. Prosperity and abundance will be yours. Excellent time to begin large undertakings.

With Saturn: Old friends and familiar pleasures absorb your attention in coming months. Your endurance and stability will bring solid, long-term benefits to your personal affairs.

With Uranus: Many beneficial changes are going on in your life in the next few months. Your innovation, invention and creativity can bring sudden and large good fortune.

With Neptune: You are particularly charitable and tolerant in coming months. Your intution and psychic abilities denote great benefits from higher guiding forces.

With Pluto: You receive karmic blessings drawn from past life deeds in coming months. Renewal, regeneration and renovation bring large benefits to all your personal affairs.

Laetitia
In the 2nd House
Alone, no planets: This is a favorable influence that remains in effect for the next few months. Finances and income can increase in a big way. Take advantage of moneymaking opportunities.

With Sun: You are radiant with good health and happiness, and filled with creative impulses. Jewelry, precious metals, finance and public utilities can bring large financial gain.

With Moon: You are happy in the limelight of public attention and cooperation. Things to do with liquids, the sea, its products, and things related to food and eating can prove profitable.

With Mercury: You take pleasure in communicating your ideas to others and gaining new information as well. Journalism, clerking, communications and messages, or detail work, can bring large profits.

With Venus: Social life, romance, cooperative dealings with others bring you great pleasure. The arts, and things to do with beauty and harmony will prove most profitable now.

With Mars: Pleasure in developing physical skills and in action for its own sake absorbs you in the next few months. Metal, tools, engineering or the military can bring great financial gain.

With Jupiter: Life is filled with pleasure and good fortune in the coming months. Dealings with professionals, department heads and bankers are favored for large financial benefits.

With Saturn: Old friends and familiar pleasures absorb your attention in coming months. Real estate, farming or mining are favored for financial gain and benefit.

With Uranus: Many beneficial changes are going on in your life in the next few months. The new, unusual, unique, inventive or creative are favored for financial gain and benefit.

With Neptune: You are particularly charitable and tolerant in coming months. Philosophy, occultism, metaphysics or magic can help you gain in financial resources.

Pluto: You receive karmic blessings drawn from past life deeds in coming months. Mining, plumbing, demolition or renovation are favored fields of monetary gain.

Laetitia
In the 3rd House
Alone, no planets: This is a favorable influence that remains in effect for the next few months. Short trips, affairs with relatives and neighbors,

and your basic studies all bring pleasure and good fortune.

With Sun: You are radiant with good health and happiness, and filled with creative impulses. Your efforts in travel and communication can bring success in personal goals.

With Moon: You are happy in the limelight of public attention and cooperation. Public speaking, a trip to the past, or communication with women are all favored now.

With Mercury: You take pleasure in communicating your ideas to others and gaining new information as well. Lectures, literature and all forms of communications bring great rewards.

With Venus: Social life, romance, cooperative dealings with others bring you great pleasure. The artistic, refined and luxurious are favored for greater pleasure and enjoyment.

With Mars: Pleasure in developing physical skills and in action for its own sake absorbs you in the next few months. You are sharp in communications, and swift in travel, and luck is with you in both of these areas of your life.

With Jupiter: Life is filled with pleasure and good fortune in the coming months. Business travel, promotion and publications can bring large rewards now.

With Saturn: Old friends and familiar pleasures absorb your attention in coming months. Communicating with authorities, and disseminating important information are favored for great benefits.

With Uranus: Many beneficial changes are going on in your life in the next few months. Research, sudden mental intuition, and originality are highlighted to bring you great rewards.

With Neptune: You are particularly charitable and tolerant in coming months. Your communications are inspired, and perhaps alluring. Stay in touch with your higher powers for rewarding guidance and good fortune.

With Pluto: You receive karmic blessings drawn from past life deeds in coming months. The genius of mental creativity is with you, and brings rewarding mental expansion.

Laetitia
In the 4th House
Alone, no planets: This is a favorable influence that remains in effect for the next few months. Activities and affairs to do with home and family bring greater benefits and enjoyment.

With Sun: You are radiant with good health and happiness, and filled with creative impulses. Home and family are the center of your attention and activity, and bring great rewards.

With Moon: You are happy in the limelight of public attention and cooperation. You are protected by women, and life in the family is caring and pleasant.

With Mercury: You take pleasure in communicating your ideas to others and gaining new information as well. Family discussions, and short trips together, lead to lively stimulation and enjoyment.

With Venus: Social life, romance, cooperative dealings with others bring you great pleasure. Favors the purchase of a home, or redecorating your home. Events in the home are pleasant and harmonious.

With Mars: Pleasure in developing physical skills and in action for its own sake absorbs you in the next few months. Apply your energies to home and family for greatest benefits and happiness.

With Jupiter: Life is filled with pleasure and good fortune in the coming months. Indulge in the luxuries of home, and enjoy the caring within the family for greater pleasure and well-being.

With Saturn: Old friends and familiar pleasures absorb your attention in coming months. Favored for establishing a permanent home, and affairs to do with your parents or elders.

With Uranus: Many beneficial changes are going on in your life in the next few months. Try new approaches to old situations in home and family, for greater success and happiness.

With Neptune: You are particularly charitable and tolerant in coming months. Spiritual and psychic harmony surround you in the home, and in family relationships.

With Pluto: You receive karmic blessings drawn from past life deeds in coming months. Renovation and renewal, in home or family, brings greater rewards and benefits.

Laetitia
In the 5th House
Alone, no planets: This is a favorable influence that remains in effect for the next few months. Luck and success in romance, gambling, creativity and the affairs of children.

With Sun: You are radiant with good health and happiness, and filled with creative impulses. Speculation, romance and social entertainment hold the promise of great rewards and pleasure.

With Moon: You are happy in the limelight of public attention and cooperation. Sweepstakes, lotteries, and speculation involving liquids, foods or the public are favored now.

With Mercury: You take pleasure in communicating your ideas to others and gaining new information as well. Amusements, conversation and short trips can bring great pleasure and enjoyment.

With Venus: Social life, romance, cooperative dealings with others bring you great pleasure. Monetary gains in gambling, and enjoyable relationships with partners are highlighted.

With Mars: Pleasure in developing physical skills and in action for its own sake absorbs you in the next few months. Your passion and ardor are great, and lead to great gains in competition and romance.

With Jupiter: Life is filled with pleasure and good fortune in the coming months. Promises great good fortune in speculation and romance.

With Saturn: Old friends and familiar pleasures absorb your attention in coming months. Conservative investments, and affairs with authorities or the elderly bring greater benefits.

With Uranus: Many beneficial changes are going on in your life in the next few months. Creative or unusual ideas can lead to greater benefits in speculation, or romance.

With Neptune: You are particularly charitable and tolerant in coming months. Romance is pleasurable and inspiring, while speculative matters in which you apply your intution are favored.

With Pluto: You receive karmic blessings drawn from past life deeds in coming months. Creative and speculative affairs can bring enormous rewards.

Laetitia
In the 6th House
Alone, no planets: This is a favorable influence that remains in effect for the next few months. Affairs related to health and work are favored for happiness and bigger benefits.

With Sun: You are radiant with good health and happiness, and filled with creative impulses. Better health, and more energy for work, bring bigger benefits and substantial gains.

With Moon: You are happy in the limelight of public attention and cooperation. You benefit from making changes in health, hygiene and dietary habits.

With Mercury: You take pleasure in communicating your ideas to others and gaining new information as well. Attention to details, and application of your mental faculties bring greater rewards in work and health.

With Venus: Social life, romance, cooperative dealings with others bring you great pleasure. Your working conditions improve, and work relationships bring luck and favor.

With Mars: Pleasure in developing physical skills and in action for its own sake absorbs you in the next few months. The vitality you show in work and duties will rebound to you with greater rewards and benefits.

With Jupiter: Life is filled with pleasure and good fortune in the coming months. You gain through generous employers, and through a more optimistic attitude toward your work.

With Saturn: Old friends and familiar pleasures absorb your attention in coming months. Steady application to the job at hand will bring larger and lasting rewards.

With Uranus: Many beneficial changes are going on in your life in the next few months. Inventiveness at work, or modern health treatments are favored now.

With Neptune: You are particularly charitable and tolerant in coming months. Follow your sensitive intuition for larger gains in affairs of health and work.

With Pluto: You receive karmic blessings drawn from past life deeds in coming months. Idealism and optimism grow, and bring large and beneficial changes in health or work.

Laetitia
In the 7th House
Alone, no planets: This is a favorable influence that remains in effect for the next few months. Relationships of all kinds improve, and you can form a fortunate alliance with another.

With Sun: You are radiant with good health and happiness, and filled with creative impulses. You are strong in competition, and can attract a fortunate partner now.

With Moon: You are happy in the limelight of public attention and cooperation. The mutual feelings in relationships are nurturing and sensitive. Fortunate for dealings with women, youth and the public.

With Mercury: You take pleasure in communicating your ideas to others and gaining new information as well. Public communications, and public relations bring greater rewards.

With Venus: Social life, romance, cooperative dealings with others bring you great pleasure. Marital happiness and pleasant associations are with you now.

With Mars: Pleasure in developing physical skills and in action for its own sake absorbs you in the next few months. You are favored in combat, and obtain large rewards by applying yourself to making relationships work.

With Jupiter: Life is filled with pleasure and good fortune in the coming months. Legal affairs, marriage and partnerships bring greater rewards and benefits.

With Saturn: Old friends and familiar pleasures absorb your attention in coming months. Taking the conservative and steady course in relationships and affairs leads to the greatest success.

With Uranus: Many beneficial changes are going on in your life in the next few months. Staying creative, and being willing to change, brings greater benefits in relationships.

With Neptune: You are particularly charitable and tolerant in coming months. You obtain the most reward and pleasure from relationships by going slow, and remaining adaptable.

With Pluto: You receive karmic blessings drawn from past life deeds in coming months. Your search for deeper relationships can lead to success. A deep relationship renews your spirit.

Laetitia
In the 8th House
Alone, no planets: This is a favorable influence that remains in effect for the next few months. You can gain in financial resources, affairs related to sex, or the mysterious and occult.

With Sun: You are radiant with good health and happiness, and filled with creative impulses. You obtain a great deal by going after what you want with purpose and optimism.

With Moon: You are happy in the limelight of public attention and cooperation. Applying psychic and intuitive talents to your affairs brings favorable results.

With Mercury: You take pleasure in communicating your ideas to others and gaining new information as well. Intense communication and interaction with others brings great rewards.

With Venus: Social life, romance, cooperative dealings with others bring you great pleasure. You can gain a great deal from the resources of others.

With Mars: Pleasure in developing physical skills and in action for its own sake absorbs you in the next few months. Your strong desire for sex, or for inner regeneration, brings large and pleasurable rewards.

With Jupiter: Life is filled with pleasure and good fortune in the coming months. Expanding and enlarging your associations will lead to greater financial benefits.

With Saturn: Old friends and familiar pleasures absorb your attention in coming months. Conservation, persistence, and a stable approach bring the largest benefits now.

With Uranus: Many beneficial changes are going on in your life in the next few months. Investigations you make now can bring sudden beneficial results.

With Neptune: You are particularly charitable and tolerant in coming months. Spiritual and occult investigations lead to good results, and large rewards.

With Pluto: You receive karmic blessings drawn from past life deeds in coming months. Your resources are renewed, and they can grow through affairs involving large groups or organizations.

Laetitia
In the 9th House
Alone, no planets: This is a favorable influence that remains in effect for the next few months. Long journeys, foreign places and higher education bring pleasure and benefits.

With Sun: You are radiant with good health and happiness, and filled with creative impulses. Success in affairs with people at a distance, and in studies that lead to a degree or diploma.

With Moon: You are happy in the limelight of public attention and cooperation. Success in travel and publication, and benefits from intuitive or clairvoyant knowledge.

With Mercury: You take pleasure in communicating your ideas to others and gaining new information as well. Advanced studies and travel for knowledge bring greater rewards.

With Venus: Social life, romance, cooperative dealings with others bring you great pleasure. You obtain greater joy and rewards from foreign travel, and relationships formed with foreigners or professionals.

With Mars: Pleasure in developing physical skills and in action for its own sake absorbs you in the next few months. Self promotion, publicity, propaganda and exploration of foreign lands and subjects are favored for rewards.

With Jupiter: Life is filled with pleasure and good fortune in the coming months. Matters far away, higher education and teachers will bring greater benefits and advancement.

With Saturn: Old friends and familiar pleasures absorb your attention in coming months. Meditation, careful judgment and conservative studies will bring stabililty and lasting rewards.

With Uranus: Many beneficial changes are going on in your life in the next few months. Prophetic messages, mental genius, or unusual contacts with people holding foreign ideas can bring great benefits.

With Neptune: You are particularly charitable and tolerant in coming months. Travel, whether physical, psychic or mental, holds great rewards. You benefit from expanding your vision.

With Pluto: You receive karmic blessings drawn from past life deeds in coming months. Learn from distant places, and former times. You reap greater rewards as you regenerate your vision.

Laetitia
In the 10th House
Alone, no planets: This is a favorable influence that remains in effect for the next few months. Promotion and honor will come to you in regard to business, career or profession.

With Sun: You are radiant with good health and happiness, and filled with creative impulses. You are more cheerful and optimistic in your business affairs, and leaders and authorities will aid your goals.

With Moon: You are happy in the limelight of public attention and cooperation. You are favored by women, and can profit greatly from business in the public.

With Mercury: You take pleasure in communicating your ideas to others and gaining new information as well. Commercial trade, science, literature or politics can bring greater benefits.

With Venus: Social life, romance, cooperative dealings with others bring you great pleasure. Partnerships, contracts and relationships in regard to business bring you popularity and success.

With Mars: Pleasure in developing physical skills and in action for its own sake absorbs you in the next few months. Taking the adventurous and courageous route in business and career brings the greatest rewards.

With Jupiter: Life is filled with pleasure and good fortune in the coming months. Your reputation and prestige are at a peak. You can obtain great favors or honors from others.

With Saturn: Old friends and familiar pleasures absorb your attention in coming months. Enlarging your responsibilities, and demonstrating your stable approach, will bring larger rewards in business and career.

With Uranus: Many beneficial changes are going on in your life in the next few months. Your ingenious ideas, and inventive creations can lead to surprising success in the business world.

With Neptune: You are particularly charitable and tolerant in coming months. Applying intuitive, visionary, and psychic energies to career and business can be very fortunate now.

With Pluto: You receive karmic blessings drawn from past life deeds in coming months. Renovation, reorganization, and renewal are basic themes you can apply for greater success in business and profession.

Laetitia
In the 11th House
Alone, no planets: This is a favorable influence that remains in effect for the next few months. Friends, social groups and social life can bring you great joy and advantage now.

With Sun: You are radiant with good health and happiness, and filled with creative impulses. Your hopes can be realized now. Excellent for association with influential friends, and cooperative group socializing.

With Moon: You are happy in the limelight of public attention and cooperation. Activities in the public, or with women or youth, can bring popularity and pleasure.

With Mercury: You take pleasure in communicating your ideas to others and gaining new information as well. Communications and short trips with friends and social groups brings happiness and lively joy.

With Venus: Social life, romance, cooperative dealings with others bring you great pleasure. Your popularity rises, in every type of relationship. Socialize for your greatest reward and benefit.

With Mars: Pleasure in developing physical skills and in action for its own sake absorbs you in the next few months. Sports and competition, of a friendly sort, are most enjoyable and invigorating.

With Jupiter: Life is filled with pleasure and good fortune in the coming months. You can obtain grants, gifts or favors from rich or influential benefactors.

With Saturn: Old friends and familiar pleasures absorb your attention in coming months. Your stable, conservative and most dependable friends and group associations are favored for greatest benefit.

With Uranus: Many beneficial changes are going on in your life in the next few months. Combine originality and socializing to realize unexpected benefits and pleasure.

With Neptune: You are particularly charitable and tolerant in coming months. Cultured, refined or esoteric socializing brings large rewards and benefits.

With Pluto: You receive karmic blessings drawn from past life deeds in coming months. You can now realize your aspirations in regard to the occult, the mysterious, or the magical.

Laetitia
In the 12th House
Alone, no planets: This is a favorable influence that remains in effect for the next few months. Your inner joy will grow, and you can obtain help or gifts from a special benefactor.

With Sun: You are radiant with good health and happiness, and filled with creative impulses. Your inner feelings of well-being and centeredness attract good fortune from others.

With Moon: You are happy in the limelight of public attention and cooperation. Application to things done in secret, out of view, or at home will be rewarding, and lead to public recognition in the future.

With Mercury: You take pleasure in communicating your ideas to others and gaining new information as well. Investigation and research into important mysteries brings success and personal benefit.

With Venus: Social life, romance, cooperative dealings with others bring you great pleasure. Inner peace and harmony are yours, and this attracts good luck in money and relationships.

With Mars: Pleasure in developing physical skills and in action for its own sake absorbs you in the next few months. Your energy can be directed inward, or to very private and personal matters. Concentrate on these for greatest benefit.

With Jupiter: Life is filled with pleasure and good fortune in the coming months. Meditation, yoga, or other spiritual/physical disciplines can bring euphoria.

With Saturn: Old friends and familiar pleasures absorb your attention in coming months. Activities you perform by yourself, or with an elder mentor, are favored for large and lasting rewards.

With Uranus: Many beneficial changes are going on in your life in the next few months. Astrology and the occult sciences are favored to bring you greater benefits now.

With Neptune: You are particularly charitable and tolerant in coming months. Meditation and consciousness development can bring inner peace, and outer benefits to your life.

With Pluto: You receive karmic blessings drawn from past life deeds in coming months. Review your inner world, and your past actions in the outer world, for successful renewal of your inner strengths, and your continued success.

CARCER

This variable symbol is given positive focus by Sun, Jupiter, Venus, and Mars; requires effort for fulfillment with Saturn, Uranus, Neptune, Pluto, Moon and Mercury.

Carcer is ruled by Saturn and associated with the sign Pisces, which represents prisons, institutions, secret enemies, fears and dreams. Saturn gives reality to both the favorable and adverse meanings of bondage—good or bad habits, a strong sense of duty, willingness to carry out responsibilities and obligations—all these are related to Carcer (Bondage). Pisces, the sign of endings, represents the "finalizing" or "completion" of a project or a situation where Carcer appears in the chart.

Carcer in the chart always represents a point of contact with reality, objective and following the rules of the material world, whether favoring or hindering the desires of the querent. Only practical action, persistence, and political maneuvering will bring the results querent desires when Carcer is the occupant of a given house. However, the results will be permanent and secure, so the benefits of the material goods, skills, knowledge and influence gained under the influence of Carcer are obviously excellent. Adversity presents a learning experience.

Carcer
In the 1st House
Alone, no planets: This influence maintains the staus quo, whether satisfactory or otherwise, for the next few months. New projects and initiatives will be stalled, while ongoing personal affairs remain the same.

With Sun: You are assured of success in your ambitions if you are patient and persistent in your efforts. Personal interests may require extra work and attention. Those in a position of power and command are important to eventual success.

With Moon: Organize and control your dealings with the public in a professional manner to achieve success. Your ties to the past, your family or your mother may create extra burdens now.

With Mercury: Careful thought, planning and organized communications are necessary for success. Matters of communication, transportation or education can limit your personal movements, or weigh heavily on your mind. Achievement comes through attention to detail.

With Venus: An old friend can be counted on for support in helping you achieve your ambitions. Social contacts, partners or lovers may be looked to in relieving the burden of personal responsibilities.

With Mars: Your energy is controlled and concentrated successfully on a specific goal in coming months. You must rely on your own initiative to obtain what is due you in personal affairs.

With Jupiter: Past restrictions are removed and you can move ahead more freely, if conservatively, in the future. You can combine wisdom and foresight to achieve your personal goals. Patient planning is essential for long term success.

With Saturn: Attention to strict realities and concentrated efforts bring lasting results in coming months. You must follow a conservative and responsible course to realize success in matters of long term personal interest.

With Uranus: You resist changes whether they are detrimental or favorable in the next few months. Past commitments may be broken, or you find new commitments do not turn out as expected. Remain calm under trying circumstances.

With Neptune: A special dream can become a reality in the next few months. Your personal vision of the future can become reality now. You will have to maintain your commitment to achieve it.

With Pluto: You have the opportunity to fulfill an obligation resulting from past life experiences in coming months. The path of life you are following had a particular point of departure. Recognize the connection between past initiatives and present realities.

Carcer
In the 2nd House
Alone, no planets: This influence maintains the staus quo, whether satisfactory or otherwise, for the next few months. Your finances remain stable. Obligations and duties will slow any attempt at acquisition or financial increase.

With Sun: You are assured of success in your ambitions if you are patient and persistent in your efforts. You may have to set a tough example of financial self-control for others to follow.

With Moon: Organize and control your dealings with the public in a professional manner to achieve success. Your home base represents the real foundation of personal financial security. Financial success requires stability in home and family affairs.

With Mercury: Careful thought, planning and organized communications are necessary for success. Messages, contacts and contracts should be carefully thought out in matters of finance or acquisition.

With Venus: An old friend can be counted on for support in helping you achieve your ambitions. Past employers, partners or business associates can present stable financial opportunities.

With Mars: Your energy is controlled and concentrated successfully on a specific goal in coming months. Financial stability and increase are directly tied to the amount of time and effort you expend.

With Jupiter: Past restrictions are removed and you can move ahead more freely, if conservatively, in the future. You may gain from matters of the law, courts and public promotion of your financial interests. Maintain a conservative course in expansive undertakings.

With Saturn: Attention to strict realities and concentrated efforts bring lasting results in coming months. Favors conservative investment and savings. Long term gain requires long term planning.

With Uranus: You resist changes whether they are detrimental or favorable in the next few months. Fluctuations in finances may require you go over old territory, and institute changes to prevent future upsets.

With Neptune: A special dream can become a reality in the next few months. Financial responsibility is required to achieve long term desires in business, income and property.

With Pluto: You have the opportunity to fulfill an obligation resulting from past life experiences in coming months. You can find a way to clear up old debts. Your future financial interests are dependent on past financial resources.

Carcer
In the 3rd House
Alone, no planets: This influence maintains the staus quo, whether satisfactory or otherwise, for the next few months. Affairs to do with local matters, relatives, messages and practical studies achieve a point of stability.

With Sun: You are assured of success in your ambitions if you are patient and persistent in your efforts. Concentration on basic ideas, and matters in the local vicinity, are important to long term success in personal affairs.

With Moon: Organize and control your dealings with the public in a professional manner to achieve success. A controlled and conservative message to the public is well received, and enhances your image in the minds of others.

With Mercury: Careful thought, planning and organized communications are necessary for success. Trips, messages and matter in your local environment require careful planning and conservative implementation.

With Venus: An old friend can be counted on for support in helping you achieve your ambitions. Public relations, and matters to do with partners are favored for solid achievement.

With Mars: Your energy is controlled and concentrated successfully on a specific goal in coming months. You are skilled at debate and persuasion in regard to practical concerns of a local nature.

With Jupiter: Past restrictions are removed and you can move ahead more freely, if conservatively, in the future. Favors communications or short trips in regard to long term interests. Double check the details of your larger thoughts and plans.

With Saturn: Attention to strict realities and concentrated efforts bring lasting results in coming months. Your communications and practical studies require time and discipline to achieve your ends.

With Uranus: You resist changes whether they are detrimental or favorable in the next few months. Lines of communications, means of transport or local affairs can present sudden upsets. Detailed analysis and planning will help you find the best response.

With Neptune: A special dream can become a reality in the next few months. Your speech and your underlying message can inspire others, and lead them to follow you in the quest for insight, understanding and practical achievement.

With Pluto: You have the opportunity to fulfill an obligation resulting from past life experiences in coming months. You may need to contact someone from your past. They hold a message or renewal and regeneration of your mind and your thinking.

Carcer
In the 4th House
Alone, no planets: This influence maintains the staus quo, whether satisfactory or otherwise, for the next few months. Family, home and basic security require a conservative and practical approach for maintenance and steady improvement.

With Sun: You are assured of success in your ambitions if you are patient and persistent in your efforts. Your power base is your home and family. Personal security requires that you honor personal commitments.

With Moon: Organize and control your dealings with the public in a professional manner to achieve success. Commitments to family members, women or the public at large can bring long term security, and a more certain foundation for the future.

With Mercury: Careful thought, planning and organized communications are necessary for success. Communications, travel and changes in regard to home and family can bring long term benefits for everyone involved.

With Venus: An old friend can be counted on for support in helping you achieve your ambitions. Relationships with parents, family and house guests are based on feelings of mutual responsibility. The outcome of public activities has its roots in your relationships closer to home.

With Mars: Your energy is controlled and concentrated successfully on a specific goal in coming months. You may undertake long term improvement projects in house or family. Go slow, and be certain of all your plans.

With Jupiter: Past restrictions are removed and you can move ahead more freely, if conservatively, in the future. You may make long term plans for security of your home and family. Home improvements, insurance or the security of children and heirs may be part of this.

With Saturn: Attention to strict realities and concentrated efforts bring lasting results in coming months. Affairs of parents, or the elderly and restricted members of the family may have to be dealt with now. Matters of retirement may be one focus of concern.

With Uranus: You resist changes whether they are detrimental or favorable in the next few months. Resistance, revolt or upsets in the home may weigh heavily on you. These may force added responsibilities on your shoulders.

With Neptune: A special dream can become a reality in the next few months. Grandparents, parents, or a more refined member of the family can be the means of special aid. You realize a particular desire.

With Pluto: You have the opportunity to fulfill an obligation resulting from past life experiences in coming months. Renovation and re-generation in family relationships, or the home environment bring lasting results for the benefit of all.

Carcer
In the 5th House
Alone, no planets: This influence maintains the staus quo, whether satisfactory or otherwise, for the next few months. Creativity, specula-tion, romance and the affairs of children require steady and certain application to maintain things.

With Sun: You are assured of success in your ambitions if you are patient and persistent in your efforts. Your restrained self-expression leads to long term benefits in romance, creativity and speculative matters.

With Moon: Organize and control your dealings with the public in a professional manner to achieve success. Deeper emotional ties with those you love will bring lasting pleasure and a sense of well-being.

With Mercury: Careful thought, planning and organized com-munications are necessary for success. Agreements with children, lovers or investment partners or agents need steady monitoring for success.

With Venus: An old friend can be counted on for support in helping you achieve your ambitions. You may meet a romantic partner through an old friend. Conserve your resources in speculative affairs.

With Mars: Your energy is controlled and concentrated successfully on a specific goal in coming months. Persistent application will finally bring positive results in a romantic interest, or a competitive venture.

With Jupiter: Past restrictions are removed and you can move ahead more freely, if conservatively, in the future. Your dedication to the one you love brings lasting joy. He or she will show appreciation far into the future.

With Saturn: Attention to strict realities and concentrated efforts bring lasting results in coming months. You may fall in love with someone older, or need to carry the responsibility in a personal relationship.

With Uranus: You resist changes whether they are detrimental or favorable in the next few months. Upsets in gambling, romance or creative ventures require a logical and emotionally reserved response.

With Neptune: A special dream can become a reality in the next few months. Someone you have been interested in for a long time may show signs of coming around. You may receive recognition for a creative production.

With Pluto: You have the opportunity to fulfill an obligation resulting from past life experiences in coming months. True love requires continual renewal. Etcrnal love is evidenced through mutual obligation.

Carcer
In the 6th House
Alone, no planets: This influence maintains the staus quo, whether satisfactory or otherwise, for the next few months. Dueties, work and health matters stabilize. Pay attention to the basics now.

With Sun: You are assured of success in your ambitions if you are patient and persistent in your efforts. Work and health have reached a temporary plateau. Maintenance is essential for long term benefit.

With Moon: Organize and control your dealings with the public in a professional manner to achieve success. You reach stable relationships with coworkers or business associates. Work in the home is favored.

With Mercury: Careful thought, planning and organized communications are necessary for success. Your analytical abilities, and your efficient working methods bring the results you are seeking at this time.

With Venus: An old friend can be counted on for support in helping you achieve your ambitions. Your income from work stabilizes, and you obtain better working conditions through the aid of an old friend.

With Mars: Your energy is controlled and concentrated successfully on a specific goal in coming months. Work requires greater effort and more serious responsibililty, but brings you to a higher level of respect among peers.

With Jupiter: Past restrictions are removed and you can move ahead more freely, if conservatively, in the future. Long term benefits come to health and work concerns. Benefits increase by taking more responsibility for yourself.

With Saturn: Attention to strict realities and concentrated efforts bring lasting results in coming months. Detailed and persistent analysis of work or health concerns may be necessary to obtain the improvements you seek.

With Uranus: You resist changes whether they are detrimental or favorable in the next few months. You may experience upsets in your workplace. Prevent accidents before they happen, and maintain your long term perspective in working relationships.

With Neptune: A special dream can become a reality in the next few months. Your long term efforts can finally pay off in your desire for improvement in health or work.

With Pluto: You have the opportunity to fulfill an obligation resulting from past life experiences in coming months. It may be your turn to aid someone in need. Honor your commitments to yourself and to others.

Carcer
In the 7th House
Alone, no planets: This influence maintains the staus quo, whether satisfactory or otherwise, for the next few months. Contracts, partnerships or marriage require responsible and consistent attention for long term stability.

With Sun: You are assured of success in your ambitions if you are patient and persistent in your efforts. Your efforts to bring balance to important relationships will show slow but steady progress.

With Moon: Organize and control your dealings with the public in a professional manner to achieve success. Maintaining a tried and true course in partnerships, marriage, or public affairs will bring the best results.

With Mercury: Careful thought, planning· and organized communications are necessary for success. Attention to the details of long term commitments or agreements is necessary to avoid future disagreements.

With Venus: An old friend can be counted on for support in helping you achieve your ambitions. A past partner may come to your aid, or a past opponent may come to his or her senses. Relationships stabilize as conflicts are resolved.

With Mars: Your energy is controlled and concentrated successfully on a specific goal in coming months. Your competitive efforts meet with success, and your efforts on behalf of partners solidify your bonds.

With Jupiter: Past restrictions are removed and you can move ahead more freely, if conservatively, in the future. You begin to obtain the benefits you hoped for from long term commitments and agreements.

With Saturn: Attention to strict realities and concentrated efforts bring lasting results in coming months. The practical realities of relationships requires you honor commitments of time and effort.

With Uranus: You resist changes whether they are detrimental or favorable in the next few months. A sudden split between you and another may not be due to any fault of your own. Accept what may have happened, and move on.

With Neptune: A special dream can become a reality in the next few months. Your efforts to gain the commitment of another may finally show results. It promises long term stability between both of you.

With Pluto: You have the opportunity to fulfill an obligation resulting from past life experiences in coming months. A contract or agreement may need to be renegotiated. Mutual benefit requires mutual aid.

Carcer
In the 8th House
Alone, no planets: This influence maintains the staus quo, whether satisfactory or otherwise, for the next few months. Resources received from others, sex, the occult or the mysteries behind matters require your deep and considered thought.

With Sun: You are assured of success in your ambitions if you are patient and persistent in your efforts. What is owed you, or what you have been seeking for a long time may finally arrive. You can discover the secrets behind intimate affairs.

With Moon: Organize and control your dealings with the public in a professional manner to achieve success. Your resources are regenerated, and occult or secret practices are intuitively used to benefit this renewal.

With Mercury: Careful thought, planning and organized com-munications are necessary for success. Contact and messages shared with another can lead to intellectual or commercial improvements.

With Venus: An old friend can be counted on for support in helping you achieve your ambitions. Your finances or most important resources benefit from the assistance and cooperation of a close partner.

With Mars: Your energy is controlled and concentrated successfully on a specific goal in coming months. High energy and intensity are applied to research, investigation or renewal of your most important partnerships, and what you can obtain from them.

With Jupiter: Past restrictions are removed and you can move ahead more freely, if conservatively, in the future. You attract the interest of generous and magnanimous benefactors. Gains may come from inheritance, or you obtain what is due you.

With Saturn: Attention to strict realities and concentrated efforts bring lasting results in coming months. You conserve and retain what you have. Future progress requires you investigate, and take the long term approach.

With Uranus: You resist changes whether they are detrimental or favorable in the next few months. Strange events impacting your resources, sexuality or occult studies may leave you uncertain. You may have to draw on past experience to see you through a period of change.

With Neptune: A special dream can become a reality in the next few months. Deep and secret desires can be fulfilled. These may relate to finances, sexuality or occult power.

With Pluto: You have the opportunity to fulfill an obligation resulting from past life experiences in coming months. Continued renewal of your deepest strengths requires that you make good on past commitments.

Carcer
In the 9th House
Alone, no planets: This influence maintains the staus quo, whether satisfactory or otherwise, for the next few months. Higher education, publishing, affairs at a distance and future plans require a stable and conservative approach.

With Sun: You are assured of success in your ambitions if you are patient and persistent in your efforts. You must take the lead in pursuit of your higher ideals and desires. Success is dependent on your good reputation and favorable publicity.

With Moon: Organize and control your dealings with the public in a professional manner to achieve success. Long term promotion and publicity efforts receive the public's approval.

With Mercury: Careful thought, planning and organized communications are necessary for success. Knowledge and understanding are essential to attaining your desires for future travel, promotion or achievement of future plans.

With Venus: An old friend can be counted on for support in helping you achieve your ambitions. Your ideals and plans for the future benefit from conservaitve and aesthetic partners, social contacts or artistic types that share your view of a more beautiful tomorrow.

With Mars: Your energy is controlled and concentrated successfully on a specific goal in coming months. Your emotional intensity in regard to matters of publicity, distant affairs or travel push you forward toward your goals and objectives.

With Jupiter: Past restrictions are removed and you can move ahead more freely, if conservatively, in the future. Carefully laid plans for the future can now be implemented. Take a reserved and cautious approach to publishing.

With Saturn: Attention to strict realities and concentrated efforts bring lasting results in coming months. Conservative and traditional institutions can benefit your long term goals and undertakings. Steady progress results from persistent application.

With Uranus: You resist changes whether they are detrimental or favorable in the next few months. Unexpected mishaps in travel, or affairs at a distance can upset your time schedule for important projects.

With Neptune: A special dream can become a reality in the next few months. Your highest ideals may be realized now. You may enter a university, take a foreign cruise or otherwise expand your perception of the world and reality.

With Pluto: You have the opportunity to fulfill an obligation resulting from past life experiences in coming months. You may contact someone in a foreign land, a religious leader or a professional. Achievement of your goals requires a broad perspective, and renewal of your philosophical ideals.

Carcer
In the 10th House
Alone, no planets: This influence maintains the staus quo, whether satisfactory or otherwise, for the next few months. Business, career and public recognition have reached a peak of attainment. Refrain from new initiatives, and concentrate on maintaining your position.

With Sun: You are assured of success in your ambitions if you are patient and persistent in your efforts. Powerful and important people have their eyes on you. A conservative approach to business assures honors and success.

With Moon: Organize and control your dealings with the public in a professional manner to achieve success. Public recognition and popularity in regard to career reach a stable plateau.

With Mercury: Careful thought, planning and organized communications are necessary for success. Success in commercial trade, communications and scientific fields. Logistics and timing are keys to productive accomplishment.

With Venus: An old friend can be counted on for support in helping you achieve your ambitions. Smooth flowing partnerships and relationships, and your general popularity among business associates bring solid gains.

With Mars: Your energy is controlled and concentrated successfully on a specific goal in coming months. Executive leadership and courage bring lasting gains in business or profession. You overcome the competition through daring and initiative.

With Jupiter: Past restrictions are removed and you can move ahead more freely, if conservatively, in the future. Long term expansion plans may now show some signs of progress. Government, institutions or professionals may be important to success.

With Saturn: Attention to strict realities and concentrated efforts bring lasting results in coming months. Take care of responsibilities and duties in business and career. Your long term success is dependent on your persistence and follow-through.

With Uranus: You resist changes whether they are detrimental or favorable in the next few months. Protect the most important foundations of business and career. Future changes may shake them.

With Neptune: A special dream can become a reality in the next few months. Your patient efforts will now see results in a long held dream of career or business achievement.

With Pluto: You have the opportunity to fulfill an obligation resulting from past life experiences in coming months. Debts, taxes or insurance matters may need attention at this time.

Carcer
In the 11th House
Alone, no planets: This influence maintains the staus quo, whether satisfactory or otherwise, for the next few months. Friends, social groups and your cooperative affairs reach a state of stability.

With Sun: You are assured of success in your ambitions if you are patient and persistent in your efforts. Take the responsibility in affairs to do with groups or friends. Your leadership keeps everyone moving in the right direction.

With Moon: Organize and control your dealings with the public in a professional manner to achieve success. Your popularity with friends and within groups is based on your solid and stable image.

With Mercury: Careful thought, planning and organized communications are necessary for success. Communications or trips with groups or friends promises a deepening of ties, and mutual respect.

With Venus: An old friend can be counted on for support in helping you achieve your ambitions. A social contact can be important to long term interests of security and achievement of life goals.

With Mars: Your energy is controlled and concentrated successfully on a specific goal in coming months. You can expend a great deal of energy in maintaining friendships, or in affairs to do with groups you belong to. Your efforts will be admired by your peers.

With Jupiter: Past restrictions are removed and you can move ahead more freely, if conservatively, in the future. Important and generous friends can aid your efforts at advancement. Social and professional contacts are important now.

With Saturn: Attention to strict realities and concentrated efforts bring lasting results in coming months. Conservative or elderly friends can be the means of advancement in a group you belong to.

With Uranus: You resist changes whether they are detrimental or favorable in the next few months. Sudden changes in the affairs of friends or groups may not please you now. Practice patience and calm, as you deal with the consequences.

With Neptune: A special dream can become a reality in the next few months. You may make a special friend that aids your long term interests, or be inducted into a group you have been trying to enter.

With Pluto: You have the opportunity to fulfill an obligation resulting from past life experiences in coming months. Lend a hand if the opportunity to aid an old friend arises.

Carcer
In the 12th House
Alone, no planets: This influence maintains the staus quo, whether satisfactory or otherwise, for the next few months. Secrets, enemies or an aspect of withdrawal can attend this influence. Maintaining your present position in life requires attention to duty, not escapism.

With Sun: You are assured of success in your ambitions if you are patient and persistent in your efforts. Success that comes slowly brings enduring results. Tap inner strengths to attain personal desires.

With Moon: Organize and control your dealings with the public in a professional manner to achieve success. Your labors in probate can bring lasting results in the field of career or public recognition.

With Mercury: Careful thought, planning and organized communications are necessary for success. Investigation and study of secret or occult matters are favored for resolution of long standing mysteries.

With Venus: An old friend can be counted on for support in helping you achieve your ambitions. Inner feelings can stabilize, and you can take the time to understand long term relationships. You achieve peace with yourself.

With Mars: Your energy is controlled and concentrated successfully on a specific goal in coming months. Dangerous duties may require your attention. You draw on inner courage in attaining your goals.

With Jupiter: Past restrictions are removed and you can move ahead more freely, if conservatively, in the future. You can lift yourself as high as your perspective and vision allow you to see. Outer realization begins with inner contemplation.

With Saturn: Attention to strict realities and concentrated efforts bring lasting results in coming months. Apply yourself to dealing with inner energies and private affairs. Time used for self improvement brings lasting results.

With Uranus: You resist changes whether they are detrimental or favorable in the next few months. Inner turmoil teaches you to take control of yourself, and not look to others as the cause of your present circumstances.

With Neptune: A special dream can become a reality in the next few months. A long sought for union of a spiritual or psychic nature can now be achieved.

With Pluto: You have the opportunity to fulfill an obligation resulting from past life experiences in coming months. Spiritual debts must be paid in order to maintain your level of development.

TRISTITIA

This adverse symbol is intensified by Saturn, Uranus, Neptune, Pluto and Mars; mitigated by Sun, Venus and Jupiter; and simply emphasized by the Moon and Mercury, which are neutral planets.

Tristitia is ruled by Saturn and associated with the sign Scorpio, an astral sign showing desire and other strong feelings, both positive and negative. Tristitia shows the negative side of Scorpio in emotinal terms—sorrow, jealousy, grief, envy, depression.

Tristitia in any chart indicates a point of negative emotions which may be caused by problems in areas of life relàted to the given house, or may create problems by limiting ability to make the most of opportunities offered by affairs of the house. Most of the feelings indicated by Tristitia are rather deep, and may require professional counseling to overcome. Inhibitions, fears and phobias, chronic emotional ailments of physical origin—all are indicated by Tristitia.

Tristitia
In the 1st House
Alone, no planets: This is an adverse influence that remains relatively unchanged in the next few months. Too many personal responsibilities, or problems in finding the right direction to your life, create depression. Make sure your physical health is up to par, then tackle your problems one at a time.

With Sun: You will rise above your sorrows through strength of will and confidence in the future. Another person may be assuming too much authority over your personal life—learn to draw the line tactfully, but firmly.

With Moon: Fleeting moods of depression can interfere with your relationships. Take care of your personal emotional needs. You may need to come to terms with the past, or be rid of negative subconscious motivations.

With Mercury: You spend too much time brooding about unfortunate situations over which you have little control. You cannot prevent others from gossiping about you. What has been said can be overcome through your personal actions from this point on.

With Venus: Friendly companions lift your spirits when life gets you down. Personal losses in finances, property or love can weigh you down. Seek friends, amusements and artistic expression to lift the discomfort.

With Mars: Make an effort to take up new activities to lift yourself out of a state of depression. Take the initiative, and work on the positive to overcome present difficulties.

With Jupiter: An end to a source of sorrow is in sight. Look forward to new successes in the near future. Place things in perspective, and you will see the good to be derived from present circumstances.

With Saturn: Your unhappiness is due to something that cannot be changed, so you must adapt your feelings. Time heals all wounds, and the cycle of life will once again lift you above your present problems. Make constructive plans for personal changes.

With Uranus: Disturbing and disruptive changes occur during the next few months. Check the details, monitor every activity, and protect yourself from accidents and unexpected upsets.

With Neptune: An undefined yearning leaves you unhappy and dissatisfied the next few months. Analyze circumstances, and deal with the concrete realities to be rid of present fears, phobias or unpleasant dreams and images.

With Pluto: The source of unhappiness is hidden in your inner self, or the result of forces from past lives. Regenerate psychic forces, and practice techniques of psychic self-healing to remove negative motivations and desire.

Tristitia
In the 2nd House
Alone, no planets: This is an adverse influence that remains relatively unchanged in the next few months. Financial concerns in regard to income, property or partners weigh you down. Analyze and organize to deal with present circumstances.

With Sun: You will rise above your sorrows through strength of will and confidence in the future. Take the lead in resolving present material difficulties. You will improve your resources as you improve your self-image.

With Moon: Fleeting moods of depression can interfere with your relationships. Clinging to the past, or refusing to let go, may be the source of present financial difficulties.

With Mercury: You spend too much time brooding about unfortunate situations over which you have little control. Come to grips with the realities of the material world, and you will be able to see your way clear from present difficulties.

With Venus: Friendly companions lift your spirits when life gets you down. Socialize, relax and evaluate, and you will achieve the balance and stability necessary to overcome present difficulties.

With Mars: Make an effort to take up new activities to lift yourself out of a state of depression. Work, construct and manufacture on the material plane to improve financial conditions that are holding you down.

With Jupiter: An end to a source of sorrow is in sight. Look forward to new successes in the near future. Your finances will eventually improve in a big way, but you must visualize before you can realize.

With Saturn: Your unhappiness is due to something that cannot be changed, so you must adapt your feelings. Long term commitments may be draining your financial or emotional resources. Analysis of how things got this way can help you change things for the better.

With Uranus: Disturbing and disruptive changes occur during the next few months. Protect property, finances and partnerships from accident, loss or disruptions.

With Neptune: An undefined yearning leaves you unhappy and dissatisfied the next few months. Things may not be as they seem in finances and property matters. Get the answers to elusive questions, to clear away present doubts.

With Pluto: The source of unhappiness is hidden in your inner self, or the result of forces from past lives. Your most important possession is yourself. Regenerate your inner resources, and your outer circumstances will improve.

Tristitia
In the 3rd House
Alone, no planets: This is an adverse influence that remains relatively unchanged in the next few months. You may experience frustration and difficulties in communications, studies, local travel or the affairs of relatives or neighbors.

With Sun: You will rise above your sorrows through strength of will and confidence in the future. Delays and frustration in communication or transportation must be overcome by force of will and personal initiative.

With Moon: Fleeting moods of depression can interfere with your relationships. A woman, child, or someone with which you are closely bonded may be the source of disappointment. Talk things out in a calm manner.

With Mercury: You spend too much time brooding about unfortunate situations over which you have little control. Hindered communications, or frustrating travels are contemporary obstacles. Practice patience and self control.

With Venus: Friendly companions lift your spirits when life gets you down. Maintain your balance if missed messages or delayed travels cost you time or money. Partners, agents and commercial transactions need to be watched.

With Mars: Make an effort to take up new activities to lift yourself out of a state of depression. You must take the initiative and work hard to keep communications and transportation on the right track.

With Jupiter: An end to a source of sorrow is in sight. Look forward to new successes in the near future. It is difficult to keep a philosophical perspective in the face of present difficulties. Resist expressing pessimistic thoughts.

With Saturn: Your unhappiness is due to something that cannot be changed, so you must adapt your feelings. You may experience morbid thoughts due to the words of a relative, neighbor or someone in your locale. You cannot change others, and must learn to accept their ways.

With Uranus: Disturbing and disruptive changes occur during the next few months. You may experience a total breakdown in communications, transportation or your rational and logical thought processes. Analyze and scrutinize important matters to catch the problems before they occur.

With Neptune: An undefined yearning leaves you unhappy and dissatisfied the next few months. Feelings of loss or limitation are tied to your locale, or to affairs of relatives or neighbors. Clear your thinking, and you will see the way out of your present mood.

With Pluto: The source of unhappiness is hidden in your inner self, or the result of forces from past lives. You may experience the destruction of outworn methods of thought, communication or transportation. This is a prelude to a powerful rebirth in the matter.

Tristitia
In the 4th House
Alone, no planets: This is an adverse influence that remains relatively unchanged in the next few months. Affairs related to the family, the home or the past may bring sadness, or frustrating and limiting circumstances.

With Sun: You will rise above your sorrows through strength of will and confidence in the future. The affairs of children or loved ones may be the source of present difficulties. Your dependability and leadership will improve the circumstances.

With Moon: Fleeting moods of depression can interfere with your relationships. Your mother, a woman or an infant may be the source of domestic problems. Take action to improve things, instead of dwelling on the negative.

With Mercury: You spend too much time brooding about unfortunate situations over which you have little control. Conversation within the family or home may be the source of pessimistic thoughts and feelings. Do something that is fun, to alleviate your blue mood.

With Venus: Friendly companions lift your spirits when life gets you down. Financial difficulties from the past, or from the affairs of family or home can be a problem. Do things with a partner to help your emotional balance.

With Mars: Make an effort to take up new activities to lift yourself out of a state of depression. Arguments or fights in the home, or with family members may be the source of present depression and frustration. Use your energies for constructive action, rather than destructive reaction.

With Jupiter: An end to a source of sorrow is in sight. Look forward to new successes in the near future. Excess or waste can be a difficulty in the home or family. Try to find some practical controls that everyone can agree to.

With Saturn: Your unhappiness is due to something that cannot be changed, so you must adapt your feelings. Signifies possible depression or withdrawal. Get out and participate, converse and socialize to relieve negative feelings

With Uranus: Disturbing and disruptive changes occur during the next few months. Protect your home and property from accident. Initiate changes after consulting everyone involved.

With Neptune: An undefined yearning leaves you unhappy and dissatisfied the next few months. Someone in your home or family may be deceiving you. Investigate to clear up any doubts you may have.

With Pluto: The source of unhappiness is hidden in your inner self, or the result of forces from past lives. Past habits may need to be altered in regard to family and home. Dig deep to discover the source of difficulties.

Tristitia
In the 5th House
Alone, no planets: This is an adverse influence that remains relatively unchanged in the next few months. You may experience frustration or sorrow in the affairs of children, lovers, creative projects or speculation.

With Sun: You will rise above your sorrows through strength of will and confidence in the future. Your efforts at romance, speculation or creativity may have met with disappointment. A fresh approach may be necessary.

With Moon: Fleeting moods of depression can interfere with your relationships. Difficulties with children, or in relationships may have caused your present emotional discomfort. Action is the antidote for depression.

With Mercury: You spend too much time brooding about unfortunate situations over which you have little control. Your thoughts may be scattered, or your feelings divided, in regard to romance, children or creative impulses.

With Venus: Friendly companions lift your spirits when life gets you down. Love or speculation may have led to recent losses. Try some pleasant diversions or amusements with congenial companions to lift negative feelings.

With Mars: Make an effort to take up new activities to lift yourself out of a state of depression. Speculation can bring losses, while romance may lead to arguments. Direct your energies in productive and non-threatening ways.

With Jupiter: An end to a source of sorrow is in sight. Look forward to new successes in the near future. Indiscriminate speculation or risk taking may lead to problems. Learn from the past, and prepare for a better future.

With Saturn: Your unhappiness is due to something that cannot be changed, so you must adapt your feelings. Delay, frustration and reversals can occur in speculation, romance or creative efforts. It is best to play the waiting game, as time will lift some difficulties.

With Uranus: Disturbing and disruptive changes occur during the next few months. An upset in speculation or romance may occur. Planning and foresight can prevent the worst.

With Neptune: An undefined yearning leaves you unhappy and dissatisfied the next few months. Cautions against illusion or self-deception in love, romance or the affairs of your children. Balance another's words with his or her actions.

With Pluto: The source of unhappiness is hidden in your inner self, or the result of forces from past lives. You may have been too trusting, or your motives sprang from negative desires. Inner renewal requires self-examination.

Tristitia
In the 6th House
Alone, no planets: This is an adverse influence that remains relatively unchanged in the next few months. Matters related to work or health can weigh you down, or result in frustration and delay. Try to rest and relax as much as possible.

With Sun: You will rise above your sorrows through strength of will and confidence in the future. Hard work may drain your energy, and bring on physical ills. Take measures to rest, relax and strengthen your body.

With Moon: Fleeting moods of depression can interfere with your relationships. Work in the home, or duties to family members, may be the source of sickness or lack of energy. Renew your strength through proper diet, and simple diversions.

With Mercury: You spend too much time brooding about unfortunate situations over which you have little control. Worry, anxiety or nervous disorders may be the result of ill health, or overwork. Try to get others to share your burdens.

With Venus: Friendly companions lift your spirits when life gets you down. Your lack of incentive, or loss of energy may be the result of hard work for little pay. The situation may be improved by the help of partners or coworkers.

With Mars: Make an effort to take up new activities to lift yourself out of a state of depression. Arguments or accidents are a potential on the job. Slow down, and you can be more productive with less effort.

With Jupiter: An end to a source of sorrow is in sight. Look forward to new successes in the near future. Work or health problems may be real, but a negative attitude will not cure them. Positive thoughts and feelings will bring positive results sooner.

With Saturn: Your unhappiness is due to something that cannot be changed, so you must adapt your feelings. Your responsibilities at work may seem overwhelming. Take care of your health first, as without it you have little.

With Uranus: Disturbing and disruptive changes occur during the next few months. Sudden upsets, or surprising changes can be a part of your present health or work scene. Turn to your stable friends to help you cope with present changes.

With Neptune: An undefined yearning leaves you unhappy and dissatisfied the next few months. Be cautious of chemicals and drugs in the workplace. There could be unseen forces working against you.

With Pluto: The source of unhappiness is hidden in your inner self, or the result of forces from past lives. You may have taken on too much work, or neglected your health. The cause resides within you, as well as the means of lifting present burdens.

Tristitia
In the 7th House

Alone, no planets: This is an adverse influence that remains relatively unchanged in the next few months. Difficulties, delays and restrictions in regard to partners, marriage or public activities are potential. Take action to resolve lingering problems.

With Sun: You will rise above your sorrows through strength of will and confidence in the future. Your personal involvement in the problems of partners can help you relieve your own difficulties.

With Moon: Fleeting moods of depression can interfere with your relationships. Lingering on the past, or maintaining over-dependent relationships can be a source of depression or sorrow. A break with the past may be called for.

With Mercury: You spend too much time brooding about unfortunate situations over which you have little control. The negative views of partners can be a part of your present pessimism. Maintaining your own optimism can work to everyone's benefit.

With Venus: Friendly companions lift your spirits when life gets you down. Joint spending can be the source of partnership disagreements. Bring in a mediator, if you cannot resolve the problem together.

With Mars: Make an effort to take up new activities to lift yourself out of a state of depression. Friction and tension in close partnerships can depress you. Trying something new together may lead to renewed closeness.

With Jupiter: An end to a source of sorrow is in sight. Look forward to new successes in the near future. Past difficulties in partnerships and relationships will soon fade. Stay on the bright side, and things will be that much better.

With Saturn: Your unhappiness is due to something that cannot be changed, so you must adapt your feelings. Delay, restriction or withdrawal on the part of a partner can be the source of present loneliness. You may turn to the social scene until this phase is over.

With Uranus: Disturbing and disruptive changes occur during the next few months. A sudden break with a partner or companion is possible. If you can possibly prevent it, you may try, but recognize you cannot totally control another.

With Neptune: An undefined yearning leaves you unhappy and dissatisfied the next few months. Deception, trickery or intoxication may be at the root of present problems in partnerships. You may have to force a confrontation to get to the truth.

With Pluto: The source of unhappiness is hidden in your inner self, or the result of forces from past lives. Your past actions have led partners or the public to perceive you in a certain way. If you do not like how you are being treated, recognize how you may have been treated.

Tristitia
In the 8th House
Alone, no planets: This is an adverse influence that remains relatively unchanged in the next few months. Joint financial affairs, inheritance, and matters of the occult can meet with delay, and result in depression or pessimism.

With Sun: You will rise above your sorrows through strength of will and confidence in the future. Your desires may be frustrated, and your purposes challenged, but you can overcome these through personal drive and leadership.

With Moon: Fleeting moods of depression can interfere with your relationships. Negative thoughts and feelings will drain your energy. Try to make emotional contact with someone who is stronger and able to encourage you.

With Mercury: You spend too much time brooding about unfortunate situations over which you have little control. Protect against lawsuits. Present frustrations require that you take the long term view.

With Venus: Friendly companions lift your spirits when life gets you down. Problems with money, property and joint financial affairs can be a point of conflict, and lead to depression. Temporary escape may be the solution, as tempers can cool down.

With Mars: Make an effort to take up new activities to lift yourself out of a state of depression. Your inner strength, or your personal resources can be depleted by frustrations in sex or finances. Step back, and discover how you can change things.

With Jupiter: An end to a source of sorrow is in sight. Look forward to new successes in the near future. Someone or something you were counting on may have let you down. Take heart, as you will recover far more than you previously hoped for.

With Saturn: Your unhappiness is due to something that cannot be changed, so you must adapt your feelings. Those in authority may be blocking your progress, and preventing you from obtaining your desires. Investigate, and you can find the means to cope with this.

With Uranus: Disturbing and disruptive changes occur during the next few months. Sudden reversals can affect your security. Protect your body, your property and your resources.

With Neptune: An undefined yearning leaves you unhappy and dissatisfied the next few months. Nightmares or frightening thoughts may plague you now. Examine your thoughts carefully, as they are the source of unfounded fear.

With Pluto: The source of unhappiness is hidden in your inner self, or the result of forces from past lives. Someone may change his or her mind, and cause you to lose something of value. Look inward to discover how you may regain what is rightfully yours.

Tristitia
In the 9th House
Alone, no planets: This is an adverse influence that remains relatively unchanged in the next few months. Higher education, distant travel or religious beliefs can lead to frustration, pessimism or depression.

With Sun: You will rise above your sorrows through strength of will and confidence in the future. Your image among professional associates may suffer. You can experience delay in travel, publishing or profession.

With Moon: Fleeting moods of depression can interfere with your relationships. Hard and restrictive limitations may be placed on you by the clergy or the courts. Losing a battle over right and wrong may be the source of present pessimism.

With Mercury: You spend too much time brooding about unfortunate situations over which you have little control. Long trips and affairs at a distance can be confused, delayed or otherwise frustrated. Check critical details to keep things operating.

With Venus: Friendly companions lift your spirits when life gets you down. Your highest thoughts and ideals can meet with opposition from partners, social contacts, bankers or the courts. Do not press your luck at this time.

With Mars: Make an effort to take up new activities to lift yourself out of a state of depression. Dangers abound in travel, and matters of speculation or risk. Conflicts can arise over religion or philosophy. Avoid friction if possible.

With Jupiter: An end to a source of sorrow is in sight. Look forward to new successes in the near future. Too much expansive enthusiasm may have led to restrictions being placed on your travels, education or legal rights. Setbacks are temporary, and you learn from the experience.

With Saturn: Your unhappiness is due to something that cannot be changed, so you must adapt your feelings. Your religious or philosophical perspective may meet with cold materialism on the part of others. Unfavorable for travel or legal actions in the courts.

With Uranus: Disturbing and disruptive changes occur during the next few months. All things at a distance are potential for upset, and your inner perspectives can completely change.

With Neptune: An undefined yearning leaves you unhappy and dissatisfied the next few months. You may experience deceptions or frauds from foreigners, clergy, lawyers or the courts. The truth will come to the light, so try to maintain your optimism.

With Pluto: The source of unhappiness is hidden in your inner self, or the result of forces from past lives. Plans for expansion or promotion may have met with setbacks. Review your plans, as the problem resides here, rather than in the outer world.

Tristitia
In the 10th House
Alone, no planets: This is an adverse influence that remains relatively unchanged in the next few months. Matters of career, profession and public standing meet with disappointment, setback or delay. Conserve and consolidate, but do not initiate.

With Sun: You will rise above your sorrows through strength of will and confidence in the future. Holding your position may require long hours, hard work and personal limitation. Executives or politicians may be a part of the problem.

With Moon: Fleeting moods of depression can interfere with your relationships. Your career image among the public may suffer. Difficulties with women, family or home may frustrate work and business.

With Mercury: You spend too much time brooding about unfortunate situations over which you have little control. Communications, transport or the affairs of agents and representatives can bring business setbacks. Check all critical details.

With Venus: Friendly companions lift your spirits when life gets you down. Cash flow can dry up, or commitments and agreements can depress finances. You may have to request aid from someone you socialize with, or a business partner.

With Mars: Make an effort to take up new activities to lift yourself out of a state of depression. Men and machinery can cause delays, frustrations and anger in business and profession. Apply your best diplomacy to resolve present difficulties.

With Jupiter: An end to a source of sorrow is in sight. Look forward to new successes in the near future. Expansion plans may have withered, and you face a period of financial decline and business retreat. You must learn to prevent similar problems in the future.

With Saturn: Your unhappiness is due to something that cannot be changed, so you must adapt your feelings. Your most important business and career foundations may be under extreme stress. There is only so much you can change, and the rest is up to fate.

With Uranus: Disturbing and disruptive changes occur during the next few months. Protect the most important areas of your business or profession. Sudden upsets, disturbances, accidents or revolts are possible.

With Neptune: An undefined yearning leaves you unhappy and dissatisfied the next few months. Cautions against deceptions in business. Do not let present difficulties weigh down your psychic and spiritual energies.

With Pluto: The source of unhappiness is hidden in your inner self, or the result of forces from past lives. Difficulties from past debts may weigh heavily on your business endeavors. Restoration and renewal are the keys to relieving the pressure.

Tristitia
In the 11th House
Alone, no planets: This is an adverse influence that remains relatively unchanged in the next few months. Your hopes may be stifled, and friends are a depressing or pessimistic influence on you. Try something that is pure fun to lift your spirits.

With Sun: You will rise above your sorrows through strength of will and confidence in the future. Your larger dreams and hopes can meet with resistance, friction or opposition. You must rely on personal strengths.

With Moon: Fleeting moods of depression can interfere with your relationships. Family life can be depressing, or past attachments can bring concern and sorrow. Do what you can, then turn to other matters.

With Mercury: You spend too much time brooding about unfortunate situations over which you have little control. Intellectual and literary matters are frustrated, and communications or transport can be delayed. Retain your perspective on the total situation.

With Venus: Friendly companions lift your spirits when life gets you down. Affectional ties, or social life and partners can present depressing circumstances. Maintain your stability in trying and frustrating situations.

With Mars: Make an effort to take up new activities to lift yourself out of a state of depression. If a woman, the men in your life may prove old fashioned or obstinate. If a man, you may face conflict with friends.

With Jupiter: An end to a source of sorrow is in sight. Look forward to new successes in the near future. Social gatherings, or activities to do with sports, religious or professional groups can be unfortunate. Friends dampen your enthusiasm.

With Saturn: Your unhappiness is due to something that cannot be changed, so you must adapt your feelings. You may feel shy and retiring among friends, or friends are negative and pessimistic now. Being your own best friend may be the only alternative now.

With Uranus: Disturbing and disruptive changes occur during the next few months. A sudden break with a group or friend may leave you frustrated or shocked. Think things through, and you may be able to repair the break later.

With Neptune: An undefined yearning leaves you unhappy and dissatisfied the next few months. Psychic and spiritual forces around friends or social groups may be depressing, or even oppressive. Fall back on logic and reason if your feelings become too inhibited.

With Pluto: The source of unhappiness is hidden in your inner self, or the result of forces from past lives. Disintegration of group ties or friendships may be the necessary prelude to more uplifting companions. You have the final word on who your companions are.

Tristitia
In the 12th House
Alone, no planets: This is an adverse influence that remains relatively unchanged in the next few months. You may arouse someone's enmity. You can be your own worst enemy, and may face a period of withdrawal or restriction.

With Sun: You will rise above your sorrows through strength of will and confidence in the future. Someone in authority may secretly oppose you. You can draw on personal courage to counter attempts to hold you down.

With Moon: Fleeting moods of depression can interfere with your relationships. Your subconscious feelings may have led you to present circumstances of limitation and withdrawal. You may have to resurrect and eliminate these from your memory.

With Mercury: You spend too much time brooding about unfortunate situations over which you have little control. Someone's communication may be continually replayed in your mind. Clear and concise reasoning is essential now.

With Venus: Friendly companions lift your spirits when life gets you down. The sorrow of one you love, or the restrictions they face, may weigh heavily on your emotions. You may need to consult someone to lift the present cloud over your feelings.

With Mars: Make an effort to take up new activities to lift yourself out of a state of depression. Beware of a personal attack from a secret or uncertain source. You may have to seek aid or asylum from a source more powerful than your enemies.

With Jupiter: An end to a source of sorrow is in sight. Look forward to new successes in the near future. You may face persecution for your religious beliefs, or face legal difficulty. You may obtain aid from a professional organization or a religious order.

With Saturn: Your unhappiness is due to something that cannot be changed, so you must adapt your feelings. You may encounter enforced restriction, or feel you must seclude yourself to cope with present difficulties. Maintain important contacts.

With Uranus: Disturbing and disruptive changes occur during the next few months. Your inner creative resources may be sapped by uncontrollable events. Maintain your self-confidence through upsets and disruptions.

With Neptune: An undefined yearning leaves you unhappy and dissatisfied the next few months. You may be falsely accused, or be the target of deception and fraud. A time to think straight, and question what others say.

With Pluto: The source of unhappiness is hidden in your inner self, or the result of forces from past lives. Suspicions run deep. Do not succumb to criminal or terrorist activity.

CAPUT DRACONIS

This symbol is essentially favorable with all of the planets, regardless of their aspects.

Caput Daraconis is the Moon's North Node and is associated with the sign Virgo, ruled by Mercury. The North Node represents the upper or spiritual kingdom, new spiritual beginnings, karmic benefits due to the person from past lives. It is a point of beneficence and fortune in astrology, and similarly in geomancy. The Head of the Dragon represents spiritual forces operating to the benefit of the querent.

Caput Draconis in a chart is always a point of benefits received through fortunate circumstances, beneficial deeds, and repayment of debts owed to you. Essentially the fates are in favor of the querent.

Caput Draconis
In the 1st House
Alone, no planets: This is a favorable influence that remains in effect for the next few months. Time to start all those optimistic new personal projects you have in mind. Reach out to meet new people, and you will benefit both spiritually and emotionally from the new horizons opening up to you.

With Sun: You find new purpose in life and the energy to pursue that purpose in coming months. Creative self-expression and opportunities to display your leadership abilities are favored.

With Moon: You gain new inspiration and support from your contacts with the public in coming months. Contacts with women and children are especially important. Whether it is your mother, daughter, sister or favorite aunt, you will gain both tangible and spiritual support.

With Mercury: New ideas inspire you to greater mental activity and interest in learning in coming months. Spend time with people who can teach you something or help you work out creative ideas. You may receive a significant personal spiritual message.

With Venus: You receive affection and approval from sources who lift your spirits in coming months. You attract affection and cooperation on both the material and spiritual planes. Carry out a daring artistic concept.

With Mars: You have an abundance of spiritual energy at your disposal. Study martial arts for spiritual discipline as well as the physical benefits. Begin a pioneering personal project with courage and daring now.

With Jupiter: Spiritual blessings in abundance are showered on you in coming months. You may have a spiritual message to share with others. Keep your mind on noble objectives and you will achieve both material and spiritual success.

With Saturn: Your sense of responsibility and devotion to duty bring long-deserved rewards in coming months. Mastery of self and circumstances opens new doors to spiritual and material success. Persistence pays off.

With Uranus: Many beneficial changes are going on in your life in the next few months. A spiritual revelation may change the course of your life. Do not hestiate to follow this vision of future fulfillment.

With Neptune: Spiritual messages inspire you in coming months. Your creative imagination is stimulated to achieve artistic success. A good time to attune your psychic self with higher spiritual sources.

With Pluto: You have the spiritual strength, energy and positivism to achieve your goals in coming months. You are filled with creative spiritual energy. You feel completely rejuvenated and dynamic. Unseen forces operate to place you on the pathway to personal success.

Caput Draconis
In the 2nd House
Alone, no planets: This is a favorable influence that remains in effect for the next few months. Excellent for starting new moneymaking projects, resurrecting forgotten resources and skills you can use again, and acquiring new possessions of lasting value.

With Sun: You find new purpose in life and the energy to pursue that purpose in coming months. Your self-confidence and aura of authority favor profits from managerial work and public political position. Investments in gold and fine jewelry are favored.

With Moon: You gain new inspiration and support from your contacts with the public in coming months. Work with public benefit groups and children's welfare organizations can be a good source of spiritual satisfaction as well as a good income.

With Mercury: New ideas inspire you to greater mental activity and interest in learning in coming months. Advertising, promotional and sales work for products that stimulate physical and spiritual well-being is highly favored. You need to believe in what you do for an income.

With Venus: You receive affection and approval from sources who lift your spirits in coming months. Start a decorating or beauty business, work in fine clothing and jewelry, or social welfare and cultural work, all are favored as good sources of income.

With Mars: You have an abundance of spiritual energy at your disposal. You enjoy working for a good cause that also provides a good income. Police, investigative and protective occupations are favored.

With Jupiter: Spiritual blessings in abundance are showered on you in coming months. Excellent for profits from publishing, especially a first effort, and the travel industry. Investments yield good early returns.

With Saturn: Your sense of responsibility and devotion to duty bring long-deserved rewards in coming months. Your experience and ability to organize efficiently bring profits in industry and government, particularly in conservation and budget control.

With Uranus: Many beneficial changes are going on in your life in the next few months. Original moneymaking ideas or an invention could be your key to financial success. Produce and sell the item yourself if necessary.

With Neptune: Spiritual messages inspire you in coming months.

Any work in healing, physical or spiritual, brings in a good and well-deserved income. You may also work in social welfare projects.

With Pluto: You have the spiritual strength, energy and positivism to achieve your goals in coming months. An occult or psychic profession may be the source of a good income and help you improve society as well.

Caput Draconis
In the 3rd House
Alone, no planets: This is a favorable influence that remains in effect for the next few months. Visit with people who inspire you to higher ambitions and lofty goals. Self-improvement books and lectures encourage you to make the most of each day and improve relations with those around you.

With Sun: You find new purpose in life and the energy to pursue that purpose in coming months. Neighbors and relatives seek you out for sound advice and moral support. You may be elected to a position of leadership in your community.

With Moon: You gain new inspiration and support from your contacts with the public in coming months. You are adept at instructing and reasoning with young children. Spend time with a local children's group in your community. Group tours can entertain and enlighten you.

With Mercury: New ideas inspire you to greater mental activity and interest in learning in coming months. Visit museum exhibits and explore other educational opportunities in your locale. You would enjoy a discussion group on a favored subject. Local travel is highly favored.

With Venus: You receive affection and approval from sources who lift your spirits in coming months. Excellent for pleasure trips. Start an art course, take tours of beauty spots, and enjoy the harmony of nature and human artifacts.

With Mars: You have an abundance of spiritual energy at your disposal. Excellent for indulging the desire to explore new places, develop special physical skills, and participate in local community action groups.

With Jupiter: Spiritual blessings in abundance are showered on you in coming months. Heal any disputes with neighbors and relatives, join a fraternal social group, and share congenial entertainment and charitable efforts.

With Saturn: Your sense of responsibility and devotion to duty bring long-deserved rewards in coming months. Visit with older friends and relatives. You accomplish a lot, as your well-organized daily routine runs without a hitch now.

With Uranus: Many beneficial changes are going on in your life in the next few months. You enjoy the new ideas, places and faces of the moment, as you are on the go on impulse now. Modern conveniences and forms of entertainment are both appealing and enlightening.

With Neptune: Spiritual messages inspire you in coming months. Start a course on psychic and spiritual development. You have many opportunities to practice your skills on neighbors and relatives.

With Pluto: You have the spiritual strength, energy and positivism to achieve your goals in coming months. Occult books or contact with a professional psychic can prove enlightening. Worries and doubts fade, and you approach your daily activities with a new attitude of positive constructiveness.

Caput Draconis
In the 4th House
Alone, no planets: This is a favorable influence that remains in effect for the next few months. A powerful sense of family solidarity and shared goals strengthens you now. You may profit from real estate investments, mining and agriculture.

With Sun: You find new purpose in life and the energy to pursue that purpose in coming months. You are the source of strength and security to family members. You prosper through managing real estate and mining ventures, and through housing construction.

With Moon: You gain new inspiration and support from your contacts with the public in coming months. Your mother is of special importance to you now, a source of strength and support. A good time to entertain at home.

With Mercury: New ideas inspire you to greater mental activity and interest in learning in coming months. Brothers and sisters are helpful in promoting both family and your own interests now. Family discussions produce fruitful ideas.

With Venus: You receive affection and approval from sources who lift your spirits in coming months. Make an effort to create a harmonious and comfortable atmosphere in your home for all family members. Interior decorating is favored.

With Mars: You have an abundance of spiritual energy at your disposal. Shared family activities release any tensions and create a positive, dynamic family relationship. A good time to make needed home repairs or undertake a move to a new locale.

With Jupiter: Spiritual blessings in abundance are showered on you in coming months. You may inherit a home or other property from a parent. Excellent for investments in agriculture, mining and real estate.

With Saturn: Your sense of responsibility and devotion to duty bring long-deserved rewards in coming months. You learn much from older family members; be sure to include them in family plans and activities.

With Uranus: Many beneficial changes are going on in your life in the next few months. An opportunity to move to a more desirable or convenient home should be grasped immediately. Strive for greater freedom and flexibility in family plans.

With Neptune: Spiritual messages inspire you in coming months.

Avoid ancestor worship, but do look back on your heritage for spiritual values and talents that may resurface in your own nature.

With Pluto: You have the spiritual strength, energy and positivism to achieve your goals in coming months. A rejuvenated family solidarity, sharing and cooperation in the home can boost the spirits and material status for all family members.

Caput Draconis
In the 5th House
Alone, no planets: This is a favorable influence that remains in effect for the next few months. You are lucky and fortunate in love, successful in carrying out creative inspirations, and satisfied with the progress of your children. You may reap karmic benefits by winning at gambling.

With Sun: You find new purpose in life and the energy to pursue that purpose in coming months. Your road to love is smooth and promising; your children give you a sense of spiritual uplift; and you can express your creative impulses successfully.

With Moon: You gain new inspiration and support from your contacts with the public in coming months. Your children are particularly important to your sense of well-being and success. You rejoice in their triumphs, romances, creative efforts as the maturation of your own desires.

With Mercury: New ideas inspire you to greater mental activity and interest in learning in coming months. Concentrate on creative self-expression, for you have a pipeline to higher sources of inspiration.

With Venus: You receive affection and approval from sources who lift your spirits in coming months. Love is an uplifting force in your life. Children are a source of pride and inspiration. Excellent for success in the art and music worlds.

With Mars: You have an abundance of spiritual energy at your disposal. Excellent for success in sporting and other competitions, investments which also require your skills and labor. Your love life is happily active.

With Jupiter: Spiritual blessings in abundance are showered on you in coming months. Highly favorable for luck in gambling and speculation, and karmic blessings in love. You may have a child soon.

With Saturn: Your sense of responsibility and devotion to duty bring long-deserved rewards in coming months. Secure investments in long-term industries and property are favored. Children are also a source of security and pride. Excellent for completing a long-term creative project.

With Uranus: Many beneficial changes are going on in your life in the next few months. Original creative inspirations lead to unexpected but deserved success. You may be lucky in games of chance. Share your windfall with loved ones.

With Neptune: Spiritual messages inspire you in coming months. The art and music give you special consolation; your creative impulses are imaginative and inspired. Romance is in the air; enjoy it. You may be lucky in a lottery or sweepstakes, or betting on the horses.

With Pluto: You have the spiritual strength, energy and positivism to achieve your goals in coming months. You may be lucky in a lottery or sweepstakes. Investments in cooperative ventures are favored. All the world loves a lover, and you feel loved.

Caput Draconis
In the 6th House
Alone, no planets: This is a favorable influence that remains in effect for the next few months. Your health is excellent, your energy level high, your efforts well-controlled, and your success on the job assured.

With Sun: You find new purpose in life and the energy to pursue that purpose in coming months. Seek advancement on the job, especially to managerial and creative activities. Your abundant self-confidence inspires coworkers.

With Moon: You gain new inspiration and support from your contacts with the public in coming months. Seek jobs with public action, or involving work with women and children. This is a period of changing job demands and interests.

With Mercury: New ideas inspire you to greater mental activity and interest in learning in coming months. Seek work that takes advantage of your mental skills and accuracy with details. Your communicative abilities are excellent, and may pave the way to advancement.

With Venus: You receive affection and approval from sources who lift your spirits in coming months. Work in social welfare, counseling, the arts, and beauty is favored. You have a special knack for getting your coworkers to cooperate to achieve success.

With Mars: You have an abundance of spiritual energy at your disposal. Excellent for work in technical and skilled fields, where physical flexibility and strength are required. You are also daring in your choice of jobs, but protected by higher powers.

With Jupiter: Spiritual blessings in abundance are showered on you in coming months. Your health is excellent. You may find your job expanding in scope, and your income improving as a result.

With Saturn: Your sense of responsibility and devotion to duty bring long-deserved rewards in coming months. Seek advancement to a managerial position, or a secure government job where your skills can deal with long-range projects. Your health and endurance are excellent.

With Uranus: Many beneficial changes are going on in your life in the next few months. This is the ideal time to grasp new career opportunities, and to change your line of work, as you will find new openings abound, and satisfactions increase.

With Neptune: Spiritual messages inspire you in coming months. A good time to launch a professional career in the psychic arts and sciences. Your health is good, and you have healing abilities that could help others.

With Pluto: You have the spiritual strength, energy and positivism to achieve your goals in coming months. Excellent for making the transition to a new line of work, or dealing with unions and other groups associated with your job. Your recuperative abilities are excellent.

Caput Draconis
In the 7th House
Alone, no planets: This is a favorable influence that remains in effect for the next few months. Ideal for a marriage of spirit as well as body. Form business partnerships with social values embodied in your enterprise. Excellent for settling any legal disputes.

With Sun: You find new purpose in life and the energy to pursue that purpose in coming months. You draw others to you with your courage, strength of will and strong purposes. Excellent for managing a business partnership. You are the dominant spiritual and driving force in marriage.

With Moon: You gain new inspiration and support from your contacts with the public in coming months. You receive much attention and enjoy the limelight when you marry. Excellent for advertising a business partnership. Legal disputes can be settled easily, as they are minor.

With Mercury: New ideas inspire you to greater mental activity and interest in learning in coming months. Excellent for signing legal agreements, discussing partnership ventures, and announcing a forthcoming marriage. You achieve excellent mental rapport with your spouse or loved one.

With Venus: You receive affection and approval from sources who lift your spirits in coming months. You have or will have a harmonious and cooperative marriage. Business partnerships give you emotional as well as financial security. Settle legal disputes in your favor now.

With Mars: You have an abundance of spiritual energy at your disposal. Initiatives in marriage and partnership are rewarded. You also succeed in competition for prizes, but should avoid legal disputes.

With Jupiter: Spiritual blessings in abundance are showered on you in coming months. You may marry wealth, or find spiritual bliss in marriage. You are successful in any legal disputes, and in competition.

With Saturn: Your sense of responsibility and devotion to duty bring long-deserved rewards in coming months. Your marriage or close relationship is secure and dependable, and business flourishes when you put your shrewdness and persistence to work. Legal disputes are lengthy, but end in your favor.

With Uranus: Many beneficial changes are going on in your life in the next few months. A sudden romance that leads to elopement turns out quite well and achieves permanence. You should avoid legal disputes, as facts come to light suddenly which could upset your cause. Similarly, put partnership ventures on hold.

With Neptune: Spiritual messages inspire you in coming months. Mutual sympathy and understanding are the basis for a strong and lasting marriage. Be cautious in partnerships, as you tend to judge by feelings rather than facts. Avoid legal disputes.

With Pluto: You have the spiritual strength, energy and positivism to achieve your goals in coming months. Your marriage is a strengthening factor in your entire life. You prefer to settle legal disputes out of court. Partnership ventures in business are highly favored.

Caput Draconis
In the 8th House
Alone, no planets: This is a favorable influence that remains in effect for the next few months. Sexual rapport is based on spiritual harmony. Occult studies are rewarded with spiritual progress. Excellent for joint financial ventures, as opportunities abound.

With Sun: You find new purpose in life and the energy to pursue that purpose in coming months. You can develop self-mastery and spiritual power for constructive purposes through occult studies. Your sexual energies are directed at someone special, and never falter. Take charge of joint financial ventures.

With Moon: You gain new inspiration and support from your contacts with the public in coming months. Excellent for developing psychic talents and practicing divination, particularly with cards. Short-term joint ventures are most profitable. You can create a romantic aura with a loved one, but your moods change swiftly.

With Mercury: New ideas inspire you to greater mental activity and interest in learning in coming months. Excellent for all studies and practices in occult subjects. You achieve true mental rapport with an intimate. Use your ideas for joint profitmaking ventures.

With Venus: You receive affection and approval from sources who lift your spirits in coming months. You can achieve true sexual rapport with someone special now. Excellent for artistic work on occult subjects. Joint ventures are profitable.

With Mars: You have an abundance of spiritual energy at your disposal. Your sexual energies can be released happily with an intimate, or directed into spiritual attainments through occult studies. Take the initiative in joint financial ventures.

With Jupiter: Spiritual blessings in abundance are showered on you in coming months. You succeed beyond your expectations in joint financial ventures. You may achieve a high level of skill and attainment in occult studies. Relations with the opposite sex are friendly and helpful.

With Saturn: Your sense of responsibility and devotion to duty bring long-deserved rewards in coming months. You achieve excellent results through the practice of high magic. You are attracted to and happiest with older members of the opposite sex. A long-term joint financial venture finally will start to pay off.

With Uranus: Many beneficial changes are going on in your life in the next few months. A sudden mutual attraction could spell bliss with an intimate. Develop your clairvoyant psychic abilities now; you may have some helpful visions of the future. Avoid joint ventures now, as results are too variable.

With Neptune: Spiritual messages inspire you in coming months.

You can develop your mediumistic and other psychic abilities to a point of excellence now. An exalting, romantic love affair has you in the clouds. Avoid get-rich-quick schemes.

With Pluto: You have the spiritual strength, energy and positivism to achieve your goals in coming months. You profit extensively from any cooperative financial ventures. You succeed beyond expectation in all occult studies, particularly healing. You also achieve rapport with an intimate, who may be your soul mate.

Caput Draconis
In the 9th House
Alone, no planets: This is a favorable influence that remains in effect for the next few months. You are attracted to exactly the studies in which you can make best progresss, for yourself and society. An excellent time to travel and make valuable contacts with those from other cultures.

With Sun: You find new purpose in life and the energy to pursue that purpose in coming months. Your strong sense of immortality turns your efforts to studies that will promote the harmony and happiness of all humankind. Excellent for travel to improve health and gain recognition abroad.

With Moon: You gain new inspiration and support from your contacts with the public in coming months. Excellent for publicity trips to promote your ideas, publications or products. Studies in public relations, advertising, sales and psychology are highly favored.

With Mercury: New ideas inspire you to greater mental activity and interest in learning in coming months. Any subject is grist for your mill and satisfies your thirst for general knowledge. Languages are especially favored if you plan any long-distance trips abroad.

With Venus: You receive affection and approval from sources who lift your spirits in coming months. Excellent for studies in the arts, music, culture, accounting, architecture, and landscaping, as well as any subject that appeals to you emotionally. Travel for pleasure is highly favored.

With Mars: You have an abundance of spiritual energy at your disposal. Travels for exploration and examination of new developments are highly favored. Excellent for technical, engineering, and metallurgical studies, as well as martial arts.

With Jupiter: Spiritual blessings in abundance are showered on you in coming months. Excellent for medical, philosophical and religious studies, and travels to promote philanthropic purposes, such as economic or spiritual development.

With Saturn: Your sense of responsibility and devotion to duty bring long-deserved rewards in coming months. Excellent for government and business travel, and for studies in history, antiques, government, politics, and business management.

With Uranus: Many beneficial changes are going on in your life in the next few months. Excellent for scientific and social studies, astrology, astronomy, and new age self-development techniques. Excellent for travel to developing countries.

With Neptune: Spiritual messages inspire you in coming months. Excellent for sea voyages and retreats for spiritual development and physical healing. Studies in psychic sciences, art, music, mathematics, are highly favored.

With Pluto: You have the spiritual strength, energy and positivism to achieve your goals in coming months. Excellent for studies in group psychology, religious cults, and occult arts. Travel for physical and spiritual rejuvenation, and to visit sites of ancient cultures, is highly favored.

Caput Draconis
In the 10th House
Alone, no planets: This is a favorable influence that remains in effect for the next few months. Excellent for starting a business of your own, entering a new line of work, and seeking advancement on the job. Your interest in public affairs may lead to public office.

With Sun: You find new purpose in life and the energy to pursue that purpose in coming months. Excellent for seeking election to a public office, or advancement to management. You may receive a public award or benefits on the job.

With Moon: You gain new inspiration and support from your contacts with the public in coming months. Excellent for seeking public support for a cause or your business; also for election to local public office. Any sales or advertising work is also highly favored.

With Mercury: New ideas inspire you to greater mental activity and interest in learning in coming months. Excellent for promoting educational causes or products, or communication and transportation equipment. You may be chosen spokesperson for a public action group.

With Venus: You receive affection and approval from sources who lift your spirits in coming months. Excellent for organizing and attending public social events to support good causes, such as charities; you may also receive recognition for work in the arts and culture.

With Mars: You have an abundance of spiritual energy at your disposal. A good time to compete for advancement on the job, or start a business of your own, particularly in a technical or repair area. Your leadership abilities are appreciated in public affairs.

With Jupiter: Spiritual blessings in abundance are showered on you in coming months. Excellent for starting or expanding a business of your own, or work in publishing or the travel and communications industries. You are assured the support and approval of superiors on the job.

With Saturn: Your sense of responsibility and devotion to duty bring long-deserved rewards in coming months. Excellent for advancement in government and industry, and for any managerial work. You may be honored for your long service to the community.

With Uranus: Many beneficial changes are going on in your life in the next few months. Excellent for starting a free-lance job or business of your own, as an astrologer, counselor, or consultant in a scientific or technical field. You may leap to public prominence supporting an issue of freedom or individual conscience.

With Neptune: Spiritual messages inspire you in coming months. Success in a psychic profession is indicated. You may also be recognized for your artistic, musical or mathematical abilities, and be prominent in supporting charitable causes.

With Pluto: You have the spiritual strength, energy and positivism to achieve your goals in coming months. Excellent for a business in the renovation or salvage business, or for professional work in psychology and union activities. You attain public prominence in supporting ecology and renewal causes.

Caput Draconis
In the 11th House
Alone, no planets: This is a favorable influence that remains in effect for the next few months. You will meet new friends who share your ideas and interest, and bring more peace and harmony into your social relationships. Join educational, inspirational and socially constructive groups.

With Sun: You find new purpose in life and the energy to pursue that purpose in coming months. You can form a positive social action group, as you have the knowledge and leadership ability to bring success to your cause. Others may elect you to group office.

With Moon: You gain new inspiration and support from your contacts with the public in coming months. Excellent for taking group ideas to the public, in lectures and personal contacts. Women are especially helpful to you now.

With Mercury: New ideas inspire you to greater mental activity and interest in learning in coming months. Excellent for starting a travel or study group, and promoting your ideas through mailings and lectures. You meet your intellectual match among new friends.

With Venus: You receive affection and approval from sources who lift your spirits in coming months. An excellent time to join or organize purely social groups, or specialized interests in the arts, music and social reform, or physical improvement and beauty.

With Mars: You have an abundance of spiritual energy at your disposal. Excellent for joining or starting a physical exercise or sports group, possibly a team of bowlers. You excel at finding new activities for friends to share.

With Jupiter: Spiritual blessings in abundance are showered on you in coming months. Excellent for forming group tours or study groups, religious discussion groups, and social action and philanthropic groups. You are especially effective with young people.

With Saturn: Your sense of responsibility and devotion to duty bring long-deserved rewards in coming months. You are especially effective in political action groups, particularly the traditional political parties. You are sought after to organize campaigns for charities and other groups. Old friends are most supportive now.

With Uranus: Many beneficial changes are going on in your life in the next few months. Excellent for starting an astrology or scientific group, becoming involved in social counseling, and making new friends independently, on your own.

With Neptune: Spiritual messages inspire you in coming months. Excellent for metaphysical groups, religious discussions, a travel group, or a dramatic club. Your imagination produces delightful activities for friends to share.

With Pluto: You have the spiritual strength, energy and positivism to achieve your goals in coming months. A spiritual revival group, an occult fraternity, or an ecology group would appeal to you now. You will meet among new friends, people you knew in past lives.

Caput Draconis
In the 12th House
Alone, no planets: This is a favorable influence that remains in effect for the next few months. Healing starts with a positive attitude and

spiritual aid, and proceeds with the best in physical medical techniques. A good time to care for teeth and any chronic ailments.

With Sun: You find new purpose in life and the energy to pursue that purpose in coming months. You can build up your natural good vitality for extra efforts. You have no secret enemies, and a positive attitude toward yourself and life.

With Moon: You gain new inspiration and support from your contacts with the public in coming months. You may have intuitive dreams that point out the best course for you to follow in dealing with inner problems and ailments.

With Mercury: New ideas inspire you to greater mental activity and interest in learning in coming months. Excellent for analyzing your inner problems and finding the right remedies. You may receive the solutions to problems in dreams.

With Venus: You receive affection and approval from sources who lift your spirits in coming months. Pleasurable dreams and harmonious solitude take you out of the mainstream, but your affections are still with loved ones elsewhere. Good for improving your appearance through development of a positive attitude.

With Mars: You have an abundance of spiritual energy at your disposal. You can resolve inner tensions and frustration through meditation and direction of energies into spiritual and magical attainment. Your health is excellent.

With Jupiter: Spiritual blessings in abundance are showered on you in coming months. You may have prophetic dreams that reflect a very optimistic philosophy of life. Meditation, health care for chronic ailments, and the practice of healing are favored.

With Saturn: Your sense of responsibility and devotion to duty bring long-deserved rewards in coming months. Attend to dental needs and build up your endurance. You enjoy meditating slowly and having the time to examine subjects of interest thoroughly. Good for examining past life experiences for valuable insights.

With Uranus: Many beneficial changes are going on in your life in the next few months. You may have clairvoyant visions of the future and should develop techniques to bring this talent under conscious control. Good for relaxing the nerves and strengthening control of them.

With Neptune: Spiritual messages inspire you in coming months. You may have visions of the future or attune yourself with spiritual messengers in dreams or meditation. Good for spiritual healing.

With Pluto: You have the spiritual strength, energy and positivism to achieve your goals in coming months. You have excellent recuperative abilities, and are charged with energies to heal others, both physically and spiritually, through the release of past-life traumas.

CAUDA DRACONIS

This adverse symbol is intensified by Saturn, Uranus, Neptune, Pluto and Mars; mitigated by Sun, Venus and Jupiter; and simply emphasized by the Moon and Mercury, which are neutral planets.

Cauda Draconis is the Moon's South Node and is associated with the sign Sagittarius, ruled by Jupiter. The South Node, and similarly Cauda Draconis in geomancy, is a point of spiritual losses and karmic debts coming due from negative behavior in past lifetimes. The Tail of the Dragon represents adverse forces, mainly spiritual and emotional, operating against the querent.

Cauda Draconis in a chart always indicates the misfortunes of circumstances or inner bad habits and unfortunate desires. It is a point of payment for past benefits, of debts coming due, of testing spiritually and materially.

Cauda Draconis
In the 1st House
Alone, no planets: This is an adverse influence that remains relatively unchanged in the next few months. Lack of purpose, limited sense of self-worth, and the nagging or boasting of others you meet can sap your energy and ability to start new projects. Work to develop a positive self-image.

With Sun: Egotism, touchy sensitivity, dictatorial attitudes and self-centered behavior are self-defeating obstacles to attainment of your goals. An authority figure in your life can make things difficult; you have difficulties dealing with the demands made on you personally. Work to develop your own sense of identity.

With Moon: Moodiness, changeability, slavish adherence to fads or popular beliefs create barriers with people who genuinely count in your life. You have difficulty identifying and dealing with the moods and needs of the new people you meet. You may also face too many distractions that hinder completion of personal projects.

With Mercury: Indecision, saying anything to please another, and carelessness with facts negate the effectiveness of your mental processes. New people may offer too many conflicting ideas or desires with which to cope. You need to develop your skill in sorting out ideas and organizing your personal projects.

With Venus: Fickleness, self-indulgence, neglect of duties in pursuit of pleasure are obstacles to the cooperation you need to attain your goals. Your desire to accommodate others may lead to making promises you cannot keep, or becoming a doormat for the feelings of others. Work on expressing your feelings creatively.

With Mars: Do not fritter your energy away pursuing unrealistic or unworthy objectives in coming months. You are more sharp and irritable with new people, especially when they sit on the fence instead of taking action, thereby hindering your own projects. Release emotional tensions with exercise and developing physical skills.

With Jupiter: Negative influences in your life will disappear in the near future. You need to avoid being too trusting or generous with new people, or slacking off on personal projects. Avoid overeating and indulging in laziness.

With Saturn: You feel depressed and passive about events in coming months, feeling there is little you can do about them. Have the courage to refuse to take on added personal responsibilities for which you do not have the time, eneregy or skills. However, do count on your own experience in life rather than the advice of others.

With Uranus: Disturbing and disruptive changes occur during the next few months. You are restless, excitable, eccentric and erratic in your personal life, due to changing desires and needs. Try to maintain some continuity and stability in your personal life, lest others decide you are unreliable.

With Neptune: Undefined negative feelings interfere with your attempts at positive action the next few months. You are caught up in vague visions of the future, not realizing the effort necessary to accomplish your goals. Try to pinpiont your genuine interests and work on them.

With Pluto: An unfortunate past life experience may be repeating itself in the near future; strengthen yourself accordingly. You tend to blame fate for the problems created by others in your life, or your own sense of isolation from the mainstream. Build up your health, and your feelings will be more positive.

Cauda Draconis
In the 2nd House
Alone, no planets: This is an adverse influence that remains relatively unchanged in the next few months. You are dissatisfied with your income, be it large or small. Avoid making important financial decisions until general economic conditions are better. Keep careful track of your possessions.

With Sun: Egotism, touchy sensitivity, dictatorial attitudes and self-centered behavior are self-defeating obstacles to attainment of your goals. A poor time to seek advancement or managerial positions, as income will not satisfy you. Get a business manager yourself if you are too inclined to spend for personal items or show.

With Moon: Moodiness, changeability, slavish adherence to fads or popular beliefs create barriers with people who genuinely count in your life. Income fluctuates now, so be flexible and plan a basic budget which will carry you through the ups and downs and insecurity. Do not carry cash in crowds.

With Mercury: Indecision, saying anything to please another, and carelessness with facts negate the effectiveness of your mental processes. Be discreet about your income and possessions, and do not rely on advice for investments. Business and financial communications may be disrupted. Keep accurate track of all cash flow.

With Venus: Fickleness, self-indulgence, neglect of duties in pursuit of pleasure are obstacles to the cooperation you need to attain your goals. Spending for personal whims or luxuries could leave you without the necessities, should your income decrease. Be more prudent with funds.

With Mars: Do not fritter your energy away pursuing unrealistic or unworthy objectives in coming months. Avoid haste in spending, and check the durability of goods you do purchase. There is a flurry of financial activity, so do not let any cash fall through the cracks of your busy routine.

With Jupiter: Negative influences in your life will disappear in the near future. Playing "hail-fellow-well-met" with your funds may have you seeking charity instead of dispensing it. Do more comparison shopping instead of buying the showiest or most expensive item.

With Saturn: You feel depressed and passive about events in coming months, feeling there is little you can do about them. You are in a situation of financial limitations which you must cope with for the time being; try to take pride in bargain hunting, coupon clipping, and generally getting the most for your money.

With Uranus: Disturbing and disruptive changes occur during the next few months. You may suddenly lose cash or an investment may fail; be sure you have secure funds to fall back on when sudden expenses arise. Avoid impulsive spending or quick purchases.

With Neptune: Undefined negative feelings interfere with your attempts at positive action the next few months. Emotional spending can put a real dent in your budget, as can loans to people who know you are a soft touch. Remember that charity begins at home.

With Pluto: An unfortunate past life experience may be repeating itself in the near future; strengthen yourself accordingly. Bad spending habits may be catching up with you now. Avoid cooperative ventures in which you end up footing most of the bill.

Cauda Draconis
In the 3rd House
Alone, no planets: This is an adverse influence that remains relatively unchanged in the next few months. You are simply not at your best dealing with your daily environment. Be discreet in speech and careful in travel while you examine your surroundings for the negative influences affecting you adversely.

With Sun: Egotism, touchy sensitivity, dictatorial attitudes and self-centered behavior are self-defeating obstacles to attainment of your goals. Avoid exceeding your authority if in a position of community prominence. Be careful in travel, as you are too self-absorbed.

With Moon: Moodiness, changeability, slavish adherence to fads or popular beliefs create barriers with people who genuinely count in your life. Too many aggravating distractions can cause traffic accidents or domestic upsets. Be discreet and ignore gossip.

With Mercury: Indecision, saying anything to please another, and carelessness with facts negate the effectiveness of your mental processes. Start making lists of things you want to accomplish or purchase, and keep your eyes on erratic traffic when traveling, as accident potential exists.

With Venus: Fickleness, self-indulgence, neglect of duties in pursuit of pleasure are obstacles to the cooperation you need to attain your goals. Watch for self-serving flattery from those around you, designed to unload negative feelings on you. Be cautious when shopping, as advertising claims are unrealistic.

With Mars: Do not fritter your energy away pursuing unrealistic or unworthy objectives in coming months. Watch for accident potential in travel and argumentative neighbors or relatives.

With Jupiter: Negative influences in your life will disappear in the near future. Do not believe all the promises made to you by now, and be cautious in travel, as you tend to trust too much to luck.

With Saturn: You feel depressed and passive about events in coming months, feeling there is little you can do about them. You will have to cheer yourself up—others around you are too busy with their own activities to have time for your problems. Travel is slow and communications delayed.

With Uranus: Disturbing and disruptive changes occur during the next few months. Watch for accident potential in travel and disruptions of your daily routines. Avoid taking up extremist ideas or expressing them to those around you.

With Neptune: Undefined negative feelings interfere with your attempts at positive action the next few months. Watch where you are going, as it is easy to get lost now, while your mind is distracted with daydreams. Messages may also be lost or garbled.

With Pluto: An unfortunate past life experience may be repeating itself in the near future; strengthen yourself accordingly. Avoid travel in bad neighborhoods, and be discreet in your discussions with those around you. Too many nosy people can create unwanted gossip.

Cauda Draconis
In the 4th House

Alone, no planets: This is an adverse influence that remains relatively unchanged in the next few months. Family dissension or feelings of insecurity can turn your home from a place of rest to a place of unrest and strife. Avoid major purchases or investments for your home.

With Sun: Egotism, touchy sensitivity, dictatorial attitudes and self-centered behavior are self-defeating obstacles to attainment of your goals. You feel your sense of authority in the home is being undermined. Try discussion rather than commands.

With Moon: Moodiness, changeability, slavish adherence to fads or popular beliefs create barriers with people who genuinely count in your life. Women in your family may be having problems which affect your own happiness and security. Watch for domestic problems and needed repairs.

With Mercury: Indecision, saying anything to please another, and carelessness with facts negate the effectiveness of your mental processes. Your family may be quite unreasonable and unwilling to discuss differences of opinion. You will have to decide if personal freedom or family harmony is more important now.

With Venus: Fickleness, self-indulgence, neglect of duties in pursuit of pleasure are obstacles to the cooperation you need to attain your goals. You should avoid trying to buy family affection with gifts or favors. Give freely, or do not give at all.

With Mars: Do not fritter your energy away pursuing unrealistic or unworthy objectives in coming months. Family frustrations lead to arguments; try to get everyone working on a constructive project, or simply out of the house for recreational activities.

With Jupiter: Negative influences in your life will disappear in the near future. Family habits of luxurious spending may need to be curbed, as your efforts may be unappreciated. Avoid real estate investments now.

With Saturn: You feel depressed and passive about events in coming months, feeling there is little you can do about them. An older family member may be creating burdens for everyone else in the family. Be reasonable, but do not become a doormat for this person. Remember that your home is designed for you, so do not become a slave to upkeep.

With Uranus: Disturbing and disruptive changes occur during the next few months. You may face sudden domestic expenses, or feel like escaping all the burdens of a home of your own. Be cautious or you may lose money if you sell too soon.

With Neptune: Undefined negative feelings interfere with your attempts at positive action the next few months. Family members may be scattered about, giving you a sense of isolation. Watch for problems with gas or the plumbing now.

With Pluto: An unfortunate past life experience may be repeating itself in the near future; strengthen yourself accordingly. Watch for problems with foundations, plumbing, and natural disasters; keep your home well secured when you are gone.

Cauda Draconis
In the 5th House
Alone, no planets: This is an adverse influence that remains relatively unchanged in the next few months. A love affair may turn out unfortunately; gambling brings losses, not profits; and investments also are not favored. Be careful of the hazards of the recreation you take up.

With Sun: Egotism, touchy sensitivity, dictatorial attitudes and self-centered behavior are self-defeating obstacles to attainment of your goals. You will lose in love because you want your own way all the time. Children also do not appreciate being bossed around all the time. Avoid gambling.

With Moon: Moodiness, changeability, slavish adherence to fads or popular beliefs create barriers with people who genuinely count in your life. Loved ones may feel you are too undependable and changeable now. Avoid gambling and investments, as the market is fluctuating too much.

With Mercury: Indecision, saying anything to please another, and carelessness with facts negate the effectiveness of your mental processes. Loved ones see through your smoke screen of words, when you do not want to commit yourself. Avoid gambling or speculation.

With Venus: Fickleness, self-indulgence, neglect of duties in pursuit of pleasure are obstacles to the cooperation you need to attain your goals. Fondness for gambling and flirtation can lose both money and a romantic attachment. Do not overindulge children.

With Mars: Do not fritter your energy away pursuing unrealistic or unworthy objectives in coming months. Avoid hazardous recreation, quarrels with loved ones, and rash demands on children. Creative efforts are full of obstacles now.

With Jupiter: Negative influences in your life will disappear in the near future. Do not be overconfident in love, or careless in keeping an eye on children, who will try to take advantage of your good nature. Gambling brings losses rather than gains, for the time being.

With Saturn: You feel depressed and passive about events in coming months, feeling there is little you can do about them. Do not expect loved ones to help you wallow in self-pity. Children will demand more attention. Avoid gambling or speculative investments.

With Uranus: Disturbing and disruptive changes occur during the next few months. A romance may be suddenly broken off; do not pursue it. Avoid gambling or speculation, and watch for sudden minor crises in the lives of your children. Original creative ideas should be put aside for better times.

With Neptune: Undefined negative feelings interfere with your attempts at positive action the next few months. Avoid get-rich-quick gambling or investment schemes, as you are living in a fool's paradise. The same may be true in your love life.

With Pluto: An unfortunate past life experience may be repeating itself in the near future; strengthen yourself accordingly. Affections of a loved one may be strained to the breaking point by your jealousy or need for constant reassurance. Keep an eye on children who may be developing some bad habits.

Cauda Draconis
In the 6th House
Alone, no planets: This is an adverse influence that remains relatively unchanged in the next few months. Your health is subject to too many varied stresses; get back to the simple basics of good diet, plenty of rest and moderate physical exercise. Do not expect too much cooperation or accomplishment on the job.

With Sun: Egotism, touchy sensitivity, dictatorial attitudes and self-centered behavior are self-defeating obstacles to attainment of your goals. Your basic vitality is threatened; do not overexert, and do balance your diet, rest and exercise more carefully. Avoid disputes with supervisors on the job.

With Moon: Moodiness, changeability, slavish adherence to fads or popular beliefs create barriers with people who genuinely count in your life. You may not be able to keep up with the moods of coworkers and the many fluctuations on the job. Do not accept split shift or overtime work now.

With Mercury: Indecision, saying anything to please another, and carelessness with facts negate the effectiveness of your mental processes. Your ideas are not welcomed on the job; save your energy for planning to change careers or jobs when conditions are better.

With Venus: Fickleness, self-indulgence, neglect of duties in pursuit of pleasure are obstacles to the cooperation you need to attain your goals. Consider the practical values of your job and avoid making changes based solely on emotional issues. Avoid overindulging your appetite for good food.

With Mars: Do not fritter your energy away pursuing unrealistic or unworthy objectives in coming months. Avoid quarrels with co-workers, and watch for accident potential on the job when you are in a hurry. You may suffer from tension headaches.

With Jupiter: Negative influences in your life will disappear in the near future. Avoid being overconfident or careless on the job, and do not indulge your appetite for good food and drink to extremes. Do not let coworkers talk you into doing their work for them.

With Saturn: You feel depressed and passive about events in coming months, feeling there is little you can do about them. Avoid taking on extra responsibilities on the job and get plenty of rest. Avoid fad diets, as you may lower your resistance to colds and the flu.

With Uranus: Disturbing and disruptive changes occur during the next few months. You may lose your job suddenly, or be faced with making quick adjustments to new equipment and job demands. Watch for insomnia and nervous tension.

With Neptune: Undefined negative feelings interfere with your attempts at positive action the next few months. You are too sensitive to the opinions of coworkers; keep your mind on the job itself, and limit personal contacts until conditions improve. Avoid drugs and alcohol, as your system is sensitized.

With Pluto: An unfortunate past life experience may be repeating itself in the near future; strengthen yourself accordingly. A backlog of work or the need to redo work may catch up with you and call for long hours and extra energy. Maintain your health with good diet and plenty of rest.

Cauda Draconis
In the 7th House

Alone, no planets: This is an adverse influence that remains relatively unchanged in the next few months. You may be in the process of a divorce, legal dispute, or separation from a loved one. Do not become too friendly with new people on the rebound.

With Sun: Egotism, touchy sensitivity, dictatorial attitudes and self-centered behavior are self-defeating obstacles to attainment of your goals. You will have to assume responsibility for meeting joint legal obligations. Avoid being too demanding of a loved one.

With Moon: Moodiness, changeability, slavish adherence to fads or popular beliefs create barriers with people who genuinely count in your life. Your popularity with too many people may cost you a more valued close relationship. Avoid seeming too changeable and restless to loved ones.

With Mercury: Indecision, saying anything to please another, and carelessness with facts negate the effectiveness of your mental processes. Avoid signing legal papers or getting involved in any legal disputes, whether your own or a partner's. Keep track of what you say to loved ones—they will remind you later of promises not kept.

With Venus: Fickleness, self-indulgence, neglect of duties in pursuit of pleasure are obstacles to the cooperation you need to attain your goals. Your affections are not returned, and you are not interested in one who is very fond of you. Avoid competition or legal disputes.

With Mars: Do not fritter your energy away pursuing unrealistic or unworthy objectives in coming months. Those close to you rub you the wrong way, either arguing or being too eager to get your attention. Avoid quarrels and legal disputes.

With Jupiter: Negative influences in your life will disappear in the near future. You may be taken advantage of in a business partnership or romantic relationship. Be forgiving, but do not let it happen a second time.

With Saturn: You feel depressed and passive about events in coming months, feeling there is little you can do about them. Do not give aid to loved ones grudgingly; either accept new duties cheerfully, or refuse to add to your own burdens with partnership problems.

With Uranus: Disturbing and disruptive changes occur during the next few months. A close relationship may be broken off or make you nervous wondering what to expect next. Avoid competition, as you will be in over your head.

With Neptune: Undefined negative feelings interfere with your attempts at positive action the next few months. You may be deceived in a supposed love relationship, or cheated by a business partner. Get agreements on paper, but do not make promises you cannot keep.

With Pluto: An unfortunate past life experience may be repeating itself in the near future; strengthen yourself accordingly. You are tired of playing the slave to loved ones and business partners; get them to shoulder their own responsibilities.

Cauda Draconis
In the 8th House
Alone, no planets: This is an adverse influence that remains relatively unchanged in the next few months. Avoid dabbling in the occult arts out of frivolous whims, or in areas where you do not know what you are doing. Again, avoid becoming intimate with someone you do not really understand.

With Sun: Egotism, touchy sensitivity, dictatorial attitudes and self-centered behavior are self-defeating obstacles to attainment of your goals. Occult experiments could subject you to adverse influences; do not be overconfident in this area of life, or in joint ventures and sexual attractions.

With Moon: Moodiness, changeability, slavish adherence to fads or popular beliefs create barriers with people who genuinely count in your life. Divination techniques may yield too many opposing insights if you keep asking the same question over and over. Avoid being moody with an intimate.

With Mercury: Indecision, saying anything to please another, and carelessness with facts negate the effectiveness of your mental processes. Spiritual messages may be deceptive; check them out against common sense and experience. Do not question an intimate too personally, or you may receive protective lies in return.

With Venus: Fickleness, self-indulgence, neglect of duties in pursuit of pleasure are obstacles to the cooperation you need to attain your goals. You are attracted where there is no hope of satisfaction. Enjoy occult entertainment for its pleasurable value, but do not take what you hear now too seriously.

With Mars: Do not fritter your energy away pursuing unrealistic or unworthy objectives in coming months. You may be subjected to sexual harassment on the job or socially. Be firm and reject such advances. Avoid joint ventures.

With Jupiter: Negative influences in your life will disappear in the near future. You are too tempted to spend on credit and lend money to deadbeats. Avoid taking a loved one for granted. Success in occult projects is assured, but you may be in for more than you bargained for.

With Saturn: You feel depressed and passive about events in coming months, feeling there is little you can do about them. You are worried about death, your own or a loved one's future. Put aside unnecessary anxieties. Avoid credit spending or borrowing money now.

With Uranus: Disturbing and disruptive changes occur during the next few months. Occult dabbling may bring unpleasant psychic experiences. Avoid being abrupt with loved ones, or a relationship may be broken off. Avoid credit spending on impulse.

With Neptune: Undefined negative feelings interfere with your attempts at positive action the next few months. Your psychic sensitivities expose you to negative feelings and influences. Avoid being unrealistic in an intimate relationship. Do not borrow or lend money.

With Pluto: An unfortunate past life experience may be repeating itself in the near future; strengthen yourself accordingly. Avoid getting in debt or lending to others. You may be attracted sexually to someone who appeals to you in no other way. This, too, shall pass.

Cauda Draconis
In the 9th House

Alone, no planets: This is an adverse influence that remains relatively unchanged in the next few months. Mental anxiety about the future, unhappy messages from distant friends and relatives, obstacles or loss of interest in studies, and delays in travel are your lot now.

With Sun: Egotism, touchy sensitivity, dictatorial attitudes and self-centered behavior are self-defeating obstacles to attainment of your goals. Do not rush in where angels fear to tread, in disputes about beliefs, or in traveling to new places. Do not make exaggerated plans for the future.

With Moon: Moodiness, changeability, slavish adherence to fads or popular beliefs create barriers with people who genuinely count in your life. Service in travel will be unreliable, other cultures difficult to understand, and travel hazardous, while your feelings and opinions are also changeable.

With Mercury: Indecision, saying anything to please another, and carelessness with facts negate the effectiveness of your mental processes. Contradictory statements by teachers may leave you in doubt about studies. Watch for confusion in travel and delays in communication.

With Venus: Fickleness, self-indulgence, neglect of duties in pursuit of pleasure are obstacles to the cooperation you need to attain your goals. You will not be happy with the results of studies or long-distance travel now. You may hear unhappy news from a friend or loved one.

With Mars: Do not fritter your energy away pursuing unrealistic or unworthy objectives in coming months. Avoid travel, as accident potential exists; and avoid disputes on matters of opinion. Your initiatives are ill-conceived, so rethink them.

With Jupiter: Negative influences in your life will disappear in the near future. Do not count on luck in your travels or studies—take care to know what you are talking about, and do not make promises you cannot keep.

With Saturn: You feel depressed and passive about events in coming months, feeling there is little you can do about them. Travel is delayed or costly, studies are arduous and sometimes unrewarding, and your general outlook for the future is pessimistic.

With Uranus: Disturbing and disruptive changes occur during the next few months. Avoid air travel, as accident potential exists. Be prepared to break off studies when duty demands. Watch for nervous tension and upsetting news.

With Neptune: Undefined negative feelings interfere with your attempts at positive action the next few months. You are in an escapist mood, but travel will prove disappointing. Avoid emotionalism in connection with your studies or discussions with those from different cultures.

With Pluto: An unfortunate past life experience may be repeating itself in the near future; strengthen yourself accordingly. Your plans for travel will be changed unexpectedly, and you will be embarking on entirely different activities. Studies in the occult seem particularly difficult to penetrate now.

Cauda Draconis
In the 10th House
Alone, no planets: This is an adverse influence that remains relatively unchanged in the next few months. Watch for losses if you run a business of your own, or a downturn in your regular work. You are unsuccessful in public action protests now.

With Sun: Egotism, touchy sensitivity, dictatorial attitudes and self-centered behavior are self-defeating obstacles to attainment of your goals. You may be saddled with authority beyond your capabilities. Not a good time to try to impress the public with your ideas or abilities.

With Moon: Moodiness, changeability, slavish adherence to fads or popular beliefs create barriers with people who genuinely count in your life. The vagaries of the public are difficult to keep up with. Avoid election campaigning or expanding any public service business now.

With Mercury: Indecision, saying anything to please another, and carelessness with facts negate the effectiveness of your mental processes. A poor time to present ideas to your employer or the public; be sure to save them for a better time. Ignore any gossip on the job, and put off any new training for a while.

With Venus: Fickleness, self-indulgence, neglect of duties in pursuit of pleasure are obstacles to the cooperation you need to attain your goals. The envy and malice of others should not influence you to leave your job or give way to the feelings of others. Strive for an attitude of professionalism.

With Mars: Do not fritter your energy away pursuing unrealistic or unworthy objectives in coming months. Do not start any new business venture, or get into disputes with supervisors on the job. You may have difficulties dealing with government authorities now.

With Jupiter: Negative influences in your life will disappear in the near future. Early success on the job should not be followed by over-confidence or carelessness. Avoid any business expansion now.

With Saturn: You feel depressed and passive about events in coming months, feeling there is little you can do about them. Your job responsibilities may be showing a diminishing reward. Make no changes now, but examine plans for a future change of job or business.

With Uranus: Disturbing and disruptive changes occur during the next few months. A sudden business loss, or loss of your job is traumatic; prepare a financial cushion in advance, if possible.

With Neptune: Undefined negative feelings interfere with your attempts at positive action the next few months. Confusion reigns supreme on the job; insist on clear instructions and a source of authority in your work. If in a psychic profession, you will have very difficult clients now.

With Pluto: You feel depressed and passive about events in coming months, feeling there is little you can do about them. Larger economic trends may phase out your job or demand a cut in pay; be prepared to decide on accepting or looking for work elsewhere.

Cauda Draconis
In the 11th House

Alone, no planets: This is an adverse influence that remains relatively unchanged in the next few months. You will run up against some devious and unfriendly people if you do not think ahead and decide exactly how you want to conduct your social life, and the kind of people with which you want to associate.

With Sun: Egotism, touchy sensitivity, dictatorial attitudes and self-centered behavior are self-defeating obstacles to attainment of your goals. You may assume leadership of a group at a point where it is disintegrating or not accomplishing anything. Scale down expectations, and save what you can.

With Moon: Moodiness, changeability, slavish adherence to fads or popular beliefs create barriers with people who genuinely count in your life. You have so many casual invitations that some worthwhile groups and individuals may get lost in the shuffle. Set some social priorities.

With Mercury: Indecision, saying anything to please another, and carelessness with facts negate the effectiveness of your mental processes. Drop groups that have changed from discussion to gossip associations. Be very discreet about your personal affairs in social life now.

With Venus: Fickleness, self-indulgence, neglect of duties in pursuit of pleasure are obstacles to the cooperation you need to attain your goals. You affections and sympathy are drawn to people who do not really deserve it. Do not get financially involved with them.

With Mars: Do not fritter your energy away pursuing unrealistic or unworthy objectives in coming months. You may meet with hostile and argumentative people while socializing. Back off with tact and avoid them in the future.

With Jupiter: Negative influences in your life will disappear in the near future. Freeloaders of all types will be pursuing you if you try to show how well-off you are. Be discreet in spending and friendly where your attentions are appreciated.

With Saturn: You feel depressed and passive about events in coming months, feeling there is little you can do about them. Social life leads you to too many depressing or greedy people. Stick with old friends who have a more balanced perspective on life.

With Uranus: Disturbing and disruptive changes occur during the next few months. Social life is a series of unpleasant ups and downs. You cannot satisfy the whims of all the groups you are part of, so go it alone for a while.

With Neptune: Undefined negative feelings interfere with your attempts at positive action the next few months. Avoid the crowds who indulge in alcohol or drugs, and stick to the artists and musicians, or people who relax you.

With Pluto: An unfortunate past life experience may be repeating itself in the near future; strengthen yourself accordingly. Be discreet while socializing, and do not get involved in groups with dubious purposes or antecedents.

Cauda Draconis
In the 12th House
Alone, no planets: This is an adverse influence that remains relatively unchanged in the next few months. Your fears about your health may be more extreme than any ailment. Stop worrying and consult a physician. Use common sense in dieting, exercising and getting enough rest.

With Sun: Egotism, touchy sensitivity, dictatorial attitudes and self-centered behavior are self-defeating obstacles to attainment of your goals. You are your own worst enemy when it comes to keeping up a good health routine. You assume nothing could ever happen to you. Build up what is essentially a good physique.

With Moon: Moodiness, changeability, slavish adherence to fads or popular beliefs create barriers with people who genuinely count in your life. Your irregular habits and emotional mood take their toll on your health because you don't have a good health regimen. Mend your ways.

With Mercury: Indecision, saying anything to please another, and carelessness with facts negate the effectiveness of your mental processes. Indiscreet speech can make you a lot of enemies. Don't talk good health, act on your own advice.

With Venus: Fickleness, self-indulgence, neglect of duties in pursuit of pleasure are obstacles to the cooperation you need to attain your goals. Self-indulgence, envy, jealousy, and self-satisfaction can ruin good relationships, and then affect your health. Beauty is in the mind as well as the body.

With Mars: Do not fritter your energy away pursuing unrealistic or unworthy objectives in coming months. Inner frustrations can lead to headaches, ulcers, and irritability. Find creative or constructive outlets for pent-up energies. Avoid hazardous places.

With Jupiter: Negative influences in your life will disappear in the near future. Excess of emotions and indulgence in excessive food and drink can leave you lethargic and overweight. Practice some self-restraint.

With Saturn: You feel depressed and passive about events in coming months, feeling there is little you can do about them. You are very susceptible to colds and the flu, or to dental problems. Build up your vitality to avoid depression.

With Uranus: Disturbing and disruptive changes occur during the next few months. You suffer from insomnia, nervous tension, and the disruptive habits of neighbors. Avoid stimulants, and develop a meditative relaxation technique.

With Neptune: Undefined negative feelings interfere with your attempts at positive action the next few months. Your psychic perceptions in sleep and dreams are depressing; avoid letting vague worries overtake you. Avoid drugs and alcohol.

With Pluto: An unfortunate past life experience may be repeating itself in the near future; strengthen yourself accordingly. You feel anxious without knowing the cause; set up a relaxing meditative technique before sleep, and use positive suggestion.

10

Interpretation of
Judges and Witnesses

Only eight of the symbols are used as Judges of the questions asked. I call these the "impersonal" symbols, in keeping with the role of a judge in a court. Symbols such as Tristitia and Laetitia, which represent emotions; Cauda Draconis and Caput Draconis, which represent primarily karmic or spiritual factors; Puer and Puella, which represent the male and female polarities; and Albus and Rubeus, which represent inner states of the mind, wisdom and anger, are not used as Judges.

The remaining symbols used as Judges are Carcer, or Bondage, representing material reality; Conjunctio, or the union of two forces, including polar opposites; Fortuna Major and Fortuna Minor, representing the Wheel of Fortune or external, non-individualized luck or fate; Acquisitio and Amissio, material gain and material loss.

Each Judge represents some external factor which can be observed and analyzed by an impartial viewer; a factor that has tangible meaning. The essence of judgment is that it results from impartially weighing observable facts, and then drawing a reasonable conclusion.

In the following pages we give a brief interpretation of each Judge; the combination of Witnesses which produce each Judge; and the planetary correlation of the Witnesses and the Judge, in order for astrology to be applied in conjunction with this part of geomantic interpretation as well as to the chart itself. The astrologically-oriented can then analyze the Witnesses and Judges more accurately by referring to the positions and aspects of the related planets in the chart.

Carcer: This Saturn-ruled Judge denotes Bondage, which includes the concepts of obligation, duty, legal contracts, habit patterns, a fixed environment or goal in life.

General meaning: The goal inquired of will be attained.

Conjunctio: This Mercury-ruled Judge denotes Union, which includes the concepts of cooperation, discussion, analysis and final conclusions, ultimately the need for more than individual action to attain the goal desired.

General meaning: The goal inquired of will be attained although the cooperation of another may be required. Ultimately the answer is "maybe."

Fortuna Major: This Sun-ruled Judge denotes Greater Fortune, which may or may not lead to a positive answer to the question, if the question involves something ultimately not to the benefit of the querent. However, in positive terms, it always denotes a favorable answer concerning the goal desired.

General meaning: An unqualified "Yes" where the Witnesses agree.

Fortuna Minor: This Sun-ruled Judge denotes Lesser Fortune, on the principle that "something is better than nothing." At the very least it preserves what the querent already has.

General meaning: A qualified "Yes," more dependent on the Witnesses than Fortuna Major.

Populus: This Moon-ruled Judge is quite variable and depends entirely on the meanings of the Witnesses for the answer to any question. Therefore, since this Judge appears more frequently in charts than most of the other Judges, you are advised to consult the interpretations each time Populus appears as the Judge for a definite answer.

Via: This Moon-ruled Judge is, like Populus, quite variable and depends entirely on the meanings of the Witnesses for the answer to any question. Therefore, you are advised to consult the interpretations given in following pages for the exact Witnesses that make up Via for your answer.

Amissio: This Venus-ruled Judge changes its nature as a Judge, and partakes more of the nature of the planet Venus, which is the Lesser Benefic, than of its own meaning as a symbol, of Loss. However, if you were to ask, "Will my new diet work?", and Amissio is the Judge, you would probably be quite happy to see Loss as the final answer to your questions. For this reason, you should consult the individual combinations of Witnesses to get an accurate answer to your query.

Acquisitio: This Jupiter-ruled Judge also changes nature slightly, and may not always be favorable; however, for the most part this Judge gives a favorable answer to your question.

Witnesses that Produce the Judge
FORTUNA MAJOR

Witness Fortuna Major		Witness Populus	Judge Fortuna Major
O O		O O	O O
O O		O O	O O
O		O O	O
O		O O	O
Sun	+	Moon	Sun

Traditionally favorable for all questions, except those concerning lawsuits and inheritances. The lunar symbol, Populus, following the Sun symbol, Fortuna Major, suggests that there are too many competitors for a legacy, and too many opponents in any lawsuit. For all other questions, the combination is favorable, and similar to a good aspect of the Sun to the Moon, such as the trine or sextile, so that the right conditions exist to attain one's desire.

Witness Populus		Witness Fortuna Major	Judge Fortuna Major
O O		O O	O O
O O		O O	O O
O O		O	O
O O		O	O
Moon	+	Sun	Sun

Traditionally favorable for all questions. Here the first Witness is variable, but the second highly favorable, and thus the results are highly favorable. Similar to a favorable aspect of the Sun to the Moon, such as the trine or the sextile, so that the right conditions exist to attain one's desires.

Witness Fortuna Minor		Witness Via	Judge Fortuna Major
o		o	o o
o		o	o o
o o		o	o
o o		o	o
Sun	+	Moon	Sun

Traditionally adverse except for questions about travel and news. Via means Pathway, so travel is favored; by such a Pathway, news also comes. Fortuna Minor is not a very good figure, and Via is variable, so there is little favorable strength to assure a favorable result. Similar in effect to the lethargy induced by the New Moon (conjunction of Sun and Moon).

Witness Via		Witness Fortuna Minor	Judge Fortuna Major
o		o	o o
o		o	o o
o		o o	o
o		o o	o
Moon	+	Sun	Sun

Traditionally favorable for all questions except those concerning career advancement. The Sun indicates ambitions, and tends to overcome the variability of the Moon-ruled Via when Fortuna Minor is the second figure. Since the Sun rules major ambitions, and the Pathway is the first figure, and external protection the second, opportunities exist for career advancement. Nonetheless effort must be made, as this combination is similar to the adverse aspects of the Sun and Moon, the square and opposition (Full Moon).

Witness Conjunctio		Witness Acquisitio	Judge Fortuna Major
o o		o o	o o
o		o	o o
o		o o	o
o o		o	o
Mercury	+	Jupiter	Sun

Traditionally favorable for all questions. Two favorable Witnesses combining to form a favorable Judge bring luck and progress in any and all areas of life. Similar to a favorable aspect of Mercury to Jupiter, such as the trine, sextile or conjunction.

Witness Aquisitio	Witness Conjunctio	Judge Fortuna Major
O O	O O	O O
O	O	O O
O O	O	O
O	O O	O
Jupiter +	Mercury	Sun

Traditionally favorable except for questions of inheritance or lawsuits. Here the Jupiter figure is first, so excessive generosity or spending may precede the news of an inheritance or eagerness to settle may precede the facts of the case, again unfavorable for lawsuits. Otherwise, this combination is similar to the above, a good aspect of Jupiter to Mercury, such as the trine, conjunction or sextile. In relation to lawsuits or legacies, more like the adverse aspects, the square and opposition of Jupiter to Mercury.

Witness Albus	Witness Tristitia	Judge Fortuna Major
O O	O O	O O
O O	O O	O O
O	O O	O
O O	O	O
Mercury +	Saturn	Sun

Traditionally favorable for all questions. Similar to the favorable aspects of Mercury to Saturn, the trine and sextile, as encouraging the materialization or realization of the goals desired.

Witness	Witness	Judge
Puella	Laetitia	Fortuna Major
O	O	O O
O O	O O	O O
O	O O	O
O	O O	O
Venus +	Jupiter	Sun

Traditionally favorable for all questions. The best possible combination, as the Judge combines the influences of Venus, the Lesser Benefic, and Jupiter, the Greater Benefic. In fact, the results may be even greater than the querent had hoped.

Witness	Witness	Judge
Laetitia	Puella	Fortuna Major
O	O	O O
O O	O O	O O
O O	O	O
O O	O	O
Jupiter +	Venus	Sun

Traditionally favorable for all questions. The best possible combination, as the Judge combines the influence of Venus, the Lesser Benefic, and Jupiter, the Greater Benefic. In fact, the results are likely to be much greater than the querent even dreamed.

Witness	Witness	Judge
Amissio	Carcer	Fortuna Major
O	O	O O
O O	O O	O O
O	O O	O
O O	O	O
Venus +	Saturn	Sun

Traditionally mildly favorable for all questions except those involving inheritances, lawsuits, and news or communications. The influence is somewhat like the minor aspects of Venus to Saturn, the semisextile of minor ease, or the quincunx of minor tension.

Witness Carcer		Witness Amissio	Judge Fortuna Major
O		O	O O
O O		O O	O O
O O		O	O
O		O O	O
Saturn	+	Venus	Sun

Traditionally mildly adverse for all questions except those regarding the ending of a venture, and communications or news. Again the influences are similar to the minor aspects of Venus to Saturn, the semisextile of minor ease, and the quincunx of minor tension.

Witness Puer		Witness Cauda Draconis	Judge Fortuna Major
O		O	O O
O		O	O O
O O		O	O
O		O O	O
Mars	+	South Node	Sun

Traditionally adverse for all questions. The first Witness is good, but the second adverse, indicating a good beginning, but the results will not be what you desire. With the South Node involved, you will lose more than you gain, materially or spiritually.

Witness Cauda Draconis		Witness Puer	Judge Fortuna Major
O		O	O O
O		O	O O
O		O O	O
O O		O	O
South Node	+	Mars	Sun

Traditionally adverse for all questions except those dealing with enemies or opponents, in which the result is favorable. With the first Witness adverse and the second favorable, a bad beginning is overcome by better results. However, with the South Node involved, you will be only partially recouping what has already been lost.

Witness		Witness		Judge
Rubeus		Caput Draconis		Fortuna Major
O O		O O		O O
O		O		O O
O O		O		O
O O		O		O
Mars	+	North Node		Sun

Traditionally mildly favorable except for questions about finances and personal affairs. The first Witness is adverse and the second favorable, so the result will be delayed, but good will come from a bad beginning. With Rubeus, the expense of energy may be so great as to be debilitating, even though the objective is gained, thus affecting personal life and general well-being; also, excessive resources may be used, affecting finances adversely.

Witness		Witness		Judge
Caput Draconis		Rubeus		Fortuna Major
O O		O O		O O
O		O		O O
O		O O		O
O		O O		O
North Node	+	Mars		Sun

Traditionally adverse for all questions. The first Witness is good, but the second adverse, indicating a good beginning, but bad results as time passes. Too many obstacles and even danger may exist. Similar to the square and opposition of Mars.

Witnesses that Produce the Judge
FORTUNA MINOR

Witness Fortuna Major		Witness Via	Judge Fortuna Minor
O O		O	O
O O		O	O
O		O	O O
O		O	O O
Sun	+	Moon	Sun

Traditionally adverse in all questions except those relating to personal affairs and travel. The first Witness is favorable, but the second variable, thus robbing the Sun of its power to do good; the tendency of the Moon is to deflect and scatter the light, or benefits, of the Sun. This deflection, as in the Full Moon, favors the traveler and enables the personality to shine out, thus favoring immediate personal goals.

Witness Via		Witness Fortuna Major	Judge Fortuna Minor
O		O O	O
O		O O	O
O		O	O O
O		O	O O
Moon	+	Sun	Sun

Traditionally favorable for all questions, as the variable first Witness is followed by a favorable Witness, thus enabling the individual to take the best advantage of what may be only average circumstances and reap a harvest as a result. Similar to the sextile and trine of the Sun to the Moon.

Witness Fortuna Minor		Witness Populus	Judge Fortuna Minor
O		O O	O
O		O O	O
O O		O O	O O
O O		O O	O O
Sun	+	Moon	Sun

Traditionally mildly favorable for all questions except those concerning lawsuits and inheritances. Neither Witness is particularly favorable, so the energies of the Judge do not reach beyond the immediate efforts of the individual to affect conflict or benefits from others favorably. The goals exceed the person's immediate reach. Similar to mildly favorable aspects of the Sun and Moon, or no helpful aspect between them.

Witness	Witness	Judge
Populus	Fortuna Minor	Fortuna Minor
O O	O	O
O O	O	O
O O	O O	O O
O O	O O	O O
Moon +	Sun	Sun

Traditionally favorable for all questions except those dealing with service from others. Similar to favorable aspects of Sun and Moon, such as trine and sextile, but very likely the phase of the waning Moon, where command over others is not so easily attained, and thus service is poor.

Witness	Witness	Judge
Conjunctio	Amissio	Fortuna Minor
O O	O	O
O	O O	O
O	O	O O
O O	O O	O O
Mercury +	Venus	Sun

Traditionally adverse for all questions, except that marriage will result if that is the question, although the outcome of the marriage may not be all that is desired. The first Witness is good, but the second adverse, so the plan or idea visualized (Mercury) has not the cooperation or support (Venus) to yield the desired results. Only good aspects are possible between Mercury and Venus, but this combination suggests no aspect between the two and Venus debilitated or afflicted.

Witness	Witness	Judge
Amissio	Conjunctio	Fortuna Minor
O	O O	O
O O	O	O
O	O	O O
O O	O O	O O
Venus +	Mercury	Sun

Traditionally mildly favorable for all questions. Here the first Witness is adverse, but the second favorable, and so the individual is able to overcome an adverse set of circumstances (Venus) through ingenuity and planning (Mercury). Similar to a favorable aspect between Mercury and Venus.

Witness	Witness	Judge
Albus	Cauda Draconis	Fortuna Minor
O O	O	O
O O	O	O
O	O	O O
O O	O O	O O
Mercury +	South Node	Sun

Traditionally adverse for all questions. The first Witness is favorable, but the second adverse, so despite the planning and thought, the project will come to nothing. The South Node always denotes a drain on resources and a negative influence on events.

Witness	Witness	Judge
Cauda Draconis	Albus	Fortuna Minor
O	O O	O
O	O O	O
O	O	O O
O O	O O	O O
South Node +	Mercury	Sun

Traditionally favorable for all questions. The first Witness is adverse, but the second is favorable, so the limited beginnings will nonetheless be overcome, and the individual will triumph and have his or her wishes fulfilled. Here the draining effect of the South Node is counteracted by quick thinking and planning.

Witness Puella	Witness Caput Draconis	Judge Fortuna Minor
o	o o	o
o o	o	o
o	o	o o
o	o	o o
Venus +	North Node	Sun

Traditionally favorable for all questions except those pertaining to love. The first Witness is variable, but the second is favorable, so the desires of the querent will be fulfilled. Puella first, followed by Caput Draconis, indicates that personal affections are left behind in favor of higher spiritual aims, and thus love is not favored by this combination.

Witness Caput Draconis	Witness Puella	Judge Fortuna Minor
o o	o	o
o	o o	o
o	o	o o
o	o	o o
North Node +	Venus	Sun

Traditionally favorable for all questions. Here love is favored as well as other questions, for from the higher spiritual fount of Caput Draconis emerges a finer form of love. Thus all questions gain a favorable nod from the stars.

Witness Puer	Witness Tristitia	Judge Fortuna Minor
o	o o	o
o	o o	o
o o	o o	o o
o	o	o o
Mars +	Saturn	Sun

Mildly adverse except for questions dealing with lawsuits and coping with enemies. The first Witness is favorable, but the second adverse, so results will not be as favorable as anticipated. Puer, ruled by Mars, shows initiative and daring, and even the depression of Tristitia cannot still the combativeness which favors success in lawsuits and dealings with enemies.

Witness Tristitia		Witness Puer	Judge Fortuna Minor
O O		O	O
O O		O	O
O O		O O	O O
O		O	O O
Saturn	+	Mars	Sun

Traditionally adverse for all questions except those having to do with marriage, which *will* take place. Although the first figure is adverse and the second favorable, this combination of Saturn and Mars is not really good. Similar in effect to the conjunction or quincunx of Mars and Saturn. The marriage which will take place may not be all that is hoped for, either.

Witness Rubeus		Witness Laetitia	Judge Fortuna Minor
O O		O	O
O		O O	O
O O		O O	O O
O O		O O	O O
Mars	+	Jupiter	Sun

Traditionally favorable for all questions. The first Witness is adverse, but the second favorable, so all things will turn out right in the end. Here the negative feelings of Rubeus are counteracted by the positive feelings of Laetitia. Similar in effect to a favorable aspect of Jupiter, such as the sextile or trine, to an otherwise afflicted Mars.

Witness	Witness	Judge
Laetitia	Rubeus	Fortuna Minor
O	O O	O
O O	O	O
O O	O O	O O
O O	O O	O O
Jupiter +	Mars	Sun

Traditionally adverse for all questions except those relating to a career in the military. Here the positive feelings of Laetitia are destroyed by the anger of Rubeus. Favorable for the military in terms of fighting anger. Similar to favorable aspect of Jupiter to an afflicted Mars. Note that the position of the Witnesses defines the difference between the similar Mars-Jupiter indications to the combination just discussed above.

Witness	Witness	Judge
Acquisitio	Carcer	Fortuna Minor
O O	O	O
O	O O	O
O O	O O	O O
O	O	O O
Jupiter +	Saturn	Sun

Traditionally favorable for all questions except those relating to marriage, career, and the final result of any project now in progress. Similar to adverse aspects between Saturn and Jupiter—the quincunx, square and opposition. Where favorable, similar to favorable aspects of Jupiter and Saturn, such as semisextile, sextile and trine.

Witness	Witness	Judge
Carcer	Acquisitio	Fortuna Minor
O	O O	O
O O	O	O
O O	O O	O O
O	O	O O
Saturn +	Jupiter	Sun

Traditionally favorable for all questions except those involving news and communications. Similar to the favorable aspects of Jupiter to Saturn, the trine and sextile.

Witnesses that Produce the Judge
POPULUS

Witness Fortuna Major		Witness Fortuna Major	Judge Populus
O O		O O	O O
O O		O O	O O
O		O	O O
O		O	O O
Sun	+	Sun	Moon

Traditionally favorable for all questions except those involving travel. Both Witnesses are favorable, but the Judge itself is variable. However, with effort the results are generally favorable. Travel is not favored because of the possible accident potential when many people are traveling at once. Similar to a favorably aspected Sun.

Witness Fortuna Minor		Witness Fortuna Minor	Judge Populus
O		O	O O
O		O	O O
O O		O O	O O
O O		O O	O O
Sun	+	Sun	Moon

Traditionally mildly favorable for all questions except those relating to the final result of a project now in progress. Both Witnesses are not really too good, and the Judge is variable. Thus success comes best when grasped swiftly, while conditions are favorable, and this combination does not favor projects that require long-term effort.

Witness Populus		Witness Populus	Judge Populus
O O		O O	O O
O O		O O	O O
O O		O O	O O
O O		O O	O O
Moon	+	Moon	Moon

Traditionally favorable for all questions except those involving the end result of a project in progress, inheritances, or lawsuits. Both Witnesses and the Judge are the same, fluctuating in effect, again not favoring long-term efforts; and not favoring lawsuits or inheritance because there is no drive or resistance in this combination. Similar to the Moon well-aspected, but with no good Mars aspect.

Witness Via		Witness Via	Judge Populus
O		O	O O
O		O	O O
O		O	O O
O		O	O O
Moon	+	Moon	Moon

Traditionally favorable for all questions except those relating to career. Both Witnesses are variable, as is the Judge; not favorable for career which demands more flexibility, while Via tends to follow the laws of dynamics: A body in motion remains in motion; a body at rest remains at rest. Similar to a Moon well-aspected, but without a Mars aspect.

Witness Conjunctio		Witness Conjunctio	Judge Populus
O O		O O	O O
O		O	O O
O		O	O O
O O		O O	O O
Mercury	+	Mercury	Moon

Traditionally favorable for all questions. This combination represents the powers of reason utilized to the greatest extent and displayed to the public, and is similar to a well-aspected Mercury.

Witness Albus	Witness Albus	Judge Populus
O O	O O	O O
O O	O O	O O
O	O	O O
O O	O O	O O
Mercury +	Mercury	Moon

Traditionally favorable for all questions. This combination represents wisdom used and displayed to the public in no uncertain terms, and is similar to a well-aspected Mercury.

Witness Puella	Witness Puella	Judge Populus
O	O	O O
O O	O O	O O
O	O	O O
O	O	O O
Venus +	Venus	Moon

Traditionally favorable for all questions. Similar to a well-aspected, powerful Venus, indicating charm, beauty, and warmth displayed to an adoring public.

Witness Amissio	Witness Amissio	Judge Populus
O	O	O O
O O	O O	O O
O	O	O O
O O	O O	O O
Venus +	Venus	Moon

Traditionally adverse for all questions. This combination indicates an afflicted Venus, possibly in Scorpio, and displaying to the public sensuality or self-indulgence.

Witness	Witness	Judge
Puer	Puer	Populus
O	O	O O
O	O	O O
O O	O O	O O
O	O	O O
Mars +	Mars	Moon

Traditionally adverse for all questions except those relating to travel. Both Witnesses are favorable, but the Judge is variable, and there is too much of Mars in this combination to favor success except in career, where dynamic energy is a requirement. Similar to a well-paced, but unaspected Mars.

Witness	Witness	Judge
Rubeus	Rubeus	Populus
O O	O O	O O
O	O	O O
O O	O O	O O
O O	O O	O O
Mars +	Mars	Moon

Traditionally adverse for all questions. Both of the Witnesses are adverse, and the Judge is variable, so nothing good comes of this combination. Similar to a dominant but afflicted Mars.

Witness	Witness	Judge
Acquisitio	Acquisitio	Populus
O O	O O	O O
O	O	O O
O O	O O	O O
O	O	O O
Jupiter +	Jupiter	Moon

Traditionally favorable for all questions but those relating to career. Both Witnesses are favorable, but the Judge is variable. There is much luck, but little drive or ambition, so career is not favored. Similar to favorable aspects of Jupiter, the sextile, trine or conjunction.

Witness	Witness	Judge
Laetitia	Laetitia	Populus
○	○	○ ○
○ ○	○ ○	○ ○
○ ○	○ ○	○ ○
○ ○	○ ○	○ ○
Jupiter　　+	Jupiter	Moon

Traditionally favorable for all questions. Both Witnesses are favorable, but the judge is variable. There is a great deal of luck and happiness, similar to the favorable aspects of Jupiter, the trine, sextile and conjunction.

Witness	Witness	Judge
Carcer	Carcer	Populus
○	○	○ ○
○ ○	○ ○	○ ○
○ ○	○ ○	○ ○
○	○	○ ○
Saturn　　+	Saturn	Moon

Traditionally favorable for all questions but love, lawsuits and career queries. Both Witnesses are essentially favorable, and the Judge is variable. Saturn tends to persistence and realism, so the results are favorable in all but Venus and Mars ruled areas of love, lawsuits and career in terms of ambition and drive. Similar to favorable aspects of Saturn, the sextile and trine.

Witness	Witness	Judge
Tristitia	Tristitia	Populus
○ ○	○ ○	○ ○
○ ○	○ ○	○ ○
○ ○	○ ○	○ ○
○	○	○ ○
Saturn　　+	Saturn	Moon

Traditionally adverse for all questions. Both Witnesses are adverse, and the Judge variable, so the combination leads to little progress or good results. Similar to adverse aspects of Saturn, causing frustration and delay, such as the square and opposition.

Witness Caput Draconis	Witness Caput Draconis	Judge Populus
O O	O O	O O
O	O	O O
O	O	O O
O	O	O O
North Node +	North Node	Moon

Traditionally favorable for all questions. Both Witnesses are favorable, stimulating the variable Judge to come down on the side of favorable results. The North Node generally indicates a point of spiritual and material benefits, sometimes considered karmic benefits from past lives.

Witness Cauda Draconis	Witness Cauda Draconis	Judge Populus
O	O	O O
O	O	O O
O	O	O O
O O	O O	O O
South Node +	South Node	Moon

Traditionally adverse for all questions. Both Witnesses are adverse, bringing no beneficial results. The South Node in the chart is a point of spiritual debts and losses, sometimes considered karmic debts from past lives.

Witnesses that Produce the Judge
VIA

Witness Fortuna Major	Witness Fortuna Minor	Judge Via
O O	O	O
O O	O	O
O	O O	O
O	O O	O
Sun +	Sun	Moon

Traditionally favorable for all questions but those relating to law-suits and career interests. A favorable Witness is followed by a less favorable, and the results are good, but not as good as possibly hoped for, especially in lawsuits and career, which demand a stronger Mars influence. Similar to favorable aspects to the Sun.

Witness Fortuna Minor	Witness Fortuna Major	Judge Via
O	O O	O
O	O O	O
O O	O	O
O O	O	O
Sun +	Sun	Moon

Traditionally favorable for all questions but those relating to personal life. The first Witness is sometimes adverse, but the second is highly favorable, so the looked-for results will materialize. A tendency to trust in luck creates some hazards to physical well-being and personal life. Similar to a good aspect to the Sun.

Witness Populus	Witness Via	Judge Via
O O	O	O
O O	O	O
O O	O	O
O O	O	O
Moon +	Moon	Moon

Traditionally adverse for all questions. Both Witnesses and the Judge are variable, so the ultimate results are adverse, as too many other people are involved, or their influence lends too much indecision. Similar to a much-aspected, but poorly placed Moon.

Witness Via		Witness Populus	Judge Via
O		O O	O
O		O O	O
O		O O	O
O		O O	O
Moon	+	Moon	Moon

Traditionally mildly favorable for all questions except those relating to legacies and career. Both Witnesses are variable and so is the Judge, but here planning and manipulation of the people leads to greater possibilities of success. Similar to a much-aspected and well-placed Moon.

Witness Conjunctio		Witness Carcer	Judge Via
O O		O	O
O		O O	O
O		O O	O
O O		O	O
Mercury	+	Saturn	Moon

Traditionally adverse for all questions but those concerning marriage, legacies and lawsuits. Both Witnesses are favorable and the Judge variable, so the results are generally good where realistic thought and business acumen are involved, similar to a favorable aspect of Mercury to Saturn, such as the trine or sextile. There is little of romance in this combination, and little of the diplomacy needed for success in lawsuits. Saturn tends to deny legacies.

Witness	Witness	Judge
Carcer	Conjunctio	Via
O	O O	O
O O	O	O
O O	O	O
O	O O	O
Saturn +	Mercury	Moon

Traditionally mildly favorable for all questions. Both Witnesses are favorable and the Judge variable, so the results are generally favorable where realistic thought and business acumen are involved, similar to a favorable aspect of Mercury to Saturn, such as the sextile or trine. Here wit overcomes the delays or hardness generated by Saturn, so all questions are favored.

Witness	Witness	Judge
Albus	Puer	Via
O O	O	O
O O	O	O
O	O O	O
O O	O	O
Mercury +	Mars	Moon

Traditionally adverse for all questions. Both Witnesses are good, but the Judge is variable, and impatience or haste generated by Mars following Mercury negates any success. Similar to an adverse aspect of Mercury to Mars.

Witness	Witness	Judge
Puer	Albus	Via
O	O O	O
O	O O	O
O O	O	O
O	O O	O
Mars +	Mercury	Moon

Traditionally favorable for all questions but those relating to new projects contemplated for the future. Both Witnesses are favorable, and the Judge variable, so results are excellent in the here-and-now. Variability of the Moon and impatience of Mars negate long-term results. Similar to a favorable aspect of Mars to Mercury, such as the sextile or trine. Here Mercury follows Mars and controls the dynamic energy of Mars, leading to favorable results.

Witness Puella	Witness Rubeus	Judge Via
O	O O	O
O O	O	O
O	O O	O
O	O O	O
Venus +	Mars	Moon

Traditionally adverse for all questions but those relating to love. The first Witness is variable, the second adverse and the Judge variable, so the results are unfavorable. Since a combination of Venus and Mars is involved, love is favored; however, this is similar to an adverse aspect between Venus and Mars, such as the square or opposition, and even the course of true love will not run completely smoothly.

Witness Rubeus	Witness Puella	Judge Via
O O	O	O
O	O O	O
O O	O	O
O O	O	O
Mars +	Venus	Moon

Traditionally favorable for all questions. Here the first Witness is adverse, and the second variable, but the combination of Mars and Venus is similar to the favorable aspects, the trine, conjunction and sextile, so the results are favorable.

Witness	Witness	Judge
Amissio	Acquisitio	Via
O	O O	O
O O	O	O
O	O O	O
O O	O	O
Venus +	Jupiter	Moon

Traditionally favorable for all questions. The first Witness is adverse, but the second highly favorable, so the results are favorable. Similar to a good aspect between Venus and Jupiter, which is the best possible combination of planets.

Witness	Witness	Judge
Acquisitio	Amissio	Via
O O	O	O
O	O O	O
O O	O	O
O	O O	O
Jupiter +	Venus	Moon

Traditionally adverse for all questions except those relating to servants or service, and communications. Here the first Witness is favorable, but the second adverse, and thus the results are unfavorable. This aspect is similar to an adverse aspect between Jupiter and Venus, causing waste, carelessness and extravagance. Jupiter rules communications in part, and the favorable Witness, so Jupiter's power is strong enough to favor communications.

Witness	Witness	Judge
Laetitia	Caput Draconis	Via
O	O O	O
O O	O	O
O O	O	O
O O	O	O
Jupiter +	North Node	Moon

Traditionally favorable for all questions but those relating to career. Both Witnesses are favorable, so the results are favorable; however, the more spiritual interests of life predominate over the things of this world, so career is not favored. Jupiter and the North Node in favorable aspect indicate karmic blessings.

Witness Caput Draconis		Witness Laetitia	Judge Via
O O		O	O
O		O O	O
O		O O	O
O		O O	O
North Node	+	Jupiter	Moon

Traditionally favorable for all questions. Both Witnesses are favorable, so the results are favorable, particularly in connection with the things of the spirit, and careers in spiritual or social areas. Jupiter and the North Node in favorable aspect indicate karmic blessings.

Witness Tristitia		Witness Cauda Draconis	Judge Via
O O		O	O
O O		O	O
O O		O	O
O		O O	O
Saturn	+	South Node	Moon

Traditionally adverse for all questions. Both Witnesses are adverse so the results are unfavorable. Similar to adverse aspects of Saturn.

Witness Cauda Draconis		Witness Tristitia	Judge Via
O		O O	O
O		O O	O
O		O O	O
O O		O	O
South Node	+	Saturn	Moon

Traditionally adverse for all questions except those relating to lawsuits. Both Witnesses are adverse, so the results are unfavorable. Similar to adverse aspects to Saturn; however, in lawsuits it is the opponent who is afflicted.

Witnesses that Produce the Judge
CONJUNCTIO

Witness Fortuna Major		Witness Acquisitio	Judge Conjunctio
O O		O O	O O
O O		O	O
O		O O	O
O		O	O O
Sun	+	Jupiter	Mercury

Traditionally favorable for all questions except those relating to dealing with enemies. Both Witnesses are favorable and the Judge favorable, so the results are excellent. Jupiter-Sun inclines to too much trust and confidence, creating hazards in dealing with enemies. Similar to a favorable aspect of Sun to Jupiter.

Witness Acquisitio		Witness Fortuna Major	Judge Conjunctio
O O		O O	O O
O		O O	O
O O		O	O
O		O	O O
Jupiter	+	Sun	Mercury

Traditionally favorable for all questions. Both Witnesses are favorable and the Judge favorable, so again the results are excellent. Here the power of the Sun, following Jupiter, remedies the problem of dealing with enemies. Similar to a favorable aspect of the Sun to Jupiter.

Witness Fortuna Minor		Witness Amissio	Judge Conjunctio
O		O	O O
O		O O	O
O O		O	O
O O		O O	O O
Sun	+	Venus	Mercury

Traditionally adverse for all questions. The first Witness is not very good, and the second is adverse, so the results are adverse, despite the fact that the Judge per se is a favorable one. Similar to an afflicted combination of the Sun and Venus, inclining to self-indulgence.

Witness Amissio		Witness Fortuna Minor	Judge Conjunctio
O		O	O O
O O		O	O
O		O O	O
O O		O O	O O
Venus	+	Sun	Mercury

Traditionally adverse for all questions except those involving love, career, and dealings with enemies. The first Witness is adverse, and the second not too good, so the results are mainly negative. Fortuna Minor represents external protection, so the combination is favorable for dealings with enemies and with career where basic retention of a job is concerned. Love is also favored because Fortuna Minor, or protection, follows the Venus figure, Amissio. Again, similar to an afflicted combination of Sun and Venus, indicating self-indulgence.

Witness Populus		Witness Conjunctio	Judge Conjunctio
O O		O O	O O
O O		O	O
O O		O	O
O O		O O	O O
Moon	+	Mercury	Mercury

Traditionally mildly adverse for all questions but those relating to legacies and lawsuits. The first Witness is variable and the second favorable, but Moon-Mercury combinations have no staying power, and so the results are not usually good or long-lasting. Moon-Mercury does favor agreements, and thus lawsuits and legacies. Similar to a mildly adverse aspect between Moon and Mercury, such as the quincunx.

Witness		Witness	Judge
Conjunctio		Populus	Conjunctio
○ ○		○ ○	○ ○
○		○ ○	○
○		○ ○	○
○ ○		○ ○	○ ○
Mercury	+	Moon	Mercury

Traditionally mildly adverse for all questions except those relating to dealings with enemies. The first Witness is good, but the second variable, and again Moon-Mercury combinations have no staying power, leading to only ephemeral results. Similar to mildly adverse Moon-Mercury aspect, such as the quincunx. Since Populus follows, indicating popularity, dealings with enemies are favored.

Witness		Witness	Judge
Via		Carcer	Conjunctio
○		○	○ ○
○		○ ○	○
○		○ ○	○
○		○	○ ○
Moon	+	Saturn	Mercury

Traditionally mildly adverse for all questions but those relating to marriage, legacies and lawsuits. Via is a variable Witness, and Carcer also, so the results are not as good as could be desired. Since Saturn relates to realization of objectives, and Mercury to agreements, marriage, legacies and lawsuits viewed as legal agreements are favored. Similar to the weak aspects of Moon to Saturn, the mildly favorable semisextile and the mildly adverse quincunx.

Witness		Witness	Judge
Carcer		Via	Conjunctio
○		○	○ ○
○ ○		○	○
○ ○		○	○
○		○	○ ○
Saturn	+	Moon	Mercury

Traditionally mildly adverse for all questions but those dealing with marriage, communications and problems with enemies. Carcer and Via are both variable, indicating little result except where legal agreements are concerned, including lawsuits and marriage. Judge is Mercury-ruled, favoring communications and the Moon-ruled Via following Saturn-ruled Carcer gives popularity, helpful in dealing with enemies. Similar to the mildly favorable semisextile and mildly adverse quincunx of Moon to Saturn.

Witness		Witness		Judge
Albus		Rubeus		Conjunctio
O O		O O		O O
O O		O		O
O		O O		O
O O		O O		O O
Mercury	+	Mars		Mercury

Traditionally adverse for all questions. Similar to an adverse Mars-Mercury aspect, as much dissension or controversy prevents the agreement or union (Conjunctio) necessary for success.

Witness		Witness		Judge
Rubeus		Albus		Conjunctio
O O		O O		O O
O		O O		O
O O		O		O
O O		O O		O O
Mars	+	Mercury		Mercury

Traditionally favorable for all questions. Similar to a favorable Mars-Mercury aspect, where dissension is overcome by reason and persuasion, resulting in agreement.

Witness Puella	Witness Puer	Judge Conjunctio
O	O	O O
O O	O	O
O	O O	O
O	O	O O
Venus	+ Mars	Mercury

Traditionally favorable for all questions. A favorable combination of Venus and Mars, such as a favorable aspect, indicates the means are at hand to satisfy all desires.

Witness Puer	Witness Puella	Judge Conjunctio
O	O	O O
O	O O	O
O O	O	O
O	O	O O
Mars	+ Venus	Mercury

Traditionally favorable for all questions. Similar to above, indicating a favorable Venus-Mars aspect which suggests that the means to fulfull desires are at hand.

Witness Laetitia	Witness Cauda Draconis	Judge Conjunctio
O	O	O O
O O	O	O
O O	O	O
O O	O O	O O
Jupiter	+ South Node	Mercury

Traditionally adverse for all questions except those relating to travel and communications, ruled by Mercury and Jupiter, which are more powerful than the South Node in the areas they directly rule.

Witness	Witness	Judge
Cauda Draconis	Laetitia	Conjunctio
O	O	O O
O	O O	O
O	O O	O
O O	O O	O O
South Node +	Jupiter	Mercury

Traditionally favorable for all questions. The first Witness is adverse, but the second very favorable, as Jupiter is the Greater Benefic, so despite initial obstacles, all will go well.

Witness	Witness	Judge
Tristitia	Caput Draconis	Conjunctio
O O	O O	O O
O O	O	O
O O	O	O
O	O	O O
Saturn +	North Node	Mercury

Traditionally favorable for all questions, as the first Witness is adverse, denoting hesitation and delay, but the second Witness is favorable and indicates elevating influences which lead to a favorable conclusion.

Witness	Witness	Judge
Caput Draconis	Tristitia	Conjunctio
O O	O O	O O
O	O O	O
O	O O	O
O	O	O O
North Node +	Saturn	Mercury

Traditionally adverse for all questions. The first Witness is favorable, denoting an optimistic beginning, but the second is adverse, denoting hesitation and delay; so the opportunity is lost, and the conclusion unfavorable.

Witnesses that Produce the Judge
AMISSIO

Witness Fortuna Major	Witness Carcer	Judge Amissio
O O	O	O
O O	O O	O O
O	O O	O
O	O	O O
Sun +	Saturn	Venus

Traditionally favorable for all questions but those involving marriage. Both Witnesses are favorable, and the Judge adverse as a symbol, but favorable as a Judge (see introduction), so the results are favorable. However, Amissio represents an afflicted Venus, so marriage is not favored. Similar to a favorable Sun-Saturn aspect; productive of material gain, but thoroughly unromantic.

Witness Carcer	Witness Fortuna Major	Judge Amissio
O	O O	O
O O	O O	O O
O O	O	O
O	O	O O
Saturn +	Sun	Venus

Traditionally favorable for all questions but those involving marriage. Both Witnesses are favorable and the Judge adverse as a symbol, but favorable as a Judge (see introduction), so the results are favorable. However, Amissio represents an afflicted Venus, so marriage is not favored. Similar to a favorable Sun-Saturn aspect, such as the trine or sextile; productive of material gain,but thoroughly unromantic.

Witness Fortuna Minor		Witness Conjunctio		Judge Amissio
O		O O		O
O		O		O O
O O		O		O
O O		O O		O O
Sun	+	Mercury		Venus

Traditionally favorable for all questions but those involving legacies and dealings with enemies. Both Witnesses are favorable, so the results are likely to be favorable. Similar to a favorable Sun-Mercury, Sun-Venus or Mercury-Venus aspect, emphasizing the personal elements in life.

Witness Conjunctio		Witness Fortuna Minor		Judge Amissio
O O		O		O
O		O		O O
O		O O		O
O O		O O		O O
Mercury	+	Sun		Venus

Traditionally favorable for all questions. Both Witnesses are favorable, so the results are favorable. Similar to a favorable Sun-Mercury aspect, the conjunction, the only aspect possible between these two planets.

Witness Populus		Witness Amissio		Judge Amissio
O O		O		O
O O		O O		O O
O O		O		O
O O		O O		O O
Moon	+	Venus		Venus

Traditionally adverse for all questions except those dealing with love, career interests and problems with enemies. The first Witness is variable, and the second adverse, so the results are generally adverse.

However, the influence of Venus is strong and favors success in careers where cooperation, personal charm, and tact are important; favors romance and indicates lessening of tensions with enemies.

Witness Amissio		Witness Populus	Judge Amissio
O		O O	O
O O		O O	O O
O		O O	O
O O		O O	O O
Venus	+	Moon	Venus

Traditionally adverse for all questions except those dealing with enemies. The first Witness is adverse and the second variable, so the results are generally adverse. However, the influence of Venus is strong and favors success in careers where cooperation, charm and tact are important; favors romance; and indicates lessening of tensions with enemies.

Witness Via		Witness Acquisitio	Judge Amissio
O		O O	O
O		O	O O
O		O O	O
O		O	O O
Moon	+	Jupiter	Venus

Traditionally favorable for all questions. The first Witness is variable, and the second favorable, so the results are generally favorable. Similar to a favorable aspect of Jupiter to the Moon, the sextile, conjunction or trine. Here again, the Judge, although adverse as a symbol, is favorable as a Judge.

Witness	Witness	Judge
Acquisitio	Via	Amissio
O O	O	O
O	O	O O
O O	O	O
O	O	O O
Jupiter +	Moon	Venus

Traditionally mildly favorable for all questions but those involving love, legacies, lawsuits, and dealings with enemies. The first Witness is favorable, but the second variable, so the power of Jupiter is diffused by the fluctuations of the Moon, and the results are not so favorable. Venus as the ruler of the Judge, however, favors love, settling lawsuits and lessening the force of enmities. Venus-Jupiter brings abundance, so legacies are favored.

Witness	Witness	Judge
Albus	Laetitia	Amissio
O O	O	O
O O	O O	O O
O	O O	O
O O	O O	O O
Mercury +	Jupiter	Venus

Traditionally favorable for all questions. Both Witnesses are favorable, so the results are favorable also. Here again the Judge is favorable as a Judge, although adverse as a symbol in general readings. Similar to a favorable aspect of Mercury to Jupiter.

Witness	Witness	Judge
Laetitia	Albus	Amissio
O	O O	O
O O	O O	O O
O O	O	O
O O	O O	O O
Jupiter +	Mercury	Venus

Traditionally favorable for all questions. Both Witnesses are favorable, so the results are favorable also. Here again the Judge is favorable as a Judge, although adverse as a symbol. Similar to a favorable aspect of Mercury to Jupiter.

Witness Puella		Witness Tristitia	Judge Amissio
O		O O	O
O O		O O	O O
O		O O	O
O		O	O O
Venus	+	Saturn	Venus

Traditionally adverse for all questions. The first Witness is variable, and the second adverse, so the results are adverse. Similar to an adverse aspect of Venus to Saturn, such as the square, opposition or quincunx.

Witness Tristitia		Witness Puella	Judge Amissio
O O		O	O
O O		O O	O O
O O		O	O
O		O	O O
Saturn	+	Venus	Venus

Traditionally mildly favorable for all questions except those involving dealings with enemies. The first Witness is adverse, but the second variable, and so there may be some mildly favorable results. However, there is no Mars influence to give strength to dealings with enemies. Similar to the mildly favorable aspect of Saturn to Venus, the semisextile.

Witness Puer		Witness Caput Draconis	Judge Amissio
O		O O	O
O		O	O O
O O		O	O
O		O	O O
Mars	+	North Node	Venus

Traditionally favorable for all questions but marriage. Both Witnesses are favorable, so the end result is favorable. However, the North Node lifts action to other planes than intimate relationships, so marriage is not favored. Similar to a favorable aspect of Mars to the North Node, the sextile or trine.

Witness Caput Draconis	Witness Puer	Judge Amissio
O O	O	O
O	O	O O
O	O O	O
O	O	O O
North Node　+	Mars	Venus

Traditionally adverse for all questions but marriage. Both Witnesses are favorable, but Mars' symbol following the Dragon's symbol tends to lower the level of action, and so results are not favorable, except for marriage, combining the Mars symbol, Puer, with the Venus judge, Amissio. Similar to an adverse aspect of Mars to the North Node, the opposition or square.

Witness Rubeus	Witness Cauda Draconis	Judge Amissio
O O	O	O
O	O	O O
O O	O	O
O O	O O	O O
Mars　+	South Node	Venus

Traditionally adverse for all questions. Both Witnesses are adverse, so the results are unfavorable. Similar to an afflicted Mars aspecting the South Node.

Witness Cauda Draconis	Witness Rubeus	Judge Amissio
o	o o	o
o	o	o o
o	o o	o
o o	o o	o o
South Node +	Mars	Venus

Traditionally favorable for all questions except those involving love and lawsuits. Both Witnesses are adverse, but for some reason, most questions are judged to have a favorable outcome. The only aspect that would agree with this is Mars opposite the South Node, which would indicate Mars in conjunction to the favorable North Node, thus possibly indicating the favorable answers. Impatience of Mars precludes success in settling lawsuits or stimulating romance.

Witnesses that Produce the Judge
ACQUISITIO

Witness Fortuna Major	Witness Conjunctio	Judge Acquisitio
O O	O O	O O
O O	O	O
O	O	O O
O	O O	O
Sun +	Mercury	Jupiter

Traditionally favorable for all questions. Both Witnesses are favorable, so the results are favorable also. Similar to a good aspect of Jupiter to Sun or Mercury, such as the trine or sextile.

Witness Conjunctio	Witness Fortuna Major	Judge Acquisitio
O O	O O	O O
O	O O	O
O	O	O O
O O	O	O
Mercury +	Sun	Jupiter

Traditionally favorable for all questions. Both Witnesses are favorable, so the results are favorable also. Similar to a good aspect of Jupiter to Sun or Mercury, such as the trine or sextile.

Witness Fortuna Minor	Witness Carcer	Judge Acquisitio
O	O	O O
O	O O	O
O O	O O	O O
O O	O	O
Sun +	Saturn	Jupiter

Traditionally mildly adverse for all questions. The first Witness is variable, the second also, so there is little good as a result. Similar to the mildly adverse quincunx aspect of Sun to Saturn.

Witness Carcer	Witness Fortuna Minor	Judge Acquisitio
O	O	O O
O O	O	O
O O	O O	O O
O	O O	O
Saturn +	Sun	Jupiter

Traditionally mildly favorable for all questions except those dealing with enemies. The Witnesses are both variable, but the power of the Sun overcomes the delays of Saturn-ruled Carcer, and most results are favorable. Jupiter ruling the Judge also adds a favorable influence. Similar to a good aspect of Jupiter to Sun or Saturn.

Witness Populus	Witness Acquisitio	Judge Acquisitio
O O	O O	O O
O O	O	O
O O	O O	O O
O O	O	O
Moon +	Jupiter	Jupiter

Traditionally mildly favorable for all questions but those involving money and retirement years. The first Witness is variable, but the second favorable, so the results are generally favorable. However, Jupiter following the Moon inclines to extravagance (like the story of the ant and the grasshopper), so not favorable for money and retirement years. Similar to the favorable sextile, trine or conjunction of Jupiter to the Moon.

Witness Acquisitio	Witness Populus	Judge Acquisitio
O O	O O	O O
O	O O	O
O O	O O	O O
O	O O	O
Jupiter +	Moon	Jupiter

Traditionally favorable for all questions but those involving career. The first Witness is favorable, but the second variable, and so the results are adverse, as the strength of Jupiter for good is diluted by the inconstancy of the Moon. Similar to adverse aspects of Jupiter to Moon, the square and opposition.

Witness Via	Witness Amissio	Judge Acquisitio
o	o	o o
o	o o	o
o	o	o o
o	o o	o
Moon +	Venus	Jupiter

Traditionally mildly favorable for all questions except those involving love and new projects. The first Witness is variable, and the second adverse, but the results are mildly favorable through the influence of Jupiter-ruled Judge, Acquisitio. Amissio is Venus debilitated, so love is not favored, nor are new projects.

Witness Amissio	Witness Via	Judge Acquisitio
o	o	o o
o o	o	o
o	o	o o
o o	o	o
Venus +	Moon	Jupiter

Traditionally adverse for all questions except those involving love and communications. The first Witness is adverse, and the second variable, so the results are adverse, as this is similar to Venus afflicted, as in the square or opposition. Jupiter is powerful enough to favor communications and fulfillment of some of Venus' indications for love.

Witness Albus	Witness Caput Draconis	Judge Acquisitio
O O	O O	O O
O O	O	O
O	O	O O
O O	O	O
Mercury	+ North Node	Jupiter

Traditionally favorable for all questions except those involving lawsuits. Both Witnesses are favorable, so the results are favorable. Similar to a favorable aspect of Mercury to Jupiter. There is no dynamic tension in this combination, so conflicts like lawsuits are not favored.

Witness Caput Draconis	Witness Albus	Judge Acquisitio
O O	O O	O O
O	O O	O
O	O	O O
O	O O	O
North Node	+ Mercury	Jupiter

Traditionally favorable for all questions. Both Witnesses are favorable, so the results are favorable, similar to a favorable aspect of Mercury to Jupiter, such as the sextile, trine or conjunction.

Witness Puella	Witness Cauda Draconis	Judge Acquisitio
O	O	O O
O O	O	O
O	O	O O
O	O O	O
Venus	+ South Node	Jupiter

Traditionally adverse for all questions except for those involving the ending of a project. The first Witness is variable, and the second adverse, so the results are unfavorable. Since this combination tends to limit things, the ending of a situation is favored. Similar to an adverse aspect of Venus to Jupiter, such as the square or opposition, creating extravagance or wastefulness.

Witness		Witness	Judge
Cauda Draconis		Puella	Acquisitio
o		o	o o
o		o o	o
o		o	o o
o o		o	o
South Node	+	Venus	Jupiter

Traditionally favorable for all questions but those involving the ending of a project. The first Witness is adverse, but the second is variable, and when the Venus symbol combines with the Jupiter Judge, the combination is excellent for good results. However, the opportunity must be grasped at once, so the ending of a project is not favored. Jupiter also favors beginnings rather than endings.

Witness		Witness	Judge
Puer		Laetitia	Acquisitio
o		o	o o
o		o o	o
o o		o o	o o
o		o o	o
Saturn	+	Jupiter	Jupiter

Traditionally favorable for all questions except those involving money, new projects, or the ending of a project. Both Witnesses are favorable, indicating favorable results, but Mars and Jupiter combined tend to action in the thick of things, so beginnings and endings are not favored. Action, not possessions, is stressed, thus this combination is not favored for money. Similar to the trine or sextile of Mars to Jupiter.

Witness		Witness	Judge
Laetitia		Puer	Acquistio
o		o	o o
o o		o	o
o o		o o	o o
o o		o	o
Jupiter	+	Mars	Jupiter

Traditionally favorable for all questions but those involving lawsuits and dealings with enemies. Both Witnesses are favorable, indicating favorable results, but there is too much haste, with Mars following Jupiter, to allow for caution in dealing with enemies. Similar to favorable aspects, the trine and sextile, of Mars to Jupiter.

Witness Rubeus		Witness Tristitia	Judge Acquistio
O O		O O	O O
O		O O	O
O O		O O	O O
O O		O	O
Mars	+	Saturn	Jupiter

Traditionally adverse for all questions except those involving war and dealings with enemies. Both Witnesses are adverse, so the results are generally unfavorable. Similar to a square or opposition of Mars to Saturn. Judge ruled by Jupiter lends success in war and dealings with enemies.

Witness Tristitia		Witness Rubeus	Judge Acquistio
O O		O O	O O
O O		O	O
O O		O O	O O
O		O O	O
Saturn	+	Mars	Jupiter

Traditionally adverse for all questions. Both Witnesses are adverse, so the results are generally unfavorable. Similar to a square or opposition of Mars to Saturn.

Witnesses that Produce the Judge
CARCER

Witness Fortuna Major		Witness Amissio	Judge Carcer
O O		O	O
O O		O O	O O
O		O	O O
O		O O	O
Sun	+	Venus	Saturn

Traditionally favorable for all questions except those relating to lawsuits. The first Witness is favorable, but the second adverse, so a good beginning nonetheless has no favorable results, except that the Judge, ruled by Saturn, favors settlement of legal disputes. Similar to Saturn adverse to Sun or Venus.

Witness Amissio		Witness Fortuna Major	Judge Carcer
O		O O	O
O O		O O	O O
O		O	O O
O O		O	O
Venus	+	Sun	Saturn

Traditionally favorable for all questions. The first Witness is adverse, but the second highly favorable, so the results are generally favorable. Similar to favorable aspects of Saturn to the Sun or Venus.

Witness Fortuna Minor		Witness Acquisitio	Judge Carcer
O		O O	O
O		O	O O
O O		O O	O O
O O		O	O
Sun	+	Jupiter	Saturn

Traditionally favorable for all questions but those involving career or dealings with enemies. The first Witness is variable, but the second is favorable, so the results are generally favorable. Similar to a good aspect of Sun to Jupiter.

Witness Acquisitio	Witness Fortuna Minor	Judge Carcer
O O	O	O
O	O	O O
O O	O O	O O
O	O O	O
Jupiter +	Sun	Saturn

Traditionally favorable for all questions but those involving lawsuits or dealings with enemies. The first Witness is favorable and the second variable, giving favorable results for most questions. Similar to a favorable aspect of the Sun to Jupiter.

Witness Populus	Witness Carcer	Judge Carcer
O O	O	O
O O	O O	O O
O O	O O	O O
O O	O	O
Moon +	Saturn	Saturn

Traditionally favorable for all questions except those involving love, marriage, legacies, lawsuits and career. The first Witness is variable, the second sometimes good, so some results are favorable, particularly those involving the ending of a project. Similar to a favorable aspect of Moon to Saturn. Relationships and favors (career) are not favored by the strong Saturn influence.

Witness Carcer	Witness Populus	Judge Carcer
O	O O	O
O O	O O	O O
O O	O O	O O
O	O O	O
Saturn +	Moon	Saturn

Traditionally favorable for all questions but those involving legacies, lawsuits and career. The first Witness is sometimes good, the second variable, so some results are favorable. Similar to a favorable aspect of the Moon to Saturn.

Witness Via		Witness Conjunctio		Judge Carcer
O		O O		O
O		O		O O
O		O		O O
O		O O		O
Moon	+	Mercury		Saturn

Traditionally favorable for all questions except those involving the ending of a project or career. The first Witness is variable, but the second favorable, so the results are favorable. Similar to a favorable Moon-Mercury aspect, somewhat ephemeral and thus not favoring the ending of a project or career. Good for immediate objectives.

Witness Conjunctio		Witness Via		Judge Carcer
O O		O		O
O		O		O O
O		O		O O
O O		O		O
Mercury	+	Moon		Saturn

Traditionally adverse for all questions except those pertaining to problems with enemies. The first Witness is favorable but the second is variable, so the results are not what is expected or desired. Similar to a mildly adverse aspect of the Moon to Mercury, such as the quincunx.

Witness Albus		Witness Puella	Judge Carcer
O O		O	O
O O		O O	O O
O		O	O O
O O		O	O
Mercury	**+**	**Venus**	**Saturn**

Traditionally favorable for all questions except those involving legacies. The first aspect is favorable, and the second sometimes variable, but ruled by a positive Venus, and thus the results are favorable. Relationships are favored over possessions, and so legacies, involving death and Saturn, are not favored.

Witness Puella		Witness Albus	Judge Carcer
O		O O	O
O O		O O	O O
O		O	O O
O		O O	O
Venus	**+**	**Mercury**	**Saturn**

Traditionally favorable for all questions except those involving legacies. The first aspect is variable but the second is favorable, and so the results are all that is desired. Similar to a Venus-Mercury aspect, the conjunction, semisextile or sextile, all of which are favorable.

Witness Rubeus		Witness Puer	Judge Carcer
O O		O	O
O		O	O O
O O		O O	O O
O O		O	O
Mars	**+**	**Mars**	**Saturn**

Traditionally adverse for all questions. Similar to an adversely aspected Mars, or Mars in the Twelfth House, where action and initiatives are too limited. The first Witness is adverse and the second

favorable, but the negative side of Mars is stronger, so the results
are adverse.

Witness	Witness	Judge
Laetitia	Tristitia	Carcer
○	○ ○	○
○ ○	○ ○	○ ○
○ ○	○ ○	○ ○
○ ○	○	○
Jupiter +	Saturn	Saturn

Traditionally adverse for all questions except those involving
legacies. The first Witness is favorable, but the second adverse, so the
results are unfavorable. The strong Saturn influence, with Jupiter, the
other economic planet, does favor legacies.

Witness	Witness	Judge
Tristitia	Laetitia	Carcer
○ ○	○	○
○ ○	○ ○	○ ○
○ ○	○ ○	○ ○
○	○ ○	○
Saturn +	Jupiter	Saturn

Traditionally favorable for all questions except those involving
marriage. The first Witness is adverse, but the second favorable, so the
results are favorable. However, the combination is entirely materialistic and economic, so marriage is not favored.

Witness	Witness	Judge
Caput Draconis	Cauda Draconis	Carcer
○ ○	○	○
○	○	○ ○
○	○	○ ○
○	○ ○	○
North Node +	South Node	Saturn

Traditionally adverse for all questions. The first Witness is favorable, but the second adverse, so the results are adverse. The influence is a little similar to the adverse quincunx or opposition being formed to the North Node, while the unfortunate South Node has the favorable semisextile or conjunction aspect from a planet of importance.

Witness	Witness	Judge
Caput Draconis	Cauda Draconis	Carcer
O	O O	O
O	O	O O
O	O	O O
O O	O	O
South Node	+ North Node	Saturn

Traditionally favorable for all questions except those involving personal affairs and marriage. The first Witness is adverse, but the second is favorable, so the rsults are favorable. Similar to an affliction of the South Node which accompanies a favorable aspect to the North Node in a chart.

STAY IN TOUCH

On the following pages you will find listed, with their current prices, some of the books and tapes now available on related subjects. Your book dealer stocks most of these, and will stock new titles in the Llewellyn series as they become available. We urge your patronage.

However, to obtain our full catalog, to keep informed of new titles as they are released and to benefit from informative articles and helpful news, you are invited to write for our bi-monthly news magazine/catalog. A sample copy is free, and it will continue coming to you at no cost as long as you are an active mail customer. Or you may keep it coming for a full year with a donation of just $2.00 in U.S.A. ($7.00 for Canada & Mexico, $20.00 overseas, first class mail). Many bookstores also have *The Llewellyn New Times* available to their customers. Ask for it.

Stay in touch! In *The Llewellyn New Times'* pages you will find news and reviews of new books, tapes and services, announcements of meetings and seminars, articles helpful to our readers, news of authors, advertising of products and services, special money-making opportunities, and much more.

The Llewellyn New Times
P.O. Box 64383-Dept. 704, St. Paul, MN 55164-0383, U.S.A.

• • •

TO ORDER BOOKS AND TAPES

If your book dealer does not have the books and tapes described on the following pages readily available, you may order them direct from the publisher by sending full price in U.S. funds, plus $2.00 for postage and handling for the first book, and 50¢ for each additional book. There are no postage and handling charges for orders over $50. UPS Delivery: We ship UPS whenever possible. Delivery guaranteed. Provide your street address as UPS does not deliver to P.O. Boxes. UPS to Canada requires a $50 minimum order. Allow 4-6 weeks for delivery. Orders outside the U.S.A and Canada: Airmail—add $5 per book; add $3 for each non-book item (tapes, etc.); add $1 per item for surface mail.

FOR GROUP STUDY AND PURCHASE

Because there is a great deal of interest in group discussion and study of the subject matter of this book, we feel that we should encourage the adoption and use of this particular book by such groups by offering a special "quantity" price to group leaders or "agents."

Our Special Quantity Price for a minimum order of five copies of *The Complete Book of Astrological Geomancy* is $44.85 cash-with-order. This price includes postage and handling within the United States. Minnesota residents must add 6% sales tax. For additional quantities, please order in multiples of five. For Canadian and foreign orders, add postage and handling charges as above. Credit card (VISA, Master Card, American Express) orders are accepted. Charge card orders only may be phoned free ($15.00 minimum order) within the U.S.A. or Canada by dialing 1-800-THE MOON. Customer service calls dial 1-612-291-1970. Mail Orders to:

LLEWELLYN PUBLICATIONS
P.O. Box 64383-Dept. 704 / St. Paul, MN 55164-0383, U.S.A.

SPECIAL OFFER

Geomancy Readings by Priscilla Schwei

Priscilla Schwei's **ASTROLOGICAL GEOMANCY READINGS** are based on the ancient geomantic divination method of Cornelius Agrippa, the famous 16th century physician, astrologer and geomantist. It is a system of divination using both the Earth and the heavens.

A) On a sheet of paper write your most pressing question at the top of the page. Then draw 16 horizontal lines of dots. Feel free to put as many dots on each line as you like, but be sure that you put some on all of the 16 lines:

    1) . . . .
    2) . . . .
    3) . .   and so on.

B) Then write down all the questions you wish answered (limit of 5).

C) If you have no specific questions, write "General Life Reading" at the top of the page.

Geomantist Priscilla Schwei will then draw up the symbols in a chart. All questions will be discussed. If you choose the General Life Reading, a detailed, house-by-house analysis will be made to cover your life.

On your sheet of paper include:
    1) Your name and full address.
    2) The date you are asking the question.
    3) A daytime phone number at which you can be reached.

Enclose a payment of $15.00 and send to:

Priscilla Schwei
c/o Llewellyn's Personal Astrological Services
P.O. Box 64383-901
St. Paul, MN 55164-0383

THE WISDOM OF SOLOMON THE KING
As interpreted by Priscilla Schwei

Now you can tap into the ancient techniques and magic of Solomon the King with this kit, which includes the 200-page *Solomon Manual of Divination and Ritual Spells*, and a 72-card deck for divination and ritual. Because this deck uses symbolism from the ancient *Key of Solomon*, you can use the cards as a powerful Tarot. Each card has valuable and meaningful symbols such as one of the 72 seals of the Spirits of Solomon, the name of the Spirit represented by the Seal, the astrological symbolism, a time period when the powers of the Spirit are at their height, the purpose and meaning of the card in divination and magic, and a symbolic figure allowing for personal interpretation.

Each card can be used as a talisman to help you claim such things as wisdom, wealth, health and love. The book gives precise and complete instructions on how to use the cards in this way, as well as instructions on how to use the cards for a variety of types of magic: spells, candle magic, ceremonial magic.

For the first time, the ancient magic of Solomon has been interpreted and codified to offer its user a complete system of divination and powerful magic!

0-87542-701-4, 200 pgs., 72-card deck   **$14.95**

ARCHETYPES OF THE ZODIAC
by Kathleen Burt

The horoscope is probably the most unique tool for personal growth you can ever have. This book is intended to help you understand how the energies within your horoscope manifest. Once you are aware of how your chart operates on an instinctual level, you can then work consciously with it to remove any obstacles to your growth.

The technique offered in this book is based upon the incorporation of the esoteric rulers of the signs and the integration of their polar opposites. This technique has been very successful in helping the client or reader modify existing negative energies in a horoscope so as to improve the quality of his or her life and the understanding of his or her psyche.

There is special focus in this huge comprehensive volume on the myths for each sign. Some signs may have as many as *four different myths* coming from all parts of the world. All are discussed by the author. There is also emphasis on the Jungian Archetypes involved with each sign.

This book has a depth often surprising to the readers of popular astrology books. It has a clarity of expression seldom found in books of the esoteric tradition. It is very easy to understand, even if you know nothing of Jungian philosophy or of mythology. It is intriguing, exciting and very helpful for all levels of astrologers.

0-87542-088-5, 560 pgs., 6 x 9, illus., softcover   **$14.95**

PLANETS IN LOCALITY
by Steve Cozzi

DIRECTION . . . it's what we all need, what we all seek. Is there a method that is clear, simple, concise and logical that will bring this needed direction to our lives? Yes. It's called Locational Astrology, a comprehensive system on the cutting edge of contemporary astrological thought and practice. Steve Cozzi, an expert in locality charts, computers, and the creator of this system of Locational Astrology, has put together a book that will show the average student of astrology as well as the professional how to use this innovative system to help not only themselves, but also their clients.

This is not only a historical analysis of Local Space Astrology—it is also a practical guide for the individual reader, applicable to most aspects of everyday activities. Did you know that your route to work each day could actually shape the way you perform or how others perceive you? That where your home is located in your town could affect your state of mind? That where you decide to relocate could change your whole sense of self or your ability to create what you desire? This is all proven fact. Cozzi shows you how to determine your own planetary lines and how to best use them to further your ideals. *Planets in Locality* has over 50 figures and maps, geomantic compasses and other illustrations to help you find and plot planetary lines within your home, town, region and on out to the country and the world. It is an essential astrological volume.

0-87542-098-2, 308 pages, 6 x 9, illus.,   **$12.95**

THE NEW A TO Z HOROSCOPE MAKER AND DELINEATOR
by Llewellyn George

This is a new and totally revised edition of the text used by more American astrologers than any other—135,000 copies sold. Every detail of: How to Cast the Birth Chart—time changes, calculations, aspects & orbs, signs & planetary rulers, parts of fortune, etc.; The Progressed Chart—all the techniques and the major delineations; Transits—how to use them in prediction, also lunations and solar days. Rectification. Locality Charts, a comprehensive Astrological Dictionary and a complete index for easy use. It's an encyclopedia, a textbook, a self-study course and and a dictionary all-in-one!

0-87542-264-0, 600 pages, 6 x 9, softcover.   **$12.95**

SPIRITUAL, METAPHYSICAL & NEW TRENDS IN MODERN ASTROLOGY
Edited by Joan McEvers

This is the first book in a new series offered by Llewellyn called the *New World Astrology Series*. Edited by well-known astrologer, lecturer and writer Joan McEvers, this book pulls together the latest thoughts by the best astrologers in the field of Spiritual Astrology.

She has put together this outstanding group with these informative and exciting topics.

- Gray Keen: Perspective: The Ethereal Conclusion.
- Marion D. March: Some Insights Into Esoteric Astrology.
- Kimberly McSherry: The Feminine Element of Astrology: Reframing the Darkness.
- Kathleen Burt: The Spiritual Rulers and Their Role in the Transformation.
- Shirley Lyons Meier: The Secrets Behind Carl Payne Tobey's Secondary Chart.
- Jeff Jawer: Astrodrama.
- Donna Van Toen: Alice Bailey Revisited.
- Philip Sedgwick: Galactic Studies.
- Myrna Lofthus: The Spiritual Programming Within a Natal Chart.
- Angel Thompson: Transformational Astrology.

0-87542-380-9, 288 pages, 5¼ x 8, softcover   **$9.95**

PLANETS: THE ASTROLOGICAL TOOLS
Edited by Joan McEvers

This is the second in the astrological anthology series edited by respected astrologer Joan McEvers, who provides a brief factual overview of the planets.

Then take off through the solar system with 10 professional astrologers as they bring their insights to the symbolism and influences of the planets.

- Toni Glover Sedgwick: The Sun as the life force and our ego
- Joanne Wickenburg: The Moon as our emotional signal to change
- Erin Sullivan-Seale: Mercury as the multi-faceted god, followed with an in-depth explanation of its retrogradation
- Robert Glasscock: Venus as your inner value system and relationships
- Johanna Mitchell: Mars as your cooperative, energizing inner warrior
- Don Borkowski: Jupiter as expansion and preservation
- Gina Ceaglio: Saturn as a source of freedom through self-discipline
- Bil Tierney: Uranus as the original, growth-producing planet
- Karma Welch: Neptune as selfless giving and compassionate love
- Joan Negus: Pluto as a powerful personal force

0-87542-381-7, 380 pgs., 5¼ × 8, illus., softcover   **$12.95**

HEAVEN KNOWS WHAT
by Grant Lewi

Heaven Knows What contains everything you need to cast and interpret complete natal charts without learning any symbols, without confusion from tricky calculations, without previous experience or training.

How does the system work? Simply look up the positions of the planets in the tables at the back of the book. Plot these positions on the handy tear-out horoscope blanks. Use the aspect wheel provided to determine the planetary aspects and then read the relevant paragraphs describing their influence.

It's easy, fast, and amazingly accurate! Grant Lewi interpets the influence of the Sun and Moon positions at birth, and describes the effects of every possible planetary aspect in language designed for the modern reader. The tables have been updated so that you can cast a chart for any birth from 1890 through 1999. *Heaven Knows What* forms an excellent astrological background for the beginner, yet Lewi's interpretations are so relevant that even long-practicing astrologers gain new psychological insight into the characteristics of the signs and the meanings of the aspects.

0-87542-444-9, 300 pages, softcover.   **$9.95**

EARTH MOTHER ASTROLOGY
by Marcia Stark

Now, for the first time, a book that combines the science of astrology with current New Age interest in crystals, herbs, aromas, and holistic health. With this book and a copy of your astrological birth chart (readily available from sources listed in the book) you can use your horoscope to benefit your total being—body, mind and spirit. Learn, for example, what special nutrients you need during specific planetary cycles, or what sounds or colors will help you transform emotional states during certain times of the year.

This is a compendium of information for the New Age astrologer and healer. For the beginner, it explains all the astrological signs, planets and houses in a simple and yet new way, physiologically as well as symbolically.

This is a book of modern alchemy, showing the reader how to work with earth energies to achieve healing and transformation, thereby creating a sense of the cosmic unity of all Earth's elements.

0-87542-741-3, 294 pp., 5¼ × 8   **$12.95**

THE GOLDEN DAWN
by Israel Regardie
The Original Account of the Teachings, Rites and Ceremonies of the Hermetic Order of the Golden Dawn as revealed by Israel Regardie, with further revision, expansion, and additional notes by Israel Regardie, Cris Monnastre, and others.

Originally published in four bulky volumes of some 1200 pages, this 5th Revised and Enlarged Edition has been entirely reset in modern, less space-consuming type, in half the pages (while retaining the original pagination in marginal notation for reference) for greater ease and use.

Corrections of typographical errors perpetuated in the original and subsequent editions have been made, with further revision and additional text and notes by actual practitioners of the Golden Dawn system of Magick, with an Introduction by the only student ever accepted for personal training by Regardie.

Also included are Initiation Ceremonies, important rituals for consecration and invocation, methods of meditation and magical working based on the Enochian Tablets, studies in the Tarot, and the system of Qabalistic Correspondences that unite the World's religions and magical traditions into a comprehensive and practical whole.

This volume is designed as a study and practice curriculum suited to both group and private practice. Meditation upon, and following with the Active Imagination, the Initiation Ceremonies is fully experiential without need of participation in group or lodge.

0-87542-663-8, 744 pages, 6 x 9, illus.   **$19.95**

TRANSITS IN REVERSE
by Edna Copeland Ryneveld
Have you wondered about whether you should take that trip or ask for that raise? Do you want to know when the best time is for a wedding? How about knowing in advance the times when you will be the most creative and dazzling?

This book is different from all others published on transits (those planets that are actually moving around in the heavens making aspects to our natal planets). It gives the subject area first—such as creativity, relationships, health, etc.—and then tells you what transits to look for. The introductory chapters are so thorough that you will be able to use this book with only an ephemeris or astrological calendar to tell you where the planets are. The author explains what transits are, how they affect your daily life, how to track them, how to make decisions based on transits and much more.

With the information in each section, you can combine as many factors as you like to get positive results. If you are going on a business trip you can look at the accidents section to avoid any trouble, the travel section to find out the best date, the relationship section to see how you will get along with the other person, the business section to see if it is a good time to do business, the communication section to see if things will flow smoothly, and more. In this way, you can choose the absolute best date for just about anything! Electional astrology as been used for centuries, but now it is being given in the most easily understood and practical format yet.

0-87542-674-3, 320 pages, 6 x 9   **$12.95**